Marginalisation, Contestation, and Change in South Asian Cities

Edited by **Nida Kirmani**

Marginalisation, Contestation, and Change in South Asian Cities

Edited by **Nida Kirmani**

OXFORD
UNIVERSITY PRESS

OXFORD
UNIVERSITY PRESS

Oxford University Press is a department of the University of Oxford.
It furthers the University's objective of excellence in research, scholarship,
and education by publishing worldwide. Oxford is a registered trade mark of
Oxford University Press in the UK and in certain other countries

Published in Pakistan by
Oxford University Press
No. 38, Sector 15, Korangi Industrial Area,
PO Box 8214, Karachi-74900, Pakistan

ISBN 978-969-7340-12-5

Typeset in Adobe Garamond Pro
Printed on 68gsm Offset Paper

Printed by The Times Press (Pvt.) Ltd., Karachi

Acknowledgements
Cover image: © Catalin Lazar/Shutterstock

Disclaimer:
The views and opinions expressed in this publication are those of the authors and do
not purport to reflect the opinions or views of the Oxford University Press Pakistan.

Contents

Introduction

Urban Transformations in South Asia: Views from Below

Nida Kirmani

The city has long been a key site of inquiry for social scientists across disciplines. Much of the research produced in the field of urban studies has centred on Europe and North America, and has viewed urbanisation within the wider framework of modernisation. However, relatively little scholarly attention has been paid to cities of the Global South, despite the fact that most of the world's urbanisation is currently taking place within the 'developing world'. As Robinson (2006) argues, work on Southern cities has tended to reproduce a binary between innovative, modern-world cities in the Global North and imitative 'third-world cities' in the South, which are assumed to be following in the footsteps of their Northern predecessors. Fortunately, recent years have witnessed a growing body of critical research on cities in the Global South by scholars based in these regions, including in South Asia.

Despite the growth in South Asian urban studies, much research remains to be done. The scale and pace of urban change in this region requires that scholars reflect on the social, political, economic, and ecological impacts of urbanisation on South Asian cities and their citizenry. This volume is one small effort to do just that. Comprised of empirically-grounded original research, this volume approaches the city as a site of multiple contestations and contradictions and aims to highlight struggles over space, resources, identities, and meaning taking place within South Asian cities in response to processes of neoliberal urbanisation. The papers in this collection are focused largely on the ways in which the adoption of neoliberal forms of urbanisation, manifested in particular ways across diverse contexts, are being

1

experienced and challenged by marginalised citizens across the subcontinent in the form of everyday and long-term struggles.

This collection comprises some of the papers from a conference held at the Lahore University of Management of Sciences (LUMS) between 4–6 March 2016, titled 'Urbanism, Exclusion and Change in South Asia', organised with the help of Ali Raza, Zaib un Nisa Aziz, and Lala Rukh Khan. This conference brought together scholars from across disciplines to explore the multi-faceted nature of urban change in the region. While we had hoped to include papers from across South Asia, the majority of contributions came from Pakistan and India, which is reflected in this volume. This is one of the few collections that include papers focusing on both Indian and Pakistani cities, highlighting similarities and differences in the nature of urban change on both sides of the border (see also Anjaria and McFarlane 2011; Ali and Rieker 2009).

Urban Transformation of the Subcontinent

While many cities in India and Pakistan have a long and rich history dating to precolonial times, both countries have witnessed accelerated urbanisation over the past two decades. While the rate of urban growth in India holds steady at 2.3 per cent per year, according to the World Bank, the number of people living in cities has grown from 20 per cent of the total population in 1971 to 34 per cent in 2019. India is also home to some of the most powerful megacities in the world. While Pakistan's urban revolution started relatively later, it is one of the most rapidly urbanising countries in the region with an urban growth rate of 3.2 per cent. More than a third of Pakistan's population live in cities while another large segment of the population live in rapidly urbanising rural areas, or what Qadeer (2013) has referred to as 'ruralopolises'. Even for those who are living in areas that appear to be clearly rural in character, their lives are in some way touched by cities, pointing to the phenomenon characterised by Janet Abu-Lughod (1991) as 'the urbanisation of everybody'.

Many of the papers in this volume draw attention to the ambiguity around what is considered 'urban', highlighting the fact that the city does not exist as a discrete entity with clearly demarcated boundaries. Rather, cities consist of circulations and flows, crossing whatever administrative borders define their edges (Amin and Thrift 2002). There are often multiple links between the rural and the urban—spatially, socially, economically, and culturally—particularly in postcolonial societies where rural areas have not de-populated and urban areas fail to completely provide means of livelihood for new migrants (Sheppard, Leitner, and Maringanti 2013). Also, much of the urbanisation that is currently taking place is located precisely within the rural, creating peri-urban spaces that are part-urban and part-rural in character, particularly in terms of the emergence of gated communities (see Ortega 2012). Hence, as Reza Ali (2013) argues, it may be more accurate to classify the rural–urban divide as a gradient rather than a dichotomy, particularly in the Global South.

Sociologists have long been concerned about the effects of urbanisation on social life, and, in fact, this was one of the foundational questions of the discipline itself. The pace of urbanisation during the early years of industrialisation in England, for example, led to a crisis of housing and sanitation. Referring to the city of London, the English pamphleteer William Cobbett went so far as to refer to the city as a 'great wen', an oozing cyst, which he saw as a drain on rural England. Similarly, although from a very different perspective, Engels (1844) wrote about the 'repulsive' nature of cities and the 'brutal indifference' that it fostered in its inhabitants. Early sociologists such as George Simmel (1903) and Louis Wirth (1938) worried about the negative social effects of cities on their inhabitants, warning about the potential fragmentation caused by the density and pace of urban life. Hence, the panic that often characterises the discourse on South Asian cities is nothing new even if the conditions under which urbanisation is taking place have shifted considerably.

The period of rapid urbanisation experienced in Western Europe and the United States occurred at a time when these regions were benefitting from uneven capitalist development, built largely at the expense of colonised and formerly colonised nations. The wealth extracted from the Indian subcontinent, for example, directly fuelled the expansion of cities in Great Britain. While the industrial workers in these cities struggled to survive the harsh realities of the capitalist economy, for much of the twentieth century, both Europe and North America maintained some form of welfare state which provided a safety net to cushion the blow for the working classes (Leitner, Sheppard, Sziarto, and Maringanti 2007). Therefore, while the urban experience was far from ideal for many urban inhabitants in these regions—particularly for new migrants and former slaves—the pace and conditions under which urbanisation took place meant that the scale of poverty was considerably less than what we are witnessing in countries of the Global South today, including India and Pakistan. South Asian cities are expanding at a time when government intervention is minimal apart from its role in paving the way for private capital.

Furthermore, these cities are indelibly marked by the experience of colonisation. During the period of colonial rule, the colonising powers often sought to reshape cities within the colonies along the lines of European urban planning, which created new forms of spatial inequality. The echoes of this period have carried over into the postcolonial period (see Sheppard, Leitner, and Maringanti 2013; Hansen and Verkaaik 2009). Therefore, as Anjaria and McFarlane (2011: 6) argue, the city must be understood as a palimpsest 'shaped by accumulations of the past and varied practices in the present.' Furthermore, these cities are expanding under conditions of continued uneven, capitalist expansion as a result of globalisation, which is characterised by growing inequality between cities in the Global North and South and within cities themselves (see Sassen 2012).

The current period of accelerated urbanisation in Pakistan and India comes at a time when neoliberal modes of urbanisation dominate, at least at the level of official discourse. These changes are creating new forms of insecurity and precarity for large segments of the urban population whose fates are increasingly tied to unpredictable market forces. These shifts are leading to an expansion of the informal sphere, with significant segments of the urban population employed within the informal economy, residing in informal housing settlements, and engaging with a range of informal actors in order to access goods and services. As AlSayyad and Roy (2004) point out, while informality may not be new in the Global South, the logic of neoliberalism creates new forms of informality—and with them new forms of insecurities—within the urban sphere.

While many have questioned the analytical worth of 'neoliberalism', which has been accused of simplifying diverse and complex processes at the local level (see Baptista 2013; Ganti 2014), the language of privatisation and efficiency has certainly been adopted by policymakers even if it has not been applied or accepted uniformly at the local level. Many governments, working in tandem with private developers, have imported some form of the 'world-class' and 'smart' city as utopian models of development with little consultation with citizens or consideration of how these models will impact the vast majority of urban dwellers (see Kuldova and Varghese 2017). This has led to a growth in 'privatopias', which cater to a particular segment of the urban population at the expense of the vast majority (McKenzie 1996). While creating more and more bubbles for the elite, this model of urban development has led to the displacement of various populations and an increased sense of insecurity amongst marginalised urban citizens everywhere.

At the same time, it is important to be wary of the flattening effects of 'neoliberalism' as a lens. Critical research must attend to the myriad ways in which this discourse unfolds at the local level, examining the extent to which this discourse is accepted or resisted by various urban actors. As the contributions to this volume so clearly demonstrate, the adoption of neoliberal modes of urban development is far from a smooth or complete process. Rather, these discourses are interpreted and applied in differing manners and to differing extents depending on the setting. Furthermore, urban citizens are not passive observers of urban development but are actively involved in these processes in the context of their everyday lives whether through their participation in these processes or through their resistance.[1]

Neoliberal urban development has been marked by a series of expulsions and displacements (see Sassen 2014) as part of what Harvey has termed the process of 'accumulation by dispossession' (2004). However, processes of dispossession rarely take place in a smooth or straightforward fashion. Rather, they are often met with resistance and are the subject of various types of political mobilisation on the part of urban citizens. The chapters in this collection highlight the myriad ways in which urban dwellers react to neoliberal modes of development, highlighting the complexity and at times the ambiguity of their responses.[2] The contributions to this volume highlight the diverse range of responses one can find amongst urban citizens, which include organised and everyday resistance, quiet encroachment, forced acquiescence, overt acceptance, and even an embrace of neoliberal models by some, depending on the circumstances.[3] An examination of these everyday negotiations demonstrates the nature of South Asian cities as works in progress that are constantly being made and remade through the contestations between multiple actors with varying degrees of power.

Tracing the Contours of Urbanism

One of the most pervasive urban forms to have mushroomed in cities across the world is the gated community or private housing scheme, which caters to the urban elite at the expense of the poor. Shahana Rajani and Heba Islam's chapter on one such gated community, Karachi's Bahria Town, carefully documents the systematic erasure of any local Sindhi or Baloch presence from the area of Gadap in order to create an urban 'utopia' for the city's elite. Their work demonstrates the ways in which the dream of 'the world class city' not only displaces local populations but even attempts to displace any cultural memory of them from the city's landscape. At the same time, this forced erasure is not a seamless process. Rajani and Islam's work highlights the resistance to this project by local residents, who are using multiple channels to claim their rights to the land. Furthermore, the authors carefully document the 'residues' of the past that remain within the local landscape, highlighting the palimpsestic nature of urbanising spaces and thus aiding the process of preserving the area's cultural memory through their own work.

Exploring the dynamics of dispossession as they unfold over time, Hashim bin Rashid and Zainab Moulvi's work on LDA City in Lahore describes the ways in which villages at the expanding edges of the city are being transformed into what developers promise will be Pakistan's largest housing scheme. Through their discussions with local residents, the authors describe the complex negotiations that took place at the local level between villagers, land developers, and the state in order to establish LDA City. Bin Rashid and Moulvi's detailed, long-term fieldwork demonstrates how resistance to the housing scheme diminished over time as many living within the village were gradually worn down and transformed into market subjects. Their research is important in complicating the binary between acceptance and resistance, with villagers exercising their agency within a changing set of constraints by simultaneously protesting and participating in the spatial transformations taking place around them. Their work demonstrates how village residents being enveloped by the city were forced to make compromises within a changing set of circumstances in order to preserve their livelihoods.

The process of displacement and dispossession that accompany the fashioning of the world-class city requires the cooperation and often the active participation of the state. In her chapter on the Jhuggi Mokhampura housing scheme in Amritsar, Helena Cermeño 'looks at the city from below' to shed light on the ways a state-led slum resettlement scheme has altered the way residents relate to the city profoundly exacerbating their social exclusion and marginalisation within the city. Using maps drawn by residents themselves, Cermeño's research documents how the forced relocation of slum dwellers has affected their access to the city. Cermeño highlights the key role of middlemen in the actual mechanics of urban development. In her case study, *pardhans* act as self-appointed representatives of the community and brokers between the slum dweller community and the state. This aspect of her research is reminiscent of Verkaaik and Hansen's notion of 'urban infra-power' (2009: 15) where certain individuals, 'the hustler, the hard man, the wheeler dealer', are able to benefit from their knowledge of the city even as the vast majority are further marginalised through processes of dispossession. Her chapter demonstrates how certain groups within the city are rendered invisible through the reordering of the urban landscape.

All three chapters highlight the ways in which neoliberal modes of urban development are increasing segregation and fragmentation within cities across the subcontinent, moving some marginalised citizens out to the peripheries and bringing others in against their will. In the case of Bahria Town in Karachi, indigenous communities are being systematically pushed off their land and their presence erased from the landscape itself. In the case of LDA City, the process is more complicated, as villagers were slowly made partners in the process of their own dispossession through their co-optation into the land market. In Cermeño's paper, she demonstrates how those living in slums for decades scattered around various parts of Amritsar were relocated to the margins of the city by the state through a long process of negotiation in a bid to refashion Amritsar into a 'smart city'. However, this refashioning only served to further exclude those who were already marginalised within the urban landscape.

A heightening atmosphere of insecurity and fear in cities is accompanying processes of fragmentation across the world, particularly amongst the urban elite. The proliferation of gated communities and of private security firms is a testament to this. Much has been written about the increased securitisation of cities over the past decades beginning with the work of Mike Davis (1990) on Los Angeles. Teresa Caldeira (2000) has documented this process in the city of São Paulo, where the fear of crime has led to the creation of what she calls 'a city of walls'. Certainly, South Asia has not been spared the fragmentary effects of this growing discourse of fear, with the architecture of insecurity radically reshaping urban landscapes.

Noman Ahmed's chapter carefully documents this hyper-securitisation in Karachi—a city that has experienced some of the highest levels of crime and political violence of any city in the region since the 1990s. Ahmed's chapter maps the emergence of multiple barriers within the city, both in terms of physical barriers such as walls and gates and 'silent barriers' such as wall-chalking and flags, which are aimed at restricting the mobility of various groups within the city who are perceived as threatening. These barriers have been erected by state and private actors, which is leading to what Ahmed refers to as a 'regime of fear' within the city, resulting in increased social distance and fragmentation in a city already scarred by decades of violence.

The growth and spread of neoliberal modes of urban development has meant an overall shrinking of 'the public' in terms of space as well as goods and services. Asad Sayeed and Kabeer Dawani document the withdrawal of the state from the arena of public transport, particularly since the 1970s in Karachi. Rather than attributing this decline to the 'transport mafia', which is popularly blamed for the failures of this sector, Sayeed and Kabeer demonstrate how the withdrawal of the state is largely due to financial logic. As the authors argue, urban public transport generally operates at a loss and hence requires state subsidisation. While the earlier Pakistani state invested in public goods, since the 1970s, the state has abdicated its responsibilities in the interests of private actors who themselves have withdrawn because of a lack of profitability. The losers in this process have been the city's vast majority who do not have access to private transport, and who are forced to crowd into unsafe forms of mass transit in order to make their daily commutes. Sayeed and Kabeer's work demonstrates how the neoliberal model of urban development and the privatisation of formerly public goods have not only dispossessed marginalised citizens of land and resources but also of their right to access the city itself.

Contestations within the city are not limited solely to the land. Rohit Negi and Prerna Srigyan's chapter documents the struggles over air that have taken place in what has come to be known as one of the most polluted cities in the world since the early twentieth century—Delhi. They highlight the increase in what they call 'toxic urbanism'—a poisonous and risky form of urban change—in Delhi, particularly since the early 2000s when the city became one of the regional epicentres of the 'India Shining' campaign, a campaign to promote neoliberal modes of development spearheaded by the Bharatiya Janata Party (BJP). The authors trace the changes in the forms of activism around air, which earlier took place in courtrooms and focused on protecting the city's elite at the expense of the poor, to gradually shifting towards environmental justice positions, which more commonly take place through public advocacy and calls for more egalitarian forms of development, placing restrictions on the elite and on polluting industries in the interests of the wider public. While many limitations remain when it comes to environmental movements within the city, Negi and Srigyan's research demonstrates the possibility of effective collective resistance to unbridled economic growth models.

Struggles over resources including land and access to public goods often take place within the electoral arena, with parties using access to these resources as a means of gaining political support. Sonal Sharma, Shahana Sheikh, and Subhadra Banda's research on electoral processes in Delhi compares the demands of those living in informal settlements for access to services such as electricity, water and sewerage, and for security of tenure, with the promises made by various political parties. Like others in this collection, their work highlights the role of intermediaries such as *pardhans* and resident welfare associations in placing demands before parties and mobilising residents in support of particular candidates. Their research finds that most of the promises regarding access to services made by parties during elections remain unfulfilled, which is why each election brings a fresh set of similar processes. This detailed analysis of the dynamic of elections in Delhi highlights how parties use the exclusion produced by neoliberal modes of urban development to maintain their power over marginalised citizens through repeated unfulfilled promises and incremental provisions.

While one can trace instances of both acquiescence and resistance to processes of urban development on the part of urban citizens, the vast majority of those living at the margins of the city are simply trying to live their lives in the best way possible within a constantly changing set of constraints. Abdoumaliq Simone (2010; 2016) documents the ways those living in urban spaces that are seemingly uninhabitable actually manage to survive through 'anticipatory politics', which encompasses a range of everyday practices and creative strategies. The work of Pinky Chandran and Kabir Arora focuses on one such case—the informal waste economy situated in the area of Nayandahalli in Bangalore. Their research demonstrates how those living on the extreme fringes of the city both socially and geographically are actually central to its economy. Those involved in the informal waste sector provide essential environmental services to the city, filling in where the state is failing. However, rather than being recognised and rewarded for their contribution to the urban economy, these workers are actually being further displaced through large-scale urban infrastructure projects and market-led gentrification.

While processes of neoliberal urban development are reshaping the urban landscape profoundly, the city itself is being made through the interaction of these processes with its citizens. Muntasir Sattar's contribution on the encounter between the city and middle-class male migrants to the city of Lahore demonstrates the dialectical relationship between the city and its inhabitants clearly. While the city of Lahore is being rapidly transformed by large-scale, top-down infrastructure projects aimed at creating a capital-attracting world-class city, Sattar's research demonstrates how young, middle-class migrants who come to the city from rural areas in order to fulfil their educational and career-related aspirations are also transforming one particular locality as they are themselves being transformed. Through a rich ethnography of a locality now dominated by hostels catering to these migrants, Sattar's chapter highlights how members of the middle class, including the owners and the residents of these hostels, are trying to make it within the new urban economy. This intervention challenges the dichotomy presented in much critical urban studies' literature between elite, gated communities and marginalised informal settlements, shedding light on the changes taking place in the middle-class spaces within the city.

What several contributions make clear is that while the majority of urban citizens are being marginalised by processes of neoliberal urban development, a select minority are not only managing to survive but are managing to thrive, particularly those groups who are capitalising on the market. These include the hostel owners presented in Sattar's chapter, the new property dealers in the areas where projects such as Bahria Town and DHA City are being established, the *pardhans* and resident welfare associations that mediate between marginalised citizens and the state, and others.

The authors describe the heated contests taking place in Pakistani and Indian cities not merely over land and resources but over the very meaning of the city itself. The contributions in this collection demonstrate how the bottom-up struggles of urban inhabitants to make it in the city are actually what make the city itself. These are not stories of passive victims but of active, creative agents who are constantly on the move (Simone 2010). These movements and negotiations are part of an emerging politics within the city, which has the potential to challenge top-down approaches to urban development. Hence, this collection is not simply a chronicle of urban tragedies. The themes of insecurity, marginalisation, displacement, and dispossession are intertwined with themes of active negotiation, resistance, and struggle. The dark side of urban development is shot through with rays of hope. Leitner, Sheppard, Sziarto, and Maringanti (2007: 2) argue that 'close, empirically-grounded analysis is essential to better understand neoliberalism and to imagine and create alternative urban futures'. This collection of carefully-researched studies of the lived realities of cities in India and Pakistan is a modest attempt to do just that.

NOTES

1. This builds on the approach taken by Anjaria and McFarlane (2011) in their edited collection on South Asian cities, which focuses on navigation as a means of understanding the ways urban inhabitants produce the city through everyday practices and contestations. It also draws inspiration from the work of Kuldova and Varghese (2017) in their collection of papers exploring the notion of 'urban utopias' in India and Sri Lanka.

2. Kingfisher and Maskovsky (2008) call for approaches to the study of neo-liberalism that highlight the instabilities and partialities of this concept as it plays out in particular contexts. Similarly, Leitner, Sheppard, Sziarto, and Maringanti (2007) argue for research that is attendant to the bottom-up contestations of neoliberalism, arguing

that top-down analyses actually serve to reinforce neoliberalism's hegemonic status.

3. While much has been written about the nature of cities as sites for collective action in the form of social movements (see Castells 1983; Harvey 2012), very often resistance can take subtler, everyday forms (see Scott 1985). Asef Bayat (2010) has highlighted the various ways that marginalised citizens in the Middle East endeavour to bring about social change through 'social non-movements' in what he calls 'the quiet encroachment of the ordinary'. This refers to the ways that disenfranchised urban citizens forge different urban realities through their everyday struggles within situations of constraint.

REFERENCES

Abu-Lughod, Janet L., *Changing Cities: Urban Sociology*, New York: Harpercollins College Division, 1991.

Ali, Kamran A., and Martina Rieker (eds.), *Comparing Cities: The Middle East and South Asia*, Karachi: Oxford University Press, 2009.

Amin, Ash, and Nigel Thrift, *Cities: Reimagining the Urban*, Cambridge: Polity Press, 2002.

Anjaria, Jonathan S., and Colin McFarlane (eds.), *Urban Navigations: Politics, Space and the City in South Asia*, New York: Routledge, 2011.

Baptista, Idalina, 'The Travels of Critiques of Neoliberalism: Urban Experiences from the "Borderlands"', *Urban Geography*, 34, 5 (2013), pp. 590–611.

Bayat, Asif, *Life As Politics: How Ordinary People Change the Middle East*, Redwood City, CA: Stanford University Press, 2013.

Caldeira, Teresa P. R., *City of Walls: Crime, Segregation, and Citizenship in São Paulo*, Oakland, CA: University of California Press, 2000.

Castells, Manuel, *The City and the Grassroots: A Cross-cultural Theory of Urban Social Movements (no. 7)*, Oakland, CA: Univ of California Press, 1983.

Davis, Mike, 'Fortress LA', in Kleniewski, N. (ed.), *Cities and Society*, Hoboken, NJ: John Wiley & Sons, 2008, pp. 267–83.

Ganti, Tejaswini, 'Neoliberalism', *Annual Review of Anthropology*, 43, 1 (2014), pp. 89–104.

Hansen, Thomas Blom, and Oskar Verkaaik, 'Introduction—Urban Charisma: On Everyday Mythologies in the City', *Critique of Anthropology*, 29, 1 (2009), pp. 5–26.

Harvey, David, *From the Right to the City to the Urban Revolution*, New York: Verso, 2012.

————, 'The "New Imperialism": Accumulation by Dispossession', *Actuel Marx*, 35, 1 (2004), pp. 71–90.

Kingfisher, Catherine, and Jeff Maskovsky, 'Introduction: The Limits of Neoliberalism', *Critique of Anthropology*, 28, 2 (2008), pp. 115–26.

Kuldova, Tereza, and Mathew A. Varghese (eds.), *Urban Utopias: Excess and Expulsion in Neoliberal South Asia*, New York: Springer, 2017.

Leitner, Helga, Eric S. Sheppard, Kristin Sziarto and Anant Maringanti, 'Contesting Urban Futures: Decentering Neoliberalism', in Leitner, H., J. Peck and H. Sheppard (eds.), *Contesting Neoliberalism: Urban Frontiers*, New York: Guilford Press, 2007, pp. 1–25.

McKenzie, Evan, *Privatopia: Homeowner Associations and the Rise of Private Residential Government*, New Haven, CT: Yale University Press, 1996.

Robinson, Jennifer, *Ordinary Cities: Between Modernity and Development*, 4, Hove, UK: Psychology Press, 2006.

Roy, Ananya, and Nezar AlSayyad (eds.), *Urban Informality: Transnational Perspectives from the Middle East, Latin America, And South Asia,* Lanham, MD: Lexington Books, 2004.

Sassen, Saskia, *Expulsions: Brutality and Complexity in the Global Economy,* Cambridge, MA: Harvard University Press, 2014.

————, *Cities in a World Economy,* Thousand Oaks, CA: Sage Publications, 2011.

Scott, James C. , *Weapons of the Weak: Everyday Forms of Peasant Resistance,* New Haven and London: Yale University Press, 1985.

Sheppard, Eric S., Helga Leitner, and Anant Maringanti, 'Provincializing Global Urbanism: A Manifesto', *Urban Geography,* 34, 7 (2013), pp. 893–900.

Simmel, Georg, *The Metropolis and Mental Life,* Chicago: University of Chicago Press, 1961.

Simone, AbdouMaliq, 'It's Just the City after All!', *International Journal of Urban and Regional Research,* 40, 1 (2016), pp. 210–18.

————, *City life from Jakarta to Dakar: Movements at the Crossroads,* New York: Routledge, 2010.

Wirth, Louis, 'Urbanism as a Way of Life', *American Journal of Sociology,* 44, 1 (1938), pp. 1–24.

1

Entangling the 'Global City': Everyday Resistance in Gadap, Karachi

Shahana Rajani and Heba Islam

Introduction

With its haphazard construction and neglected infrastructure, an urban utopia is hard to imagine in the sprawling metropolis of Karachi, Pakistan. But with little land to spare for grand visions in an increasingly congested space, real estate ventures now look to the peripheries of the urban landscape to create the 'world-class city'. One such venture is the mega real estate project of Bahria Town, marketed as Asia's largest real estate company. Spread over 23,300 acres, this project is based in Gadap Town, a vast region that encircles most of the city and is home to indigenous Sindhi- and Balochi-speaking communities (Ali and Zaman 2019). A Bahria Town advertising campaign was organised in 2015, with eager consumers responding speedily to what was bound to be either a profitable investment, or a comfortable home away from the squalor of the city. From the media campaign, one might never have known that Gadap was already settled by a local population long before real estate's foray into the area.

Our research in Gadap began with an interest in exploring the excessive use of force involved in the making of Bahria Town's imported and secure geography (Ali and Zaman 2019) and the erasure and exclusion of indigenous pasts and presents. Our essay draws on research and fieldwork conducted between February and July 2016. We participated in a collective research project titled 'Gadap Sessions', organised by the Karachi Art Anti-University[1] in collaboration with the Karachi Indigenous Rights Alliance (KIRA).[2] Over six months, along with 11 other participants, we began to document Gadap's disappearing and emergent ecologies, new architectures, disappearing

14

histories, and persevering struggles. In the process of documentation, however, it became clear that the 'vanishing' that Bahria Town engaged in (Ali and Zaman 2019) was neither total, nor passively received. Rather than the imposition of a 'new' geography upon an old one, we witnessed 'an entangled landscape in which multiple spatialities, temporalities, and power relations combine' (Moore 2005: 4), producing a more complex narrative than the one we originally conceived.

This chapter approaches the new future envisioned for Gadap as an entanglement rather than a clear-cut process by which 'progress' and 'development' enact violence and erasure. We find that non-linear temporalities continue to operate on the edges of the city, leaving behind residues of a local geography that is not only cherished but acts as an agent of resistance. In the first section, we explore the ways in which the construction and development of Bahria Town is performing a simultaneous forgetting and erasure that not only relegates the indigenous to the past but attempts to render the latter's spatiality non-existent. Specifically, we do so by examining the architecture, visuality and accompanying materialities of the new geography being carved into Gadap, analysing both its form and function. We place this in the context of similar developments taking place in new megacities that aspire to be 'global' such as Dubai, which is a central inspiration for Bahria Town and, more widely, the political and economic elite of Pakistan.

In the second section, we challenge this positing of Gadap as 'empty' by highlighting the rich sediment and layering of histories that are both local and widely connected to trans-regional networks of trade and religion. We describe the ways in which Gadap has long been a nourishing spatiality rather than a barren one, which has historically made it the target of both structural and brute violence. In the final section, we examine how the spectral traces of the indigenous landscape—specifically saintly graves—have been 'allowed' to remain while barriers, gates, and artificial lakes have replaced homes, fields, and entire mountains.

We read these less-assuming structures, the graves, through the lens of texture, as a more granular form of opposition to large-scale erasures of indigenous life, a means by which agency saturates everyday existence. The enduring presence of these graves allows for fissures and disturbances in the new landscape and creates avenues and narratives for resistance, community building, and indigenous mobility where other such attempts have failed in the face of Bahria Town's construction and destruction. Through this chapter, we emphasise that, while Bahria Town and similar global city utopias aim to identify themselves as the future and the local as the past, it is these ventures in themselves that are phantasmatic, using a glossy exterior to, only partially successfully, hide the phantoms in the materialities left behind by previous residents (Navaro-Yashin 2012: 14).

Architectures of Forgetting

The Bahria Town map provided to us by an enthusiastic realtor presents a fantasy-scape of an elite, utopic city. The promotional pamphlet in which this map appears informs us that Bahria Town Karachi is Pakistan's most luxuriously planned project, integrated with world-class infrastructure and amenities, where each sector has its own park, sports area, mosque, and school: 'Welcome to Futuristic Living!'. Jinnah Avenue, a 400-feet wide main boulevard, serves as the backbone of this picturesque geography, weaving together the international theme park, cineplex, zoo, botanical gardens, golf course, lakes, universities, hospitals, and stadiums. The only reference on the map to what Gadap looked like before Bahria Town's incursion into real estate on the margins of Karachi is the Langeji River, a tributary of the Malir River, snaking its way alongside, but not quite inside, the gated city-to-be. It is not labelled, unlike every other place on the map. It remains an innocuous blue line. The remaining landscape presents itself as a pastiche of proudly imported elements that are cut-and-pasted onto Gadap to create a vision of this new 'world-class' city.

The map provided by the realtor bears almost no trace of indigenous presence, no mention of the Sindhi and Baloch communities who have been living on this land for generations. Their villages, homes, agricultural fields, and pastoral lands are denied representation and have disappeared from our view. The unmarked river, therefore, is the sole element that hints at another phenomenon altogether—that the real estate development taking place in the area is as much about construction as it is about destruction; a future built upon the erasure of a past and a present, its proudly 'memorable' new structures simultaneously practicing how to forget.

The map presupposes Gadap to be a blank, ahistorical site. The panoramic views on an official promotional video available online show a barren and empty landscape, accompanied by a voiceover that describes the location before Bahria Town's development as *'ghairabad, banjar, aur ghairmehfooz'* (unpopulated, barren, and unsafe). The rendering of Gadap as a blank text waiting to be inscribed by development continues the colonial myth of *terra nullius*, a no man's land of dry dusty paths and thorny bushes waiting to be ordered and made productive (Tiffin and Lawson 2002: 5). While the urban is conceived as a space that is full of historical meaning, the rural is represented and experienced as a void, an absence of historical significance. This juxtaposition hides the violence of urban development, which is based on rural expropriation and indigenous dispossession in order to create 'high-yield real estate'. Chattopadhyay explains that, 'Cities and villages in this world view occupy two different times, not just spaces, and it assumes that rural "backwaters" must be brought within the time and spatial regime of the urban' (2012: 16). In a similar vein, the Karachi Strategic Development Plan 2020 implemented a new growth strategy in 2007 to redevelop Karachi's periphery by incorporating villages and reconfiguring 'empty land' (Anwar 2013: 4). This plan opened up the rural land and villages of Gadap for privatisation and development. Bahria Town's private venture is set within this larger trend of suburbanisation and the implementation of a world-class city vision.

The promotional video highlights the role of Bahria Town in transforming this supposed barren wasteland into a 'secure and complete, gated city'. This contrast is perpetuated constantly through its use of monuments, place-naming and place-marking. The naming of Bahria Town's main boulevard, 'Jinnah Avenue', appeals to a nationalist memory, which, by invoking the founding father of Pakistan, excludes and removes indigenous histories and claims of belonging that stretch back beyond 1947. Similarly, the entrance wall of Bahria Town Karachi displays an image of Jinnah alongside two flags—one with Bahria Town's icon, the other with Pakistan's flag. This smooth incorporation of Jinnah draws upon existing nationalist visual tropes, which, as Iftikhar Dadi explains, creates a hegemonic popular spectacle of continuity and legitimation (2007: 17). Bahria Town is strategically marketed not as a profit-driven, privatised venture, but one that is magnanimously continuing the nation-building project. The promotional video ends by exclaiming that this new development is 'a gift by Bahria Town to the people of Karachi, and to Pakistan'. Such narratives are essentially 'organised forgetting as a keen operation to construct a bourgeois nationalism' (Sargin 2004: 664). It seems as if memory (or rather, its erasure) is utilised by real estate interests in Gadap to provide legitimacy to its venture, to turn destruction into construction, in the name of nation building and progress.

Similar to Bahria Town projects in Lahore and Rawalpindi, Bahria Town Karachi houses a mini Eiffel Tower and Stonehenge, Corinthian columns, and a Trafalgar Square with a twist, where the central figurative statue is replaced with a large 'Allah' sculpture. If there are 'no more obvious markers of memory in a city than its monuments and no more obvious sites for crises of memory' (Crinson 2005: xvi), what do we make of the monuments that seem to invoke a non-memory, a symbolism almost completely foreign? This unanchoring of Bahria Town from the historically and geographically specific landscape of Gadap isolates the planned entity from its physical and social surroundings in an attempt to connect it with regions remote and Western. As Chattopadhyay explains, this dual move underscores 'a pattern based on the idea that forms developed in other parts of the world can be cut and pasted in the new locale without significant change.' In this equation, any reference to the local 'is unnecessary and indeed undesirable' (2012: 34). Sargin's note on bourgeois nationalism is thus particularly relevant, keeping in mind that much of the corporation's architecture consists of a motley of iconic monuments that appropriate global symbols within a larger nationalist framework. The organised forgetting is the erasure of Gadap's dynamic history and present, its longstanding indigenous population, and its place as a source of livelihood earned through livestock and farming.

What may appear as bizarre and kitsch at first sight is in fact a call to a future that is evoked through the replication of Western icons. Rather than rewriting history, the construction of what Bahria Town calls a luxury 'lifestyle destination' treats the landscape as a blank text on which to write the future. This evocation does not merely create an aesthetic utopia but serves the function of placing Bahria Town, not Gadap, on the proverbial map. The 'rural backwaters' of Gadap are washed from the slate of memory. It is far more convenient to inscribe future aspirations on the landscape when the monuments seem to say: there is nowhere to look but forward, and simultaneously westward, towards 'progress'. Trafalgar Square and the Eiffel Tower are the icons of cities that have already placed themselves on the map; Paris and London are viewed universally as global capitals.

Jennifer Robinson explains that urbanism in the Global South takes its inspiration from these Western cities precisely because they are assumed to be at an advanced stage of development, occupying a future time zone (2006: 3).

These hierarchies formulate fixed codes of urban modernity, embedded in colonial and neo-imperial power relations, and force non-Western cities into playing a punitive game of catching-up. The erasure and replacement of Gadap's local landscape with an entirely foreign, Westernised landscape is, therefore, in line with these biases inherent in global (read: Western) urbanism. By importing a Western pictorialisation of space and time through a 'cut-and-paste' matrix of picturesque tourist icons, Bahria Town presents an alternate reality that is easily identifiable, consumable, and compatible with elite desires for modernity.

Thus, while the monuments littered through the gated city's landscape seem like a pastiche of imitative urbanisms, one must view them as a careful ordering of space, power, and a global vision. This becomes apparent when observing this view in person; this is uncannily similar to that described by Timothy Mitchell where everything is 'arranged before an observing subject into a system of signification, declaring itself to be a mere object, a mere "signifier of" something further' (2002a: 500). Though Mitchell is referring to the colonial era, his conceptualisation of 'the world-as-exhibition as a place where the artificial, the model and the plan were employed to generate an unprecedented effect of order and certainty' (2002a: 496) finds deep resonance within the exhibitionary order of Bahria Town. Its monuments are not merely a collection of knick-knacks or viewing experiences, but also a carefully curated organisation of the world into a system of objects that enables it to evoke some larger meaning of progress and modernity.

In this sense, Bahria Town's aspirations are strikingly similar to Dubai's, and the corporation proudly declares its hope to exceed Dubai one day. According to a press release on their official website, the patriotically named Jinnah Avenue is inspired by Sheikh Zayed Road in Dubai. Given this inspiration, it is pertinent here to examine what exactly the landscaping of Dubai entails:

> Everything must be world-class [a term often used in promotional materials by Bahria Town] ... Dubai is building the world's largest theme park, the biggest mall, (and within it, the largest aquarium), the tallest building, the largest international airport, the biggest artificial island, the first sunken hotel and so on. (Davis 2006: 47)

Bahria Town's promotional video makes similar claims: the world's third largest mosque, along with Pakistan's largest cricket stadium, shopping mall, and golf course. This description of form is important because it speaks to function. Dubai, too, is noted for its efforts to establish itself as a transnational urban hub. Like Gadap, Dubai's story has been presented as one of an empty desert, waiting to be monetised and made productive. The irony, of course, lies in how the architecture and monumentality of Bahria Town and cities like Dubai have redefined 'productivity' itself through their organised erasing and forgetting. Whereas Gadap has historically been home to farms, livestock, and a fresh water supply, the new landscape's idea of productivity is one actually embedded in hyper-consumption. This section earlier speaks of the need for Bahria Town to place itself on the world map, but the deliberate amnesia induced by the monuments also normalise consumption and speculative capital over the kind of historical connectivity and productivity to which Gadap has been witness. Bahria Town is therefore not merely an imitation of 'global cities' but a simulation twice removed from reality, an imitation of an imitation, i.e. Dubai, a city that has built itself as a reflection of other global cities.

In describing an iconic building in Malaysia, Sklair describes how the Islamic motifs and Malaysian design elements do not hinder the functioning of the shopping mall on its ground floor, one of the most well-known transnational spaces in the continent (2010: 5). Similarly in Bahria Town, the Islamised Trafalgar Square and the multi-domed Grand Jamia Mosque—set to be the largest mosque in the world after those in Mecca and Medina— do not contradict but rather complement the 'idyllic neighborhood [sic] where children play in the streets and homeowners stroll to the local health club or mini-mart' (Cochrane 2008). While the Islamic motifs may seem odd in a landscape so focused on evoking a sense of the international and foreign, it reflects a limited flexibility in the codes of global urbanism to cater to specific audiences. On one level, it softens the overt Westernisation through a tint of religious symbolism, making the project more consumable in the context of Pakistan. However, the eclectic hodgepodge of recognisably Islamic elements within the world-class aesthetics of Bahria Town is more than just an attempt to balance modernity with religious symbolism. Moser (2012), in her discussion of trends in contemporary Malaysian urbanism, connects the adoption of High Islam—a generic Middle Eastern architectural idiom—to broader transnational religious change. She argues that the inclusion of overtly Muslim symbolism should be understood in the context of growing connections between Malaysia and the Middle East. In adopting this Islamic idiom, however artificially, Bahria Town is positioning itself to attract attention and more importantly the investment of Pakistanis abroad and the wealthy Arab elites. A *Newsweek* article linked on the corporation's official website makes visible Bahria Town's target audience, stating that it is drawing 'Pakistan expats and a smattering of wealthy Arab Muslims away from places like Dubai' (Cochrane 2008).

Similar to Dubai's malls, seven-star hotels, and clubs, Bahria Town's amenities are available for consumption to a privileged class who can afford to live within its secured, monitored boundary walls. The exclusion is one not just of historical representation but of current accessibility. The monuments and architecture of Bahria Town arguably represent a more structural exclusion. Forgetting in and of itself would not be so significant if it did not result in deliberate segregation. Hence, the function of the new Bahria Town landscape, we argue, is not merely one of transforming the local into the transnational, of normalising hyper-consumption as progress, and of encouraging global capital and investment, although all these aspirations play a role. It also plays a role of fragmentation and division (Acuto 2010), where global connectivity and symbolic exhibitions render invisible and exclude entire populations based on what is considered culturally relevant, what is affordable/unaffordable, and what is perceived as secure.

Katheryne Mitchell (2003: 444) argues that patriotism is vital in the production of public memory, because it can navigate both vernacular loyalties to local and familiar places and official loyalties to national and imagined structures, but in the case of Bahria Town in Gadap, there is no local, or familiar. Only the blandly named Jinnah Avenue and the gigantic Grand Jamia Mosque placate 'official loyalties', while vernacular loyalties are ignored. This is fitting for the larger narrative Bahria Town perpetuates through its construction/destruction: real estate developers and corporate interests are less interested in producing public memory than they are in acting as if there is nothing to remember.

Histories and Practices of Place-making

Beneath the new tar and concrete of Bahria Town lie spectral traces of a local geography of belonging that is being violently erased by the new development. While Bahria Town presents Gadap as *'banjar'* and *'ghairabaad'*, this area is settled by at least 45 villages belonging to Sindhi and Baloch communities with ancestral claims to the land. Residents from affected villages explained to us that their everyday life has historically centred on Pahwaro Mountain, which is fast disappearing as Bahria Town gouges and levels the land to construct a more suitable and pruned landscape for Phase 1 and 2 of Bahria Town. Spanning over 3,000 acres, Pahwaro is considered common land, where communities have collective ownership of these areas, with equal rights of access and use. Deen Mohammad, from Nabi Bakhsh Gabol Goth (village) explained:

> Pahwaro is our whole way of life. It has protected and sustained us, providing water and pasture. The village lands on which our homes are built are not so important. Much more valuable is the pastoral land and mountains around us that sustain our livestock … Bahria Town is not just usurping our lands, but destroying our way of life.

Mah Bibi from Jumma Khan Goth elaborated further: 'All us women would go together to Pahwaro to wash our clothes there. We would go with our goats and roam around there in the day. Children would go to play there, they would climb Pahwaro.'

As Donald Moore has suggested, contemporary struggles over land remain 'crucially dependent on the diverse ways land comes to be inhabited, laboured on, idiomatically expressed, and suffered for in specific moments and milieus' (2005: 2). 'Pahwaro' is a Sindhi word which means to struggle in the face of difficulties and hardships. Its name is a testament to the communities' relationship to this land—the spatial and temporal practices of struggle and place-making that have marked this landscape with meaning and memory over centuries. Moore argues that the indigenous Kaerezians in Zimbabwe invoked memories of suffering for territory to stake claims to postcolonial land rights. In doing so, they fused notions of persevering and enduring struggle to territory. In this conception, place has a history of becoming, where land bears both material and symbolic 'traces of historically sedimented processes—the drying and hardening of soil as well as situated struggles' (Moore 2005: 2). Similarly, the evocation of hardships in the name Pahwaro acquires a renewed significance in response to ongoing dispossession, where communities can stake claims and exercise agency through histories of 'suffering for territory'.

During our interviews, as residents referred to the material features of their everyday life, we became aware that the mountain and surrounding landscapes are dotted with local landmarks that bear witness to indigenous histories, practices, and mobilities. Mando Taraii, Thango Chakhor, Savesar Taraii, and Lala Pir are Baloch place-names that preserve memories of their predecessors who settled in these areas after digging wells and finding water. These place-names record and remember these histories of becoming, locating them not just in memory but also in the material landscape. However, these places are not simply containers of history but are made meaningful through everyday socialities of work, leisure, and conviviality, as highlighted by Deen Mohammad and Mah Bibi. Padaraii Chhab is another place in the mountains where every year after the rains, people of Nabi Baksh Gabol Goth would go live with their livestock. '*Padar*' in Balochi means temporary/nomadic, and '*chhab*' means a small waterway. There would be enough pasture and water to last three to four months, and they would live in temporary homes here for that period. These place-names are embedded and implicated in the way people engage and inhabit their land. They enable an oral transmission of genealogical histories and practices of settlement, an inter-generational sharing of familiarity and knowledge about the memorial narratives embedded in the landscape.

Interestingly, place-names not only record human actions upon land but also the natural landscape and ecology of Pahwaro. '*Roz*', '*Kaccha*', and '*Chakor*' are Balochi names given to streams and places where water would collect after rains. While Bahria Town has catastrophically decimated the natural landscape, these landmarks recall a nourishing mountain with an abundance of water and life, bearing witness to the dense interconnections between people and nature, to a practice and politics of care and respect for the ecology and natural orders of landscapes. Within this indigenous geography, textures of ecology and everyday life are inextricably entwined.

The network of place-names is not merely limited to familial or genealogical connections to the land; it also stretches past to incorporate longer histories. Pahwaro was located at the crossroads of a historic trade route to China and the Middle East that connected the coast of Makran to Bhambore. It is also part of the ancient pilgrimage route to Hinglaj Mata (an important Hindu temple located in Balochistan). Hence, Pahwaro was not an isolated locality of indigenous inhabitation but a site of passage, connected to a vast network of regions. Local place-names bear witness to this history of travel and mobility. Dotting the landscape are anonymous graves of such travellers. In an interview conducted on 7 June 2016, the archaeologist

Kaleemullah Lashari dated some of these graves back to the fourteenth and fifteenth centuries.

The local landmark of Bhagi, which means 'to run' in Sindhi, is named after the journey of Sussui who crossed the mountains of Pahwaro in search of her lover, Punhu, in the twelfth century—a history that also survives in popular folklore. Deen Mohammad elaborated that this site was named Bhagi by those who witnessed the suffering Sussui as she crossed Pahwaro. While writing *Shah Jo Risalo* in the eighteenth century, Shah Abdul Latif Bhittai decided to trace the footsteps of Sussui in order to excavate and experience the spectral traces of her suffering embedded in the landscape. Memories of his journey also survive; the place where Bhittai rested for the night became a site of pilgrimage. According to local narratives, today, on this site, stand the toilets of the Grand Jamia Mosque.

These landmarks bear witness to a radically different conception of place, to borrow from Doreen Massey, where relations are not contained within the place, but 'stretch beyond it, tying any particular locality into wider relations and processes in which other places are implicated as well' (1994: 120). For Massey, such a conception of place offers a counterargument to inward-looking, exclusive, or reactionary places such as gated communities. While Bahria Town's monuments short-circuit the local and regional, emulating and exhibiting a global/Western aesthetics derived from London, New York, and Paris, these local landmarks are reminders of a landscape that was/is anchored in regional networks. In contrast to the violent laying down of colonial/postcolonial boundaries, precolonial place-making in Gadap was the result of an accretion of diversity and connectivity.

The border-making and boundary-drawing project of the Bahria Town is not simply denying indigenous communities access to their lands, but actively destroying and erasing it. Mahnoor Bibi told us, 'Now when we remember Pahwaro, our heart hurts. Our lands, our Pahwaro—everything is snatched from us. These memories haunt me daily.' Pointing to the Bahria Town wall that now separates their village from their ancestral lands, Deen Mohammad exclaimed, 'We watch helplessly as Pahwaro is torn down, rock by rock.' The destruction of the indigenous geography of Pahwaro is an integral part of what we earlier refer to as organised forgetting, which repackages Gadap as a *tabula rasa*. The obliteration of the material indigenous landscape, torn down 'rock by rock', is an attempt to inscribe Gadap with emptiness. This destruction erases (and legitimises the erasure of) existing social and geo-cultural formations in preparation for the projection and emplacement of a new order. Gadap thus becomes an empirical 'object of development' presented as a space distinct from history and economy, while Bahria Town presents itself as an objective entity seeking to transform the land through scientific and technological means (Mitchell 2002b: 230). The textures of everyday life are cauterised, replaced with the gloss of Bahria Town's new, imported, and secured geography.

Gadap's residents view Bahria Town as a militarised terrain of occupation, where the destruction of Pahwaro is accompanied by a new infrastructure of walls, roads, and policing systems. Deborah Cowen explains that, 'in colonial and settler colonial contexts, infrastructure is often the means of dispossession, and the material force that implants colonial economies and socialities' (2017). Kanda Khan from Jumma Goth, one of the residents we spoke to, invoked this colonial legacy when he explained to us that 'Bahria Town has entered Gadap, just like the East India Company'.

Deen Mohammad also referred to Bahria Town's violence as the most recent manifestation of a long history of spatial reorganisations resulting from colonial restructuring and resettling of nomadic indigenous communities. Through surveys and enclosures, indigenous communities were colonised and forced to settle on land redefined as private property. The British built their property system on 'a vision of the environment that made a fundamental distinction between productive land and what the British called waste' (Gilmartin 2015: 80). These wastelands—arid areas of pastoral wandering that carried the potential promise of future state-initiated transformation—were held in general or public interest as state property. The postcolonial development of Bahria Town, in transforming indigenous lands into prime real estate, is mobilising the colonial rhetoric of Gadap as standing-reserve. Therefore, historical and contemporary violence in Gadap reveals the persistence of colonial and capitalist systems in sustaining and facilitating urban development through indigenous dispossession.

The material reordering of Gadap through new infrastructure began in 2015, when Bahria Town started constructing *chowkis* (land markers) on indigenous lands. These were five-by-five feet, white structures on which 'Bahria Town' was written. When we first visited Bahria Town, we found hundreds of these *chowkis* dotting the landscape. These were an attempt to de- and re-territorialise the land—material and symbolic re-inscriptions that made visible Bahria's new control over the land. The infrastructure of roads and walls followed soon after to enact containment, disconnection, and dispossession. This remaking and renaming of territory not only usurped land but has also resulted in an extreme sense of spatial disorientation.

Faiz Mohammad Gabol from Noor Mohammad Gabol Goth told us that it now takes them endless hours to move through their land because the new roads are built only to facilitate mobility within this gated city. The older network of roads that connected villages to each other, routes through which they travelled to other neighbourhoods in Gadap and the adjacent settlement of Malir, have been completely destroyed. He elaborated,

> How do I visit my relatives in Konkar now? There are no routes left. The new Bahria Town roads are all topsy-turvy, we think we're going in one direction, but then the road turns and takes us back. It takes us over an hour to navigate through this new maze.

Despite the 'organised forgetting' of Bahria Town's architecture and monumentality, and the burying of precolonial history of the region, the indigenous communities of Gadap actively resist this hegemonic apparatus. They employ various strategies, often co-opting legal-political institutions such as courts and the mainstream media to give voice to their concerns. In addition, they have consistently organised politically to present their demands as a collective body. KIRA itself, the organisation with which the Gadap Sessions collaborated on its research, was formed in March 2015 in response to the unchecked real estate activity underway in the area. Although our conversations with residents highlighted that it was their contemporary living conditions that were under dire threat, the issue was presented to the media as an issue of preserving heritage sites, a decision that displays awareness that this narrative was likely to gain more sympathy over the narrative of everyday indigenous life (Albro 2006: 393).

Further, many residents have utilised the state's legal apparatus to resist the Bahria Town takeover. Faiz Mohammed, at the time of writing, had a case pending in court against Bahria Town's usurpation of his land. Kanda Khan filed 12 cases in court and 54 police cases against the real estate expansion on behalf of various residents whose homes had been demolished. The villages in Gadap are not informal, and the homeowners have leases from the time of colonial rule to legitimise their claim to the land. Thus, they should have recourse to justice through legal means. The residents we spoke to were well aware of when their land was formally recognised. Kanda Khan's village was formalised in 1927, although, as he emphasised, his predecessors lived there earlier.

As Alfred and Corntassel emphasise, 'colonial legacies and contemporary practices of disconnection, dependency and dispossession have effectively confined indigenous identities to state-sanctioned legal and political definitional approaches' (2005: 600). This explains their emphasis in media briefings on historical legacy over contemporary livelihood. But the approaches referred to in the quotation and examples above have, despite their use of the language and rationale of the state, been thwarted time and time again. In the media coverage, for example, KIRA's protest, which blocked traffic along the highway adjacent to Bahria Town, was absent, as was the real estate company's name altogether in the coverage of KIRA's launch, effectively erasing from the story those who were threatening these historical sites in the first place. The clout of construction and development interests and their ability to influence public narratives stymied this attempt at public awareness. In our interview with Faiz Mohammad, the extent to which these possible sites of action have been compromised became apparent when he told us that survey markings—stones with survey figures—from the colonial era that littered the area and hint at its formalisation were also bulldozed and removed in the process of land seizing.

Material Residues of a Spectral Landscape

Figure 1: Grave of Misri Shah Bokhari
Source: Shahana Rajani

Figure 2: Grave of Dadar Pir
Source: Shahana Rajani

Despite the ravaging of Gadap by Bahria Town and the limited success of attempts to resist it, some material residues of indigenous life remain embedded in the landscape and by mere virtue of their continuing presence in the face of unabated erasure, are worthy of being studied. In the final section of this essay we ponder on this idea of persistence as resistance, which manifests itself in Gadap through material forms, particularly graves which have been left behind within the walls of the gated complex. As we approached one of these gravesites on our tour led by the realtor, we asked him, 'What is that?' He dismissively replied: '*Woh? Woh hai kuch...*' (That? That is ... something). The grave of Misri Shah Bokhari, a saint who was once the slave of a king, according to Faiz Muhammad, now lies, ludicrously, on Jinnah Avenue, close to the entrance. Further into the complex, near the famed world-class golf course, is a nondescript-looking low stone wall circling a few old trees and several graves enclosed within. One of these is the grave of Dadar Pir (Fig. 2), so called because the soil surrounding his grave is known to cure skin allergies (*dadar* in Sindhi refers to skin breakouts).

The abrupt appearance of graves amidst a golf course creates an 'eeriness discharged by a territorial space and material objects left behind by a displaced community' (Navaro-Yashin 2012: 20). Drawing on Teresa Brannan, she explains that these lingering phantoms and spectres transmit an 'effect' through their material presence and endurance within a phantasmatically crafted space and polity. We further draw on Navaro-Yashin's notion of 'irritability' to explore the affects invoked by these graves. She explains irritability as a 'dis-resonating feeling produced by environments that harbour phantoms' that works 'against the grain of an imaginary harmonious attunement' (2012: 20). The jarring visuality of Misri Shah Bokhari's grave confined and contained within the newly-laid pavement fissures the carefully curated foreign landscape. In cities undergoing dramatic social and political change, 'these trans-generational phantoms inhabit particular places and constitute their social realities, particularly where the city and society are "out of joint in terms of both time and space"' (Pile 2004: 217). The affects and charges that emit from this grave are of tension and disturbance; an irritability that itches at the glosses of Bahria Town, something the realtor did not want to confront.

During our time spent with people in Gadap, it became clear that the shrines of Misri Shah Bokhari and Dadar Pir are incredibly important sites of agency in the indigenous landscape of Gadap, where everyday socialities are practiced, rituals elaborated, oral histories and memories transmitted, and communities formed and sustained. As Nile Green has argued, saint-shrines serve as active spaces of memory and belonging (2012: 264). They connect local communities to memories of the distant places from which the saints came, as well as embedding them in local sacred geographies and local histories. Kanda Khan explained that the grave of Dadar Pir is a sacred site of veneration not only for the neighbouring communities, but for 'all sorts of people, whether Sindhi, Baloch, Urdu-speaking, Memon, Kathiawari, who come to visit Dadar Pir for blessing and healing from all over Sindh and Pakistan.' People on whose lands these saint-shrines are located told us that Bahria Town had full intentions of levelling these graves.

Faiz Mohammad said that when Bahria Town illegally usurped 50 acres of land that belonged to his family, he obtained a stay order from the court to temporarily halt construction. However, the developers, relying on the brute force of the police to enable their occupation, paid no attention to these orders. While Faiz Mohammad's agricultural fields, wells, roads, and trees were gouged and razed with ease, the bulldozer came to a halt when it approached the grave of Misri Shah Bokhari. The construction workers (mostly brought in by Bahria Town from Punjab) tried several times to proceed with its demolition, but each time they would try to move forward, the bulldozer would freeze. Faiz Mohammad credited this miracle to saintly power and divine protection.

Rani Bibi, who lives in Jumma Khan Goth, narrated similar miracles that occurred at the grave of Dadar Pir. When the bulldozers approached the gravesite, its engines caught fire. She explained that after a few attempts the labourers too became convinced that this was indeed a powerful saint, and refused to destroy his grave, afraid to invoke the wrath of Dadar Pir. These stories illustrate that the saintly-graves, which were an integral part of everyday rituals and indigenous life, continue to be sites of presence, resistance, and action in Bahria Town's new territory. The remains and presence of different pasts in the landscape as graves and ruins, ghosts and ancestors, are 'active' in the varying ways that they materialise, constrain, enable and structure different, entangled discourses and practices of belonging at play in the reconfiguration of authority over land (Fontein 2011: 708).

Nawaz Ali, during our visit to Dadar Pir, showed us a makeshift stone border made by the workers, in the wake of the miracle, to mark the sacred land that was not to be transgressed. Rani Bibi deduced that, 'the Bahria Town [administration] realised that work would not proceed here with ease and so they let it be, and moved on.' After the incident, people from

Mohammad Ali Goth built a wall around Dadar Pir and the familial graves surrounding it to further protect this sacred site, stirred to action and responding to Bahria's reworking of the geography with their own material transformations. In the face of the unrelenting erasures of Bahria Town, these graves are thus not limited to acting as containers of memory and connectors to the history of the land, but as active agents in the contemporary every day, giving meaning and form to contests of belonging in the face of widespread dispossession.

In this way, object-centred agency (the affects emanating from the material) and human-centred agency (the community-building and story-telling around the graves) form not just fissures in the social and physical cityscape of Bahria Town but also alternative loci of resistance. While the on-going militarised development continues to destruct and reconstruct the material landscape, erasing indigenous dwellings, fields, and lands, its project of re-territorialising is far from totalising. The eeriness discharged by the material presence of the leftover graves of Misri Shah Bokhari and Dadar Pir in the newly carved out territory of Bahria Town is a refusal to conform to dominant narratives of Gadap as an untouched territory and signposts a deeper history. These lingering phantoms resist the organised forgetting of the towering monuments and the imposing Grand Jamia Mosque.

Bahria Town, however, does not perceive these graves to pose a future threat. On the other side of town, in the posh Defence area of Karachi, Bahria Town was also in the process of constructing the aptly named 'Icon Tower', a skyscraper right next to a well-known local landmark, the shrine of Abdullah Shah Ghazi. Rather than attempting to raze the structure, Bahria Town transformed its façade, replacing its blue and white tile work with a cleaner, starker sandstone. Given the corporation's pseudo-Islamic and nationalist veneer, their co-option of holy spaces is not surprising; they do not recognise their potential as sites of agency. As Katherine Ewing explains, Sufi doctrine has often been appropriated to conform to the goals of the nation-state in building a new 'national orientation' rather than a local one (1983: 267). It thus follows that there is a precedence of saint-shrines surviving within development projects. On the Islamabad Motorway and in the Korangi Industrial Area and Steel Mills, saintly graves remain, enclosed by concrete. They do the job of dislocating indigenous time and materiality, which at worst is not worthy of being noted and at best consigns them 'to the past, but not to history' (Attwood 1996: xii).

These essentialist assumptions continue to exclude indigenous people from city life by presenting their symbolic paralysis as spatial outcasts—as people 'out there' or historical figures 'back then' (Watson 2014: 406). Their everyday geographies of belonging have been obliterated from the landscape to cement this view. The leftover shrines enable Bahria Town to recast the indigenous not as contemporaneous inhabitants but as mystic others from a forgotten past. In addition, the graves, in their capacity as historical/sacred sites, represent possible tourist hubs as exemplified by Port Grand's co-optation of the adjacent Lakshmi Narayan Hindu temple in Karachi (Anwar and Viqar 2014: 340). One such shrine in phase IV of Bahria Town has been incorporated into the official map—the sacred thus appears contained through a secular, scopic appropriation. But as is apparent from the various stories of memorialisation and miracles we discuss above, despite the apparently non-threatening nature of these holy sites, Bahria Town cannot wholly consume either these materialities or their connected socialities.

We can see the community-building and mythical narratives of supernatural interventions as well as the affective presence of the graves as a kind of 'infrapolitics'—'circumspect struggles that remain like "infrared rays beyond the visible end of the spectrum"' (Scott 1990: 183). Chattopadhyay elaborates on this, explaining that 'invisibility here ... is intentional (not an effect of practice), a tactical move on the part of subordinated groups in response to the recognition of the imbalance of power' (2012: 53). In the context of Bahria Town Karachi and the tombs of Misri Shah Bokhari and Dadar Pir, this statement is particularly relevant. The graves may be surrounded by new, alien concrete structures but they allow a narrative that slips beneath the totalising, aggrandising gestures of Bahria Town. This reflects the notion of entanglement, where indigenous and globalising landscapes interweave into one another. This often-uneasy interaction and inextricable connection manifested through graves is what creates 'texture', what Donald Moore refers to as 'knots, gnarls, and adhesions rather than smooth surfaces' (2005: 4).

Graves are sites of presence that enable an interactive relationship between the dead and the living in contemporary everyday life in Gadap. In opposition to the naturalised colonial conceptions of linear temporality, where the dead are firmly placed in the past, in Gadap 'the historical is given meaning and value by the presence of the sacred' (Taneja 2013a: 7). This non-linear temporality is apparent in the dreams and visions that Misri Shah Bokhari often occupies—Faiz Mohammad explained to us that the saint endows blessings and healing through appearing in such visions. Such dreams operate on two levels; they are an affective manifestation emerging from the presence and materiality of the graves and they rework Bahria Town's fictions that fix indigenous life in the past. However, these spectres should not be read as an anomaly, nor confined to an inscrutable indigenous world. Taneja links such affective presences of saintly graves to a longstanding Islamic tradition of valuation of the imaginal—a cosmology of the imagination where dreams and visions are considered inherently meaningful forms of knowledge (2013a: 95).

Such visions elicit a sacred politics of alternative times against 'the magical art of forgetting of the state' (Taneja 2013b: 160). In the face of state neglect and forgetting, we find in Gadap alternate and imaginal modes of knowledge transference. Kanda Khan explained to us that his grandfather did not know any factual details about Dadar Pir. When his grandfather decided to get a tombstone made, and to cement this sacred grave, Dadar Pir appeared in a vision to the tombstone maker. He provided his name, Syed Hussain Shah, and the year of his burial, 1150 AH. It is through these knowledge transferences that the graves and imaginal beings challenge the state project of forgetting and erasure. They form a tissue of nominal connections between the imaginal world of immutable entities and the historical world of changing places and times (Ho 2006: 137). These histories exist as texture, in a 'localised weave of kin and proximate spirit and human relationships, not removed from but subsisting below the threshold of national-colonial histories' (Singh 2012: 398).

The past and present come together in such fashion to challenge Bahria Town's erasures, and bear witness to the intervention of the sacred in the everyday. The stories of miracles are the transmittance of an affective presence that directly responds to and engages with the contemporary violence of displacement and dispossession. The violence of this development project, therefore, leads not only to erasures and disenchantments of the world, but also 'to renewed forms of re-enchantment' (Taneja 2013a: 25) which present new possibilities for agency. As Grunebaum describes, '[on] the fault lines where multiple temporalities of change are entangled with normative modes of domination, subordination, and disavowal, the opportunity for a counter-temporality, a time of the dead, open[s]' (2011: 130). The here and now becomes dislocated as traces thought safely buried or erased re-emerge as revenants.

The affective sacrality and non-linear temporality mentioned above is not only phantomic or imaginal but is embedded in the material landscape. Pilgrims who come to the grave of Dadar Pir rub soil from around his grave on their skin to cure allergies. The saint's grave posits a different relationship to the land. His power to heal is linked to the land and soil, to the materiality of place. Graves are not simply burial sites that are simply passive and inert criteria for the assertion of belonging; they have a more active and affective presence through the transferences and merging of materials/substances of body, clay, and soil (Fontein 2011: 713). Through this merging, the saint's blessing are directly linked to the material landscape, permeating the soil and textures of everyday life, an intertwining of sacred, ecological, and the everyday. Such interweaving once again sees a collaboration of object-centred and human agency: Deen Mohammad explained, laughing, that Bahria Town has been trying to landscape the terrain around Dadar Pir to set up Golf City, the golf course within the complex. However, every time Bahria tried to lay down their imported grass on the land, the grass would not take root and die. In this instance, the textures of indigenous landscape, imbued with saintly blessings, are understood to be actively resisting material transformation.

Conclusion

In their persisting materiality, these graves and sacred sites bear witness to the geographies of loss and exclusion that continue to structure contemporary urbanisms. The ongoing erasure of the indigenous landscape and histories is part of a much longer history of structural violence, where the postcolonial state continues to enact policies of discrimination and displacement against the indigenous population of the city. The wider project of modernising the city has been accompanied by a state-sanctioned erasure of the city's precolonial pasts. This legitimises and sanitises the violence of development by removing any claims that indigenous communities have to the present/ presence in the homogenous space and time of the new city. Gadap is not only located at the outskirts of Karachi, but also occupies a peripheral location in the public imaginary, which is the result of the formulation of a historical narrative of the nation that neglects indigenous pasts and presents. This rewriting is also evident in heritage conservation, where selective pasts are recouped into public memory as national heritage. Indigenous historical sites are neglected, while seemingly unlimited funds are spent to protect and preserve colonial building to reify state narratives that the story of Karachi begins with colonial conquest, before which it was a wasteland.

The story of Gadap and its rapidly transforming geography is, of course, not a unique one. As we note in section 1, it is a story of exclusion, a story playing out repeatedly as megacities around the world fulfil their global aspirations by progressively erasing the local. In our final analysis, however, we want to emphasise that the resultant anxiety and nostalgia for 'the past' we may experience, while grounded in legitimate concerns, is myopic. Transnational and speculative capital have transformed cityscapes dramatically, but as we have attempted to show in this essay, this transformation has remained contested and incomplete. While indigenous communities in Gadap have suffered displacement and been the target of 'organised forgetting', material 'leftovers' and saintly interventions continue to texture the landscape in a way that prevents a smooth overlay of a 'world-class city' constructed by Bahria Town on an apparently empty geography. A significant point to consider in light of our analysis, therefore, is that if such agency is active in the present, then the future too holds a myriad of possibilities. While the graves remain within the 'secure' gates and walls of Bahria Town, opportunities for mobility also remain. If the recognition of the graves as sacred has resulted in preservation and possible appropriation, entanglements and infrapolitics ensure that this sacrality also allows for possible pilgrimage by indigenous communities and thus continued connections to the land. As long as such materialities continue to exist and resist, Bahria Town's hotels, homes, and theme parks will have to make space for those who seek more from the land.

NOTES

1. The Karachi Art Anti University was founded in May 2015 by Zahra Malkani and Shahana Rajani, and is an Anti-Institution based in Karachi seeking to politicise art education and collectively explore new radical pedagogies and art practices.

2. The Karachi Indigenous Rights Alliance was founded in March 2015 by Gul Hasan Kalmatti, Saleem Baloch and other indigenous community leaders in direct response to Bahria Town's incursion into Gadap.

REFERENCES

Acuto, Michele, 'High-rise Dubai urban entrepreneurialism and the technology of symbolic power', *Cities*, 27, 4 (2010), pp. 272–84.

Albro, Robert, 'The Culture of Democracy and Bolivia's Indigenous Movements', *Critique of Anthropology*, 26, 4 (2006), pp. 387–410.

Alfred, Taiaiake, and Jeff Corntassel, 'Being Indigenous: Resurgences against Contemporary Colonialism', *Government and Opposition*, 40, 4 (2005), pp. 597–614.

Ali, Naziha Syed, and Fahim Zaman, 'Bahria Town Karachi: Greed Unlimited', *Dawn*, 8 April 2019.

Anwar, Nausheen, 'Planning Karachi's Urban Futures', *Asia Research Institute Working Paper Series*, 203, (2013), pp. 3–29.

_____ and Sarwat Viqar, 'Producing Cosmopolitan Karachi: Freedom, Security and Urban Redevelopment in the Post-colonial Metropolis', *South Asian History and Culture*, 5, 3 (2014), pp. 328–48.

Bain, Attwood, 'The Past as Future: Aborigines, Australia and the (Dis)course of History', in *In the Age of Mabo: History, Aborigines and Australia*, St. Leonards, Australia: Allen and Unwin, 1996, pp. viii–xxxviii.

Chattopadhyay, Swati, *Unlearning the City*, Minneapolis: University of Minnesota Press, 2012.

Cochrane, Joe, 'Safe Behind Their Walls', *Newsweek*, accessed 10 February 2017 <http://europe.newsweek.com/safe-behind-their-walls-93819?rm=eu>.

Cowen, Deborah, 'Infrastructures of Empire and Resistance', Verso Books, accessed 10 February 2017 <http://www.versobooks.com/blogs/3067-infrastructures-of-empire-and-resistance>.

Crinson, Mark, *Urban Memory: History and Amnesia in the Modern City*, London: Routledge, 2005.

Dadi, Iftikhar, 'Political Posters in Karachi, 1988–1999', *South Asian Popular Culture*, 5, 1 (2007), pp. 11–30.

Davis, Mike, 'Fear and Money in Dubai', *New Left Review*, 41 (2006), p. 41.

Ewing, Katherine P., 'The Politics of Sufism: Redefining the Saints of Pakistan', *The Journal of Asian Studies*, 42, 2 (1983), pp. 251–68.

Fontein, Joost, 'Graves, Ruins, and Belonging: Towards an Anthropology of Proximity', *Journal of the Royal Anthropological Institute*, 17, 4 (2011), pp. 706–27.

Gilmartin, David, *Blood and Water: The Indus River Basin in Modern History*, Berkeley, CA: University of California Press, 2015.

Green, Nile, *Making Space: Sufis and Settlers in Early Modern India*, Delhi: Oxford University Press, 2012.

Grunebaum, Heidi, *Memorializing the Past*, New Brunswick, NJ: Transaction Publishers, 2011.

Ho, Engseng, *The Graves of Tarim: Genealogy and Mobility across the Indian Ocean*, Berkeley, CA: University of California Press, 2006.

Massey, Doreen, *Space, Place, and Gender*, Minneapolis: University of Minnesota Press, 1994.

Mitchell, Katharyne, 'Monuments, Memorials, and the Politics of Memory', *Urban Geography*, 24, 5 (2003), pp. 442–59.

Mitchell, Timothy, 'Orientalism and the Exhibitionary Order', in: N. Mirzoeff (ed.), *The Visual Culture Reader*, New York: Routledge, (2002), pp. 495–505.

———, *Rule of Experts: Egypt, Techno-Politics, Modernity*, Berkeley: University of California Press, 2002.

Moore, Donald S., *Suffering for Territory*, Durham: Duke University Press, 2005.

Moser, Sarah, 'Circulating Visions of 'High Islam': The Adoption of Fantasy Middle Eastern Architecture in Constructing Malaysian National Identity', *Urban Studies*, 49, 13 (2012), pp. 2913–35.

Navaro-Yashin, Yael, *The Make-Believe Space: Affective Geography in a Post-war Polity*, Durham, NC: Duke University Press, 2012.

Pile, Steve, 'Ghosts and the City of Hope', in: L. Lees (ed.), *The Emancipatory City?*, London: SAGE, 2004.

Robinson, Jennifer, *Ordinary Cities: Between Modernity and Development*, New York: Routledge, 2006.

Sargin, Güven A., 'Displaced Memories, or the Architecture of Forgetting and Remembrance', *Environment and Planning D: Society and Space*, 22, 5 (2004), pp. 659–80.

Scott, James, *Domination and the Arts of Resistance*, New Haven: Yale University Press, 1990.

Singh, Bhrigupati, 'The Headless Horseman of Central India: Sovereignty at Varying Thresholds of Life', *Cultural Anthropology*, 27, 2 (2012), pp. 383–407.

Sklair, Leslie, 'Iconic Architecture and the Culture-ideology of Consumerism', *Theory, Culture & Society*, 27, 5 (2010), pp. 1–25.

Taneja, Anand, 'Jinnealogy: Everyday Life and Islamic Theology in Post-Partition Delhi', *HAU: Journal of Ethnographic Theory*, 3, 3 (2013a), p. 139.

———, 'Nature, History and the Sacred in the Medieval Ruins of Delhi', PhD dissertation, Columbia University, 2013b.

Tiffin, Chris, and Alan Lawson, *De-scribing Empire: Post-colonialism and Textuality*, London and New York: Routledge, 2002.

Watson Mark K., 'Cities: Indigeneity and Belonging', in L. Graham and H. Glenn Penny, (eds.), *Performing Indigeneity*, Lincoln, NE: University of Nebraska Press, 2014.

2

The Case of LDA City: How a Public–Private Partnership Fractured Farmers' Resistance in Lahore

Hashim bin Rashid and Zainab Moulvi[1]

Introduction

About ten men were sitting underneath a banyan tree in the Warraich village. Toor Warraich is one of the seven revenue villages that have been marked for acquisition as part of the Lahore Development Authority (LDA) City housing scheme. The other six revenue villages included in the scheme are Thay Panju, Rakh Jaidu, Kahna, Halloki, Kacha, and Sidhar. Announced in 2011, the LDA City scheme promised to be Pakistan's 'biggest housing scheme', spread over an area of over 64,000 kanals in southwest Lahore. The areas to be acquired were notified under Section 4 of the Land Acquisition Act, 1894. Drawing on the star power of the Pakistani cricket superstar Shahid Afridi, advertisements for buying plots in LDA City flooded national newspapers and TV channels in the months of March and April 2015. The advertisements sketched an alluring picture of a luxury residential housing scheme with high-end shopping malls, state of the art medical and educational facilities, an eighteen-hole golf course, a commercial centre, and even a diplomatic enclave along the lines of the one in the capital city of Islamabad.

Fields of wheat crop filled up the landscape beyond the banyan tree. The crop was delineated into small blocks. To the right, two new houses were being built. A little further down, solar panels were being installed. On the surface, it did not seem like the housing scheme had impacted the village yet but talk of it dominated our conversation. The ages of the men sitting underneath the tree varied from the elderly, middle-aged, and young. They talked to us about the LDA's housing scheme, their opposition to it, and also of land issues their village was facing.

'The land in the villages of Warraich and Toor is under dispute,' one of the older men told us:

> In the last government, one of the ministers tampered with the land record of the villages. On paper, no one knows which piece of land belongs to whom. Over 100 acres has been transferred into his and his son's name. The dispute has been in the courts for about ten years now.[2]

Given the problems with the land record, we were told that the land of the two villages could not be sold at the moment. The same story was repeated by the residents of Toor. However, the men told us that they were part of protests against the LDA City scheme a few years ago. The protests took place in early 2012 when thousands of landowners and peasants assembled outside the Prime Minister and Chief Minister's residence in southern Lahore. After protests in January 2012, one of the men alleged, Chief Minister Shahbaz Sharif had agreed to stop the project altogether and publicly declared the rolling back of the project, only to renege on the promise post-elections.* The project was even expanded from its original size of 45,000 kanals to around 64,000 kanals.

The majority of the villagers are small to medium sized farmers with anywhere between 8–12 acres of land. The villagers complained about what they characterised as more insidious techniques to induce sale. While most of these were precolonial villages, they were now dependent on waterways built during the colonial period. They claimed that this water had been suspended on purpose to make it impossible for them to grow their crops.

During our discussion, one of the men called a former nazim[3] of the area who, he said, was involved in resisting the housing scheme. Arriving by car, the middle-aged man told us that his main gripe was the compensation they receive. He said, 'If we are compensated well, we will sell. The problem is that the LDA is saying only Rs 5 million per acre while other schemes in the area, including DHA Rahbar, have been paying Rs 15 million per acre.'

---

* Newspaper reports on the protest did not report an agreement to stop the scheme <https://www.pakistantoday.com.pk/2012/01/08/%E2%80%98but-we-don%E2%80%99t-want-a-plot-in-your-lda-city%E2%80%99/>.

The arrival of the former nazim silenced everyone else who had been part of a lively discussion on the merits and demerits of, and strategies being used to deal with, the housing scheme. After he left, one of the old men led us to the side and whispered, 'Get in touch with me if you want to get involved here.' We felt it was too early to make any such commitment, but what was clear from our discussion was that the response to the LDA City scheme was much more complex than the villagers-against-developers story we had expected.

**

The scenario described above is by no means an unusual occurrence in the city; over the past two decades, Lahore has undertaken a pattern of development that echoes what Andy Merrifield describes as the Neo-Hausmannisation of the city. Under this pattern, 'land takes on the pure character of fictitious capital ... circulating through the property market, enhancing the value of land, and redeveloping and upscaling that land for "higher" and better "capitalistic" uses' (Merrifield 2014: 23). This pattern of development, based on accumulation or 'speculative urbanism', echoes that of other cities around the world (Banerjee-Guha 2010; Menon and Nigam 2007; Goldman 2010). It involves the plunder of rural land on the fringes of the city by acquiring it at cheap prices and converting it into high-value real estate—usually in the shape of high-end residential enclaves.

The voracious growth in real estate has been the central feature of Lahore's development for the past decades but its roots reach back further as well. Mohammad Qadeer (1996) argues in his appraisal of Lahore's urban policies through the 1950s to the late 1990s that urban development in Lahore has always taken place through the idiom of 'plots and public works'. By the 1990s, urban land markets had become highly speculative, and co-operative housing schemes—acquired and built by the Pakistan Army, universities, Pakistan Railways, Water and Power Development Authority, and other public corporations and private groups—also entered the urban land market. The real estate market boomed again in the 2000s as remittances flooded in from overseas Pakistanis after 9/11 due to the tenuous circumstances abroad. The LDA has also now entered the highly lucrative game of housing schemes, putting itself in the suspect position of both regulator of housing schemes and a profiteering developer.[4] While one of its initial goals as per its 1975 charter was to facilitate low-cost housing schemes, it seems to have changed directions under the tutelage of the Pakistan Muslim League-Nawaz (PML-N) government, which sought to transform Lahore into a 'world-class city'—a transformation driven largely by mega projects.

David Harvey's (2003) concept of 'accumulation by dispossession' can prove useful when trying to think through the forms and role of land grabs in contemporary capitalism. Harvey (2003) reworks Marx's theory of primitive accumulation and argues that far from a historical precursor to full-fledged capital relations, it has a salience in contemporary industrial and financial capitalism. However, while this concept seems to fit excellently with the variety of dispossessions that are proliferating in today's day and age as a result of financialisation, privatisation, real estate development, SEZs, and the growth of intellectual property rights to name a few, some have questioned the explanatory value of this concept which collapses a number of processes under one banner.

Harvey (2003) focuses on the function of accumulation by dispossession, which he argues is absorbing over-accumulated capital in the global economy. Yet Michael Levien (2015) raises the contention that this does not explain why this impulse of global capitalism translates into dispossession in a particular case. He argues that at different stages, states have dispossessed people for different reasons. For example, in colonial India, communities were displaced for the building of railways while the Nehruvian state dispossessed primarily for public sector and industrial purposes. Thus, at any given point in time, the question to ask is 'how and why do states restructure themselves to dispossess land for different purposes and different classes in different periods' (Levien 2015: 149).

Given this context, we will examine one particular instance of dispossession—LDA City—to illuminate how this specific dispossession unfolded and to underscore how the mechanism chosen to undertake the dispossession shapes resistance at different junctures. When it comes to understanding the prospect of struggle formation, it becomes paramount to examine the actual mechanics of particular instances of dispossession. Under what circumstances can dispossession most likely encounter successful resistance? What are the strategies used to overcome resistance? Who are the losers and winners? Over the course of the paper there are three things we would like to keep in mind:

1) Dispossession in this case is not the sweeping, forceful, and violent separation of communities and their land, but a product of the state deploying various strategies and instruments to ensure dispossession.

2) Through an ethnographic exposition of the dispossession process in the LDA City housing scheme, we wish to re-examine the categories of 'urban/ rural' and 'peasant' to situate the logic and practice of dispossession.

3) Academic writing on agrarian land grabs has tended to give the figure of the peasant an almost static subjectivity. Closer attention to the specifics of a dispossession will allow us to appreciate peasants as dynamic, varied, and agential actors who engage with their specific changing circumstances in varied ways.

We will argue that the dispossession involved in building the LDA City must be located in a larger history of the seven revenue villages in south-eastern Lahore from the colonial to the postcolonial period. We will also argue that the process is aided by laws such as the Land Acquisition Act 1984 that facilitates state dispossession under the guise of 'public purpose', urban policy that focuses on real estate development as the preferred form of urban development, the prolific rise of private and semi-private housing schemes in Lahore (e.g. DHA),[5] the expansion of Lahore into an urban agglomerate or 'city-region', and the empowerment of the Lahore Development Authority to facilitate the processes of dispossession and development.

The first section provides a sketch of the rural relations, transformations in them, and how they set up a complex response to the housing scheme. This sets the context for why the state has to rely on force in addition to using the market to expropriate land. The second section traces some of the changes already underway in the area and provides some sense of the peri-urban space which plays a key role in circumscribing the future that villagers in the area are able to envision for themselves. The third section will outline some key restructuring in urban governance to rescale state sovereignty and consolidate state control in urban affairs. It will, at the same time, point to the resistance to state force which compels the state to re-strategise its approach to dispossession. The fourth section details the role of the private developers and the nexus between state power and private firms and how it compels people to sell.

Section One:

VILLAGE ECONOMIES AND THE LOGIC OF RESISTANCE

Rural land markets have proven remarkably resistant to the commodification of land. This is not due to villages somehow being outside of capital relations—far from it. Individual property rights have long been deeply entrenched in the villages around Lahore. There are two key historical junctures that significantly structured the property regime in these villages. The first is the British settlement of Punjab. After the conquest of Punjab in the late 1840s, the British conducted a survey of the villages and recorded existing arrangements. The settlement process conferred private property rights to various classes and introduced the alienability of land. The Punjab Alienation of Land Act 1900 served to institutionalise an 'agricultural caste'. Agricultural tenants, labourers, and other non-cultivating castes (such as *nayi*, *kumhar*, *mocha*, *mirassis*) that traditionally had certain rights and claims to produce were now dispossessed of any rights (see Ali 2014 and Gazdar 2009).

The second key juncture was the partition of the subcontinent. As many of these villages are old Sikh villages (with the notable exception of Toor), the majority of the original landowners migrated to India and migrants from India came and settled in the evacuated villages. Thus, there was a major demographic shift in these villages after 1947, when new *biradaris* such as Rajput, Mewati, Joiye, Arayein, Gujar, and Barwalay entered the social matrix. The difference between the 'old and non-agricultural castes' and 'new' inhabitants becomes important when considering who owns land in the villages and who does not.

In Halloki, there is a significant Christian population who trace their roots to before Partition. These Christians do not own land and have historically tended to the cattle of the Muslims and worked on their lands. Their response to the rise in housing schemes and acquisition was thus been significantly different. While many non-tenants were a part of the 2012 protests, the Christians adjusted to the changes in different ways. Many were working in construction in their own village and surrounding areas, factories, or as domestic labour in the nearby housing schemes. These shifts seemed to opened up new opportunities for them and many embraced the relative freedom that these new job opportunities afforded them.

The majority of the landowners in Halloki, Toor Warraich, and parts of Punju[6] were middle-sized farmers who owned anything between 8–12 acres.

They mostly grew wheat, rice, and fodder on the land. They also owned cattle, with selling milk in the city is a significant source of income, which was coming under threat. The creeping urbanisation means that it became increasingly hard to grow fodder, and with the acquisition of the land, this is becoming impossible. Fodder would have to be acquired from other villages, and at the rate and expanse of the surrounding housing schemes, this would soon be untenable.

Yet villagers were less inclined to view their land as a commodity to be alienated and floated on the market as they treated it as a source of food. In Halloki, villagers we spoke to told us that while some people had sold land, they were few and far in between. The reasons they cited for lack of sale were the difficulty in acquiring agricultural land elsewhere and competing claims between family members who all had an interest in the land, which made sale a cumbersome process fraught with tension and conflict. The fact that they owned not more than ten acres also meant that the money they received would not be a substantial amount necessary to secure a steady source of income. One villager wryly put it, 'They'll probably spend it all on one function for the child's marriage', gesturing to the risk inherent that such a lump sum will be floundered away in consumption. This concern was echoed by a number of villagers. Another villager pointed out that it only benefits those who do not have many dependents.

This gestures towards a few key realities of the area: first of all, since most of the families supplemented their agricultural work with wage labour in the factories, dispossession would not suddenly convert them into an industrial working class. In all likelihood, it would increase the strain on daily finances as the cost of buying food from the market would now have to be factored in. Thus, the fact that majority of the farmers were small to middle-sized farmers and there were no major landlords in the area was a significant impediment to real estate developers seeking to set up housing schemes. Not only was the sale of their land less profitable for them, but convincing a large number of peasants with such fragmented landholdings was a formidable task.

While discussions around agrarian relations have often focused on static traditional value systems that mediate relationships to land, what needs to be highlighted is that peasants make interpretive and predictive claims when analysing the issue—factoring in not only economic viability but also engaging in discussions and analysis of what will come to pass as a result of sale, responsibilities such as marrying children and dependents, the state of non-landowners, their own disadvantaged position with respect to knowledge of urban markets, and access to information and connections that will facilitate this process. However, these conversations, calculations, and analysis of their own situations and prospects do not remain static; we noted subtle shifts during our subsequent visits in our discussions even as villagers continued to oppose the scheme. As Allen (2003) puts it, the challenge is to study how power works to form subjects through 'a variety of modes playing across one another. The erosion of choice, the closure of possibilities, the manipulation of outcomes, the threat of force, the assent of authority or the inviting gestures of a seductive presence' (196). The next section explores the larger spatial, social and economic relations within which these villages were embedded, compelling us to revise our notions of what it means to be a 'villager' on the peri-urban fringe of a megacity like Lahore.

Section Two:

THE GEOGRAPHY OF CAPITAL IN THE 'URBAN FRINGES'

The landscape around Warraich has already undergone major transformations in the last four decades. These villages had close relations with the city since as far back as the Sikh rule of Punjab. In the British era, a fruit and vegetable market was built at Kahna, which has since been a source of food for the city. But the scale of change in the landscape in the last two decades has been unprecedented and the relationship between the 'city' and its urban hinterlands has undergone a fundamental shift. New roads, new infrastructure, new housing schemes and factories—all of these are visual symbols marking the area for transformation.

When traveling to Warraich Village from Lahore, the scale of change can be witnessed depending on which route one takes. If you take the Kahna Kacha Road, it leads to the factories near Kahna Village, which cropped up in the 1980s and have brought with them an in-migration of factory labourers. Go the opposite direction and it takes you to the New Fruit and Vegetable Market built in 2011 and a number of housing societies built over the last decade. Drive towards Toor Village and you hit the double road constructed to facilitate the LDA City project. The factories and housing societies have changed the area. Hundreds of informal housing schemes have cropped up to accommodate factory workers and household servants. Families of landless peasants have begun to take up factory and household labour. To the right of Warraich Village is the Audit and Accounts Housing Society, which was built on land purchased from agricultural landowners in the early 1990s.

Ahmed (name changed), who we met in his real estate office in Punju Gaon, described these changes to us at length. A long-time resident of the village and owner of land as well, he turned to the real estate business a few years back while his uncle now tends his agricultural lands. Real estate is an increasingly viable and popular occupation for a lot of residents in the area; the number of real estate offices that can be seen dotting the roads is a testament to this fact. The city of Lahore is naturally bounded by the River Ravi to the north and the Indian border to the east. The southern and western borders of the city, between Multan Road and Bedian Road, form a natural growth corridor for the expansion of the urban fabric. The Master Plan of Lahore 2021 explicitly marks out this area as the direction of further growth,[7] especially for residential purposes. A drive down Ferozepur Road will confirm the direction of the sprawl that is taking place around Lahore. The housing and land market in the area is thus a complex game and Ahmed and others like him are located at the heart of these processes.

While a number of the estate agents who operate in the area are from elsewhere, a fair amount are local villagers who have turned to the business. Ahmed's shop is small and sparsely furnished, with a couplet by the poet Iqbal sprawled across the wall. In the grounds opposite, children are playing and a large group of men sit around in groups of four and play cards. Yet despite being in real estate, Ahmed has little to no role in the massive housing project that is sweeping his locality. In fact, he is quite categorically against it and a majority of his conversation with us is dominated by his vocal opposition to the scheme. Ninety per cent of the people in Punju, he claims, are not landowners and stood to suffer the most from the sale of land as they were not entitled to any compensation. His work in real estate is also highly circumscribed in scale and he recently attempted to enter the rental market bolstered by the influx of migrants aiming to sell their labour in the surrounding factories and brick kilns. He swears to not try that again as his experience with 'outsiders' trying to live on rent in the village was not good and he now thinks it best to not intervene.

As the case of Ahmed demonstrates, relations and socio-economic realities in this area are far from straightforward. Ahmed defies easy shelving in any of the standard categories involved in the discourse around dispossession of resistant peasants and a brutal state. He actively engages in the land market while at the same time retaining links with the land and rural life. He is also bound in the webs of social and economic changes that come with the industrial influx in the area. Yet despite his occupational interest in land prices, he overtly criticises the LDA scheme by pointing out the danger to the non-landowners (of which there are plenty), and he participated in the protests against the scheme. While he actively responds and transforms along with larger economic and social shifts in the area, his is not a teleological transformation; he constantly interprets different shifts and predicts the effects of these changes, moulding his attitude and approach accordingly. Ahmed is not enthusiastic about the influx of industrial labour, but is able to reconcile himself with it as a much more 'natural' change. His response to the housing scheme is much more vehement as it would involve a complete and drastic transformation of their livelihoods.

Located on the main Kahna Kacha Road was another such office, but a considerably larger one with an LDA city advertisement donning the entrance. Inside, the office was divided into two portions—one selling medication and one which is locked. Adnan, who sits at the shop, proudly explained that he had done a course in pharmaceuticals and received accreditation from the government. While originally from the village Punju, he no longer resides there. He owns a small square of land in the village which has been leased to tenants. The office is his uncle's, who had been the *numberdar*[8] of the village and owns a significant amount of property in the area. Over the years, his uncle had been buying and selling land in the village and even made a small housing scheme there. While he said that the LDA officially banned the sale or transfer of land to anyone other than the private urban developers they partnered with, slightly more powerful individuals were attempting to buy up land which they could sell to the developers at a profit.

Levien extends Harvey's argument 'by showing how accumulation by dispossession does not always simply pit capital versus peasants—or "commoners" for that matter—but can create a whole chain of rentiership that incorporates well-placed fractions of the peasantry.' (Levien 2012: 942). This chain becomes even more complex when one places dispossession in the context of a peri-urban area. The villagers who anticipate the sudden entry of billions of rupees into the area by buying up land and setting up real estate agencies are the ones who adapt to the new capital flows in the area. With capital aiming to convert agrarian land into an instrument of speculation, and then, perhaps, urban land, there is a killing to be made by those who can read the market correctly. Bigger landowners, who have never done manual labour before and have others working their land, are able to use their structural power to consolidate the mediating position for themselves. This structural power in empirical terms translates into substantial land-ownings and links with local politicians and bureaucrats. This, in turn, often increases access to information about the property markets, leads to moderate amounts of education, which can ensure employment, and a steady flow of money leading to a lack of dependency on the land for food. For these reasons, both in Halloki and Punju, the *numberdars* of the village have become property agents. These players profit by convincing people to sell to them at a cheaper rate before selling to the LDA's property dealers at a profit. The inevitability of the process of acquisition has converted institutions critical to sustaining the colonial agrarian structure, such as the *numberdar*, into active agents for the break-up of the agrarian economy of the area. In the transition between agrarian space and urban space, these actors smoothen the transition by facilitating the rupture.

Section Three:

STATE, LAW, AND URBAN GOVERNANCE

The evolution of the Lahore Development Authority has also been an interesting trend. It came into being in 1975 as a new version of the Lahore Improvement Trust and was, largely, a toothless organisation assigned the task of making master plans and developing low-income housing schemes but without the finances or clout to do so. Through an amendment in its Act in 2013, the organisation now has extended its jurisdiction to the entire Lahore Division, not just the district, which includes neighbouring towns such as Nankana, Kasur, and Sheikhupura. This expanding urban conglomeration echoes observations by urban theorists that the old idea of the city as a clearly delineated block of space is no longer tenable. Creating master plans, zoning, land use, land classification, and reclassification are now concentrated in the hands of this organisation, rendering local elected bodies, such as town municipal administrations, relatively powerless. It also holds the powers to approve all private housings schemes (this is despite its own housing schemes being accused of not following proper procedures like getting an approval from the concerned environmental department). The transfer of these functions has also resulted in the transfer of fees that these local bodies received to carry out these functions. Its internal structure was also changed with then Chief Minister of Punjab, Shahbaz Sharif, heading it. The changes in structure have resulted in the LDA intervening in urban governance in new ways.

Neil Brenner (2004) calls attention to the role of urban governance in making and remaking state spatiality. Urban governance, he argues,

> is a key institutional arena in which states attempt to influence the geographies of capital accumulation and everyday social reproduction within their territories ... urban geographies of state space may also be reconfigured in conjunction with distributional pressures that emerge as competing localities, cities and regions within a national territory struggle to channel public resources and private capital into their jurisdictions (Brenner 2004: 457).

Following these lines, the government diverted development funds from other cities in Punjab towards Lahore, provoking an outcry from the other regions.[9]

Lahore as a city has become central to the spatiality of state power as cities are 'increasingly viewed as dynamic growth engines through which national prosperity could be secured and as an essential national economic asset' (Brenner 2004: 470–1). Writing about Europe, Brenner (2004) argues that welfarist functions and local democratic institutions took a back-seat and public–private partnerships became increasingly prevalent since the 1980s. A similar situation was evident in Lahore as the Punjab government and the LDA partnered with selected urban development firms and construction companies (leaving ample room for patronage and *biradari* [caste]-based politics in the assigning of tenders) and in certain instances courted Chinese investment for mega projects ('Chinese Banks ...' 2015).

Indeed, LDA has since become active in managing mega projects,[10] and this is the second residential scheme it has launched in 11 years. Yet for many on the ground, it is one of the most 'corrupt' organisations (a reputation buttressed by the recent LDA Avenue debacle[11]) and a 'mere smokescreen for accumulation by powerful individuals'.

Yet while the organisation has been empowered in certain ways, resistance to it on the ground has been fierce. Locals tell us that in 2013, LDA officials attempted to demolish a few houses and forcibly acquire the land in the village of Thay Punju. This caused an uproar in the village as the villagers fought back. The story of the fight is told to us with relish by a local resident of Punju who describes the scene with a glint in his eye, 'The LDA officials had to be escorted out of the area by us. Their clothes were torn and they abandoned their vehicles and fled.' He went on to say of the surrounding villages, 'Historically, the police has been too scared to venture into these villages. Every family in the village has weapons and they are *badmash log* [lawless people]. How can they forcibly take their land from them? It is not possible.' It seems as though the LDA has also realised the futility in using force and has since rethought its techniques as the furore of the three years past gave way to an uneasy silence. Under the cover of this silence, land was changing hands slowly in the case in the village of Punju. LDA had not so much backed off as shifted techniques.

Section Four:

PUBLIC–PRIVATE PARTNERSHIPS: THE NEW STRATEGY APPROPRIATED

Faced with protests, the LDA saw that forced acquisition could not work. It decided to use 'middlemen' (Sud 2014) to broker the deal. In January 2014, the LDA announced it would partner with six private development firms[12] who would take care of the acquisition for them. The sale and purchase of land by any party or individual other than these firms was banned. To get a better idea of the acquisition process we sat down with Hamza (name changed), the son of the owner of one of these firms. The area under acquisition was divided into five zones and each zone assigned to each firm. This strategy was adopted after the five partners recognised that they were pushing the prices up for each other. Later, no other firm was allowed to acquire land in the other firm's zone. This had the effect of limiting competition by establishing a monopoly over that zone and keeping prices down as no other firm could make an offer.

Detailing how their firm got involved, he told us that the LDA published an advertisement in 2014 for developers to partner with it in developing the LDA City housing scheme. Acquisition, contrary to what we had been hearing, was going rather well according to him. With a target set of acquiring 18,000 kanals of land by January 2016 to build the first phase of the housing scheme, he told us that they had already acquired over 11,000 kanals. The area demarcated for the first phase covered the villages of Panju, Sidhar, and Rakh Jaidu. The noise and confrontation of the previous years had given way to the quiet sale and acquisition through private means. The government had shifted the four *patwaris*[13] of the area to the main LDA office, further facilitating the smooth transfer of land. We asked Hamza how people were selling land to them when they had previously protested against the scheme. He shrugged and simply said, 'People always sell. They were scared at first but the people have started selling. They see that others are selling and we also offer a better price than the government so they are happier selling to us.'

His simple statement, which takes human behaviour as rational economic actors almost as axiomatic truth, glosses over the role of their strategy of acquisition in compelling people to sell. He does not take into consideration the fact that the area had already been notified for acquisition under the Land Acquisition Act, a fact of which the people were well cognizant, being faced with visual reminders in the form of advertisements everywhere. The law set up a complex pricing mechanism by appointing lower level revenue officials (the District Commissioner) to decide a rate for the land based on previous agricultural value. The mechanism ensured pricing that was well below current urban market rates, and stifled the ability of landowners to be able to negotiate the value of their land.

The price that was offered under the Act was below the private developers' offers, and people were aware of this. Yet the agreement between the developers prevented the market prices of the land from reaching the rate that it would in the event of an open competitive market. This shift, in a sense, fractured the collective political subject. The new player in this game is the individual property owner who must make pragmatic decisions regarding the sale of his land if he is to benefit at all and not have to face the eventuality of having his land forcibly acquired from him under government rates. Once the property agent convinces a property owner to sell his land, the property owner must come to the LDA office and present the proof of ownership. A file is made and handed over to the LDA. The LDA issued an advertisement in newspapers for claimants to contest the ownership of land within two weeks. The land is then transferred to the LDA, and the payment is made to the landowner. This entire process was, of course, facilitated by the co-option of the *patwaris* who had, as mentioned before, been transferred to offices near the LDA main office. This entire procedure itself was in stark contrast to the collective bargaining and negotiating at the time of the initial protest.

Hamza went on to tell us, 'Our target is to acquire 75 per cent of the land. Once we do so, the LDA will use the Land Acquisition Act to acquire the rest of the 25 per cent.' Prices steadily increased as the buying continued. In the early days of acquisition, he told us he would buy someone's land for around Rs 3 million per acre. The average price increased to around Rs 8 million. The doubling of land prices took place within a year. The result was a secondary land market, where local influential actors used their capital to buy land from small farmers, hold on to it, and sell it to the LDA at a premium.

The urban developers gained quite spectacularly from this. Hamza alleged that the LDA agreed to give them 31 per cent of the residential plot files to sell and a significant number of files for the commercial plots. Files for plots were being sold despite acquisition for the first phase of the LDA City scheme not being completed. The marketing company managing the project had apparently made over Rs 1 billion while Hamza admitted that their own firm made a good amount of profit. By selling files for the project before the acquisitions were complete, the capital to finance the acquisition was being generated on the go. This situation raised the eyebrows of corruption authorities, with the National Accountability Bureau stepping in to investigate the project to ensure that those buying files for the housing scheme were not cheated.[14]

Profits were being made before the acquisition process was finished—and much before the actual development process began. Files for the project were already available on the market with prices continuing to waver. Despite the unwanted attention the project attracted, including the NAB inquiry and media reports alleging mass fraud, Hamza was certain that the project would reach fruition. 'People will eventually sell their lands,' he promised.

Conclusion: A Fractured Resistance

Dispossession in this case must be seen as a larger part of a conjuncture—a spatially and temporally specific set of relations, practices, and processes that shape the potential for resistance. The first such set of relations we discussed were the processes that have shaped this area in particular and different circuits of land capital that are already circulating in the area and slowly shifting relations. The case of Ahmed is an interesting one because in one way his rootedness in the rural sets of relations has allowed him to awkwardly straddle two different sets of relations towards the land. Moreover, his engagement in the informal rental market shows how rural communities are engaging in the processes facilitating the influx of migrants. Often families are renting out rooms or upper portions in existing houses, and this close use of intimate space at times results in everyday arguments and tensions as the village struggles to engage with the influx of 'outsiders'.[15] This is a far cry from the image so often presented of upper middle-class buyers gentrifying the landscape along simple rural–urban and poor–rich divisions.

However as mentioned earlier, the commodification of land in the area has created yet another cadre of local villagers who are market savvy and have managed to profit from this circuit of capital. Their interventions involve selling and buying land in areas where there is a chance of schemes getting built. These villagers have picked up the language of the market; they are often those who already held relatively more amount of land or were in positions of power (the *numberdar*) or were prominent in local politics. The process of the market—unlike the process of direct dispossession—excludes the voice and the agency of the lower classes and economically weaker castes. For example, the Christian population of Halloki does not get a say in the process of the commodification and selling of land to LDA appointed developers, simply because they do not own property.

The rise of a new class of villagers who are ready to make the most of the commodification of land, and the markets' silencing of the landless residents' claims to the social and economic space of the village becomes key to making the land acquisition process smoother. Marketisation allows for the silencing of non-economic claims to the land in the village of Panju in particular, which is the largest of the villages presented here and the one that is closest to major road infrastructure and hence more integrated in urban modes of production, which makes it easier to convince people to sell their land. This is also the village where the collapse of the category of peasant is most visible. Landowners have begun to see land as a financial relation, instead of their earlier relationship to it as a means of production. The villages of Toor and Warraich, who were more militantly against the scheme, are also the villages where these processes have not taken root as deeply; in fact, they had actively been sidelined by these processes.

Yet over subsequent visits to Toor and Warraich, we noticed that residents had increasingly become keen to the shifting vicissitudes of the market and remain up to date not only on their case but on market prices as well. Their future is uncertain as the fate of the LDA City project was settled in court. For almost five years, the question of whether the LDA City scheme would go ahead or not remained up in the air; however, the purchase of land continued on the ground. In late 2019, the LDA began to bring the housing project back on track by promising plot allocations and advertising the scheme once again.[16] On the ground, the villagers still saw no way out of the scheme. One man resigned, 'We will have to sell; there is no choice. Look at the area around us; the road has come all the way up till here. It is just a matter of time.'

What does infrastructure do to resistance? Having physically fought, resisted, and even thrown out the LDA at one point, it is not the Land Acquisition Act or the prospect of state force that has so much compelled these people as it is the more insidious infrastructural changes and the knowledge that in the village right next door, people are selling with little fuss. With no fodder to feed their cows, irrigation channels turned off, surrounding villagers absorbed by cement and bounded up by walls, the prospect of a direct confrontation with the state became a less tenable strategy. The new double-road going into the area from the north-western part of the city and a flyover built to connect the area to the south-eastern part of the city contribute to the sense that the agrarian future of the marked area has little life in it.

Yet despite these changes, the sheer scale of the project and acquisition would have proven idle grounds for a ferocious resistance; indeed we saw sparks of them initially. Yet the nexus between the urban developers and the LDA ensured that the area was fragmented and that people got drawn in by the prospect of better prices than those the government was giving. Furthermore, operating under the knowledge that land had been notified under the Land Acquisition Act, the prospect of the state snatching their land from them at throwaway prices was a likely one. The consortium formed by the urban developers limited a competitive market to dictate prices, and this monopoly allowed the developers to reap in billions in profits. The case of LDA City lays bare how increasingly the state, rather than clearing the way for capitalists, is becoming indistinguishable from them. Urban development authorities have thus usurped power from local governments.

The case presented demonstrates the ways in which the new urban citizen in Lahore is one whose political subjectivity increasingly becomes moulded into a market subject. This feeling is encapsulated in the words of one of the elderly Christian men who remarked sadly, 'In the old days we valued relations, not land. If people did not abide by the communal water sharing system, they would be deprived of their land. Yet those days are gone now.'

NOTES

1. The authors would like to thank Bilal Anwar, Zahid Ali and Umar Zamran for helping with our research.

2. The interviews were conducted in Urdu and Punjabi and have been translated by the authors.

3. A nazim is an elected local councillor. Local councillors were introduced under the Local Bodies Ordinance 2001.

4. For the LDA's rules of approving private housing schemes, see: Lahore Master Plan 2016, Annex to Chapter 7, pp. 1–4. <https://www.lda.gop.pk/images/final_report_volume_i.pdf>.

5. Lahore has seen the entry of a number of public and private actors in developing new housing schemes. One of the biggest actors is the Defence Housing Authority (DHA), which is directly run by the Pakistan Army.

6. Land that was historically used in common as pastoral grazing grounds and other communal uses (in local parlance, called 'rakh' land) have also been subsumed by state land, and now multiple politicians own land there. Thus in Rakh Jedu the acquisition process is substantially different from that of the other villages.

7. The Lahore Metropolitan Area Master Plan 2021 explicitly marks out this area as the new corridor for industrial and housing growth <https://www.lda.gop.pk/images/Integrated_Master_Plan_of_Lahore.jpg>.

8. Village headman, a state appointed figure introduced in the colonial period.

9. A report in the *Daily Times* on 6 August 2016 cites that Lahore gets the lion's share of Punjab's development budget. <https://dailytimes.com.pk/65767/lahore-gets-lions-share-of-punjab-development-budget/>.

10. Other mega projects include the Ravi River Development Front, the New City project, a central business district in Gulberg, the Metro Line, and the Orange Line.

11. In 2001, the LDA decided to launch another scheme. After acquiring the land possessed by an earlier housing scheme, it declared the acquisition footprint to come under the label of LDA Avenue 1. Despite building the road infrastructure and emptying the land of the earlier agricultural plantations, the scheme became a hallmark of the failure of the LDA as a land developer fit for the contemporary environment. The LDA Avenue 1 scheme remains mired with litigation from villagers, land speculators, and other housing schemes. Even until 2019, the matter remains unresolved as shown in the following report in *Dawn* on 2 August 2019 <https://www.dawn.com/news/1497581>.

12. These are Millennium Land, Urban Developers, Paragon City, Alfa Estate, Pak Estate and Maymar Housing Service.

13. Rural land record keepers.
14. In 2018, the then LDA Director, General Ahad Cheema, was arrested by NAB over alleged corruption in the LDA City project. NAB withdrew the said case in September 2020 <https://www.dawn.com/news/1579342/court-allows-nab-to-close-lda-city-corruption-probe>.
15. AbdouMaliq Simone reminds us that in the absence of state provision of low-income housing, people develop their own resources to cope with the absence of these provisions—what he calls 'people as infrastructure' (2004).
16. LDA attempted to resurrect the scheme by promising plot allotments after the controversy surrounding it, especially after NAB arrested the then LDA DG Ahad Cheema. Dawn, 'LDA City House Scheme: Land arranged to allot plots to 9,700 file holders'. 31 December 2019 <https://www.dawn.com/news/1525339>.

References

Ali, Imran, *The Punjab under Imperialism, 1885–1947*, Princeton, NJ: Princeton UP, 2014.

Allen, John, *Lost Geographies of Power*, Malden, MA: Blackwell Pub., 2003.

Banerjee-Guha, Swapna, *Accumulation by Dispossession: Transformative Cities in the New Global Order*, Los Angeles: SAGE, 2010.

Brenner, Neil, 'Urban Governance and the Production of New State Spaces in Western Europe, 1960–2000', *Environment & Policy the Disoriented State: Shifts in Governmentality, Territoriality and Governance*, (2004), pp. 41–77.

'Chinese Bank to Provide Rs162mn Loan for Orange Line', *Dawn*, 12 December 2015, accessed at 30 June 2016 <http://www.dawn.com/news/1228044>.

Gazdar, Haris, *Residential Security as Social Protection*, SPA Working Papers, 2009.

Goldman, Michael, 'Speculative Urbanism and the Making of the Next World City', *International Journal of Urban and Regional Research*, 35, 3 (2010), pp. 555–81.

Harvey, David, *The New Imperialism*, Oxford: Oxford University Press, 2003.

Levien, Michael, 'Six Thesis on India's Land Question: From Primitive Accumulation to Regimes of Dispossession', *Economic and Political Weekly*, 50, 22 (2015).

———, 'The Land Question: Special Economic Zones and the Political Economy of Dispossession in India', *Journal of Peasant Studies*, 39, 3–4 (2012), pp. 933–69.

Menon, Nivedita, and Aditya Nigam, 'Globalization 1: Accumulation by Dispossession', *Power and Contestation: India since 1989*, Halifax: Fernwood Pub., 2007.

Merrifield, Andy, *The New Urban Question*, Pluto Press, 2014.

Qadeer, Mohammad A., 'An Assessment of Pakistan's Urban Policies, 1947–1997', *The Pakistan Development Review*, 35, 4 (1996), pp. 443–65.

Simone, AbdouMaliq, 'People as Infrastructure: Intersecting Fragments in Johannesburg', *Public Culture*, 16, 3 (2004), pp. 407–29.

Sud, Nikita, 'The Men in the Middle: The Missing Dimension in Global Land Deals', *Journal of Peasant Studies*, 41, 4 (2014), pp. 593–612.

3

Looking at the City from Below: How 'Access' Approach and 'Cityscapes' Contribute to the Understanding of Marginalisation in Amritsar

Helena Cermeño

Introduction

Cities represent for each of their residents a different and complex overlapping of past and present experiences, needs, and aspirations. Precast urban development programmes, recycled from a set of already existing repertoires resulting from global paradigms of development, are unlikely to acknowledge the complexity and variety of urban experiences worldwide. Ethnographies of small and medium-sized cities continue, nevertheless, to be scarce. In the city of Amritsar in Indian Punjab, as in many other South Asian cities, how ordinary residents make sense of the city from their own positionalities remains largely ignored, both in the processes of urban planning and academic knowledge production. Euro-North American urban theory not only persists in academic and everyday imaginaries around the globe (Amoo-Adare 2017), it is also generally uncritically embraced by planners and policymakers, resulting in concepts such as 'world class cities', 'global cities', 'creative-', and 'smart cities' being held up as the ideal model for Indian cities. Decolonial scholars have critiqued the epistemic violence intrinsic in the 'tyranny of abstract universals' (Mignolo 2007) such as these recurrent buzzwords steering urban planning in India and elsewhere today. Still, except for a few significant works (e.g. Sandhu 2006; Sandhu and Singh 2011; Sandhu 2013; Sandhu and Teoria 2013), there is little systematic research that critically examines processes of urban development and dominant neoliberal trends governing urban planning in Amritsar and the role of the resulting development ventures in (re-)shaping the everyday life of ordinary residents.

In order to reflect on the effects—and calculations—of urban development programmes, particularly how they shape or limit the ability of residents to access and benefit from urban resources (i.e. housing, services, and the city space at large), it is necessary to take a critical stance on urban development, planning, and housing projects. New methodological approaches need to bring to the forefront the perspective and voice of those targeted as 'subjects of development' that these programmes intend to 'benefit'. Based on the case study of Jhuggi Mokhampura[1] (Amritsar)—a resettlement low-income housing scheme sponsored by the Municipal Corporation of Amritsar[2]— and extensive fieldwork conducted in 2015, I explore in this chapter the potential of an 'access' approach (Ribot and Peluso 2003) and the concept of 'cityscapes' (Cermeño and Mielke 2016) as lenses to 'look at the city from below' and unveil ongoing processes of marginalisation. The case study featured in this chapter demonstrates how development planning and low-income housing projects, which aim to improve the lives of marginalised city residents, actually often hinder access to resources and the city space at large, shaping urban landscapes and livelihoods in ways that create sites of conflict and contestation and (re-)produce further social exclusions.

I begin this chapter by reviewing the policy background and national 'missions' under which the Jhuggi Mokhampura housing scheme is framed, reflecting on the aims and logics of their development calculus. Subsequently, I explore the effects of urban planning and development rationalities in this case study through engaging those whom these programmes intend to benefit. For that purpose, participant observation, and in-depth and structured interviews were conducted with residents of Jhuggi Mokhampura.

The concept of 'access' facilitates the investigation and operationalisation by guiding the researcher to look at practices that enable or hinder residents' ability to gain, control, maintain, transfer, and improve their houses and services, and how these practices are intertwined with the development process of the housing scheme and the power relations and power resources of different actors involved (e.g. residents, municipal corporation officers, and local politicians) influencing these practices. The access approach refers here not only to the capacity of residents to 'benefit' from the sponsored housing scheme, but also to the ability of residents to benefit from the city space from their new positionality after the resettlement.

During fieldwork, 'access to the city' was explored through a process of cognitive mapping. Drafted along with the residents and subsequently redrawn and interpreted, these maps serve as a visualisation of different resident's 'cityscapes', representing the range of everyday practices that construct the experienced and imagined space of the city for each individual. The cityscape approach is based on the assumption that the lived and imagined life-worlds of residents express and at the same time also produce themselves through everyday social practices. Hence, I argue, it is through the exploration of these routinised social practices that we can better understand how residents situate themselves in the urban social and spatial grid, and ultimately unveil patterns of social exclusion and marginalisation.

Policy Background and the Nehru National Urban Renewal Mission

In recent decades, Indian cities have undergone fast social and spatial transformations. According to the last census (GOI and MoHA, 2011), more and more settlements are acquiring urban characteristics, and peri-urban areas in particular are witnessing processes of rapid urban transformation. One significant phenomenon is the development of middle- and high-income exclusionary housing schemes in the urban peripheries. These fully serviced satellite settlements contrast with the scarcity of resources in other urban locations and highlight the uneven access to resources, growing polarisation, and spatial segregation between high-class urbanites and the urban poor.

The response from the Indian government to the challenges of urban growth and urban poverty over the years has produced several centrally sponsored national 'missions' and development projects. These programmes have been pushed forward by international aid institutions like the World Bank pursuing, since the 1980s, a clear neoliberal urban agenda (Sandhu and Singh 2011). The subsequent implementation of urban development strategies at both the national and city level, although 'benevolent',[3] for they envisage improving the lives of the urban poor, have either triggered a limited output (Sivaramakrishnan 2011) or, as underlined in this chapter, produced further exclusions.

Decentralisation in India, since the 74th Constitutional Amendment Act (CAA) of 1992, establishes that the responsibility over the design and execution of housing and development schemes falls mostly on each state or union territory. Therefore, within the federal framework, respective local governments are entitled to determine their needs and priorities and set their own development agendas. In practice, however, local urban planning efforts are often aligned with national plans inspired by global agendas and the latest urban fashions. Underlying neoliberal rationalities of dominant urban 'visions', e.g. 'sustainable-', 'world-class-', or 'global cities', foster competitiveness between cities over access to international capital markets and foreign direct investments (FDI). Under the emblem of 'good governance' (Kessides 2000), urban planning in Indian cities has increasingly shifted to a logic of 'competitiveness' and 'bankability' that produces urban visions and planning strategies removed from the socio-political realities of urban life. The Amritsar City Development Plan (CDP 2006–2025)[4] and the Amritsar Master Plan: 2010–2031 (PUDA 2010) also the include 'world class-' (Trust of India 2014) and 'smart city' vision (GOI and MoHUPA 2015). These planning instruments, which are modernisation-inspired and include planning visions derived from non-Indian contexts, have failed to implement innovations for addressing the situation and the needs of low-income residents. In fact, as Mahadevia, Joshi, and Sharma (2009) put it, it is mostly through the non-implementation of Master Plans that the poor seem to find the ability to access resources. Against this backdrop, I argue in this paper that it is through the implementation of current planning visions and policies—largely inspired by dominant neoliberal trends—that marginalised residents are often precluded from accessing urban resources, thus further generating exclusions. The same urban poor that find their way through the non-implementation of the Master Plan are made 'legible to the state' (Scott 1998) as 'subjects of development' under a variegated range of 'missions' and improvement projects which are proclaimed as initiatives for social inclusion. By bringing the example of the Jhuggi Mokhampura housing scheme, I intend to highlight how these development ventures frequently tend to (re-)produce marginalisation and unjust spaces in the city under the emblem of legality.

Although originally initiated under previous poverty alleviation and urban development programmes, the Jhuggi Mokhampura housing scheme was mostly developed under the Jawaharlal Nehru National Urban Renewal

Mission (JNNURM) in Amritsar—a central government-sponsored programme. JNNURM was rolled out in India in 2005 as a subsumption of many initiatives undertaken over the years[5] (Sivaramakrishnan 2011). Given its scale and ambition, JNNURM spawned greater expectations than its predecessors. It was, however, also received with strong criticisms by scholars who considered it 'the official carrier of neoliberal urbanism' in India (Banerjee-Guha 2009: 95).

To understand these criticisms, one has to look back to the development of previous poverty alleviation programmes that subsequently resulted in the JNNURM. A number of poverty reduction and urban development programmes had been introduced over the years under the slogan 'Garibi Hatao!' ('Remove Poverty'). One of the more important ones was the establishment in 1970 of the Housing and Urban Development Corporation (HUDCO), whose mandate was to create affordable housing finance with low interest loans and longer repayment periods (Sandhu 2013). Similarly, the Urban Land Ceiling and Regulation Act (ULCRA) in 1976 represented a major effort to limit the development of luxury housing, control urban land property, and provide land and resources for low-income housing and public interest (Banerjee-Guha 2009). Interestingly, ULCRA was progressively repealed in several states. The abrogation was set as a pre-requisite to access particular funding lines such as 'technical assistance programmes' and 'incentive-based grants' and, later, also a pre-condition to 'benefit' from JNNURM. Similarly, the Urban Reform Incentive Fund (URIF)[6] conditioned aid to neoliberal structural reforms[7]— including repealing the ULCRA and the subsequent opening up of vacant land to the market (Banerjee 2002; Mahadevia 2006; Banerjee-Guha 2009; Sivaramakrishnan 2011).[8]

Within the JNNURM framework, different development projects were framed from 2005 onwards. The mission established different guidelines to improve 63 Indian cities, Amritsar being one of them.[9] It required the coordination between different ministries[10] which ultimately led to the development of two main—partly overlapping—'sub-missions':[11] the Urban Infrastructure and Governance (UIG) and the Basic Services to the Urban Poor (BSUP), both dealing with water supply, sanitation, sewerage, drainage, and roads (GOI and MoHUPA 2007). The latter became the main funding frame for the Jhuggi Mokhampura housing scheme. Initially deployed for a period of seven years, JNNURM was extended and concluded in 2014.

By then, the Jhuggi Mokhampura housing scheme had not yet been fully developed. Since 2014, new programmes have taken over with new labels and acronyms but with similar approaches, fostering mainly the 'development-economic growth' tandem.[12] The focus on economic growth and competition as drivers for 'more inclusive urban planning' and 'affordable housing' does not constitute a particularly innovative approach. They are a continuation of modernisation-driven approaches and neoliberal policies in the realm of planning and development that often create contradictions and social tensions (Jessop 2002).

Conceptual Premises

'Access' Versus 'Rights' Approach

Following the same rationale as JNNURM and soon after the framing of a new National Urban Housing and Habitat Policy (NUHHP-2007), the national government developed the 'Affordable Housing—2010' guidelines and subsequently the Rajiv Awas Yojana (RAY) programme. These entailed bringing in the private sector to provide formal housing to the urban poor through the extension of loans and cash grants and with explicit stress on tenure security as property rights (Mahadevia 2011). Based on the assumption that provision of tenureship through urban land titles and property rights might facilitate access to credit, increase social inclusion, and provide residents with certain social protections (Soto 2000), it is often believed that regularisation or resettlement of informal low-income settlements would benefit the urban poor. A wide range of scholars, however, have challenged De Soto's (property) 'rights approach'—Mitchell (2009), Payne, Durand-Lasserve and Rakodi (2009), and Gilbert (2002), among others. The latter argues that policies based on titling programmes are merely strategies for winning votes during election time and trigger political patronage and dependency of the urban poor on political elites, constraining the capacity of residents to access resources.

In line with these authors and taking a cue from Ribot and Peluso (2003), I argue that the often used (property) 'rights approach' (à la De Soto) fails to provide a comprehensive view of how people de facto access (i.e. gain, control, maintain, transfer, and improve) urban resources—whether under given circumstances they have the ability or not to benefit from housing and services and the city space at large. Although a rights approach implies that certain claims are formally recognised by an institutional framework, many forms of access are not secured the same way (Sikor and Lund 2010). There are cases in which people do not have rights but have the ability to access resources and vice versa; being granted property rights can entail further constraints for the beneficiaries and not necessarily ensure access to resources.

Both could be illustrated in the case of Jhuggi Mokhampura. The first represents particularly the situation before the Jhuggi[13] community resettled and lived informally in different locations in Amritsar; deprived of legal ownership, residents were able, nevertheless, to negotiate access to shelter and resources in the city for decades. The latter relates to the situation after relocation into the Jhuggi Mokhampura housing scheme, where the Jhuggi community struggles on an everyday basis for access to housing and services (i.e. water supply, electricity, sewage, and drainage)—whether they hold property rights to their current houses or not.

Mechanisms of access to urban resources in, and from, Jhuggi Mokhampura are understood here as social practices enabling or hindering the ability of residents to gain, control, maintain, transfer, and improve their houses and services on an everyday basis. Through these 'everyday organising practices', residents negotiate within the Jhuggi community and with different actors in order to derive benefits from the development project. The Jhuggi Mokhampura housing scheme, with its own developmental rationalities and rules, can, therefore, be considered a field in which different actors, as agents with particular social (dis-)positions, take part in the conflict over and competition for urban resources. This approach is informed by Bourdieu's theory of practice and the concept of field (*champ*) and force fields (*champ de forces*) in which habitus[14] and forms of capital (sources of economic, social, cultural, and symbolic power) held by agents structure the social space (Bourdieu 1977; Bourdieu and Wacquant 1992; Bourdieu 1994; 2002; Eichholz et al. 2013; Bourdieu 2015). In this chapter I suggest that forms of capital(s) and the concept of habitus constitute a 'bundle of powers' (Ribot and Peluso 2003) and 'power resources' (Uphoff 1989; Mielke 2015) that can be possessed by individuals and ultimately shape power relations between actors. These power resources can be seen as force fields (Nuijten 2003; 2005)—'forms of dominance, contention and resistance' that can be mobilised to improve one's positionality within a particular field of conflict and to keep a particular sort of resource access (see Fig. 1).

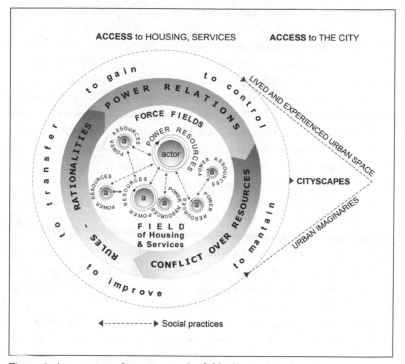

Figure 1: Access as social practices in the field of housing and services
© Helena Cermeño, after Eichholz et al (2013)

As depicted in Fig. 1, the access approach refers here not only to the capacity of residents to benefit (or not) from the sponsored housing scheme (housing and services), but also to the ability of residents to access and benefit from the city space according to their own positionality once displaced from their original settlements and relocated. In doing so, I aim to look at not only patterns of exclusion and marginalisation on the micro scale within the Jhuggi Mokhampura settlement but also at the city scale.

'CITYSCAPES' AS IMAGINARIES AND ENACTED EVERYDAY PRACTICES[15]

For that purpose, 'access to the city' is explored here through a 'cityscapes' lens. This theoretical perspective enables us to not only look at enacted everyday practices in Jhuggi Mokhampura and beyond that shape the lived and experienced urban space, but the spatial imaginaries as well. This theoretical approach takes cue from Appadurai's conceptualisation of '-scapes'[16] referred to as 'imagined worlds'.[17] Nurtured by global flows of ideas, funding, and people (Appadurai 2005 [1996]), imaginaries transcend realities and even imagined communities (Anderson 2006 [1983]). The concept of 'cityscapes' implies that the way residents make sense of the city space and their everyday urbanism is not the result of objectively given relations but the output of perspectival constructs, modulated by their spatial, historic, linguistic, and political positionality. Instead of looking at Jhuggi Mokhampura as a locality, we understand it from a relational perspective, as a complex of localities: this includes the memories of the previous residences of the Jhuggi community, their current living space, and from there, their experience and images of the city space at large, and their imagined future aspirations within the city of Amritsar. As Appadurai puts it: '[T]he work of imagination allows people to inhabit either multiple localities or a kind of single and complex sense of locality, in which many different empirical spaces coexist' (Appadurai 2002: 43).

Since both lived and imagined life-worlds express—and at the same time produce—themselves through everyday social practices, it is through the study of these routinised practices that we can explore the individuals' 'cityscapes', visualised here as cognitive maps. In line with the previously elaborated access approach, residents' urban imaginaries too act as a sort of organised field of social practices that enables entering negotiation between spaces of agency and arenas of opportunities. Individual 'cityscapes', representing the social practices that produce and express the lived and imagined city, can reveal how their beholders access resources and situate themselves in the urban social and spatial grid at the city scale and hence inform about patterns of marginalisation and social exclusion.

Looking at the City from Below: Housing, Services, and the City Space

Based on an 'access' and 'cityscapes' perspective and in order to investigate how urban planning and housing development ventures shape the everyday life of ordinary residents, I combined qualitative and quantitative research methods in a mixed methods design. The focus was set on the ethnographic part of the research, using quantitative data as a way of triangulation and to complement the narrative accounts. Participant observation, informal, in-depth and structured interviews, and cognitive mapping were conducted with selected residents, local politicians, and municipal corporation officers and were later analysed. The schematic representations of the cognitive maps were drawn based on drafted maps developed in participatory sessions during the interviews, tracing the everyday social practices that shape access to housing, services, and the city space.

JHUGGI MOKHAMPURA HOUSING DEVELOPMENT PROJECT: RELOCATION OF JHUGGIS TO A MARGINAL LAND

The Jhuggi Mokhampura low-income housing scheme was developed by the Municipal Corporation on the northern side of the 'Challih Khuh' (Forty Wells) area along with the railway line to Batala. Initiated in 2005 under the BSUP funding programme, it aimed to relocate residents of jhuggis—mostly migrants—who had lived in different areas of the city for more than thirty years. At the time of this research, the Jhuggi Mokhampura locality encompasses those residents who have been able to benefit from a municipality-sponsored flat and those still residing in jhuggis in the immediate vicinity of the housing scheme (Fig. 2). The representation of the cognitive map (Fig. 2) of one of the interviewees, a Hindu widow and mother of two working as a waste-picker and residing in a flat in Jhuggi Mokhampura, exemplifies the current situation of the housing scheme.

The Challih Khuh area is known in the city for its proximity to the Leisure Valley cum Rose Garden, which used to be one of the main green spaces in the city after the Ram Bagh Gardens. Under British rule, a complex hydraulic engineering system comprising forty wells, that supplied water to the city of Amritsar, was constructed in this location which progressively became the centre of a popular park. Since 1902 and for about 70 years subsequently, the forty wells spread over 40 acres along the Rose Garden not only provided water to the city but also a space for leisure to the neighbouring residents of the densely populated 'Jaurah Fatak' ('railway intersection') area. Subsequently, this water supply system was replaced and, gradually, the park was abandoned. Despite different initiatives to create a heritage park in Challih Khuh, the area has remained largely disregarded by

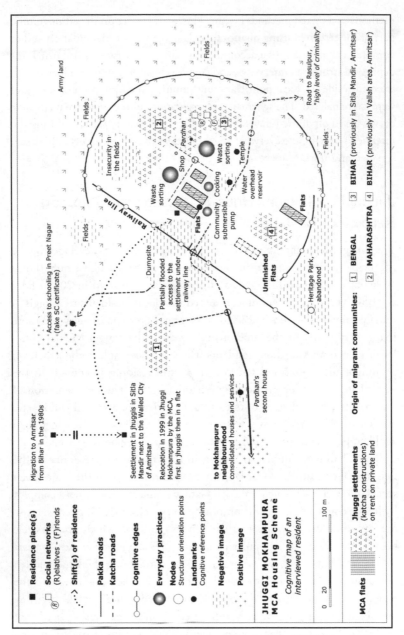

Figure 2: Cognitive map of an interviewed resident in Jhuggi Mokhampura
© Helena Cermeño

the municipality. Two railway lines, the abandoned park itself on the south and an extensive military area on the northeast, act as physical borders to the settlement (Fig. 2). Over time, the isolation of the housing scheme from the city space as well as its perceived insalubrity and insecurity has contributed to the negative image of the area among Jhuggi Mokhampura residents and inhabitants of nearby localities.

The municipality selected this marginal location in the city as the site for the resettlement project in the 1990s. Following the 1990 National Housing Policy (NHP–1990) that had promised housing for the poor, the Municipal Corporation of Amritsar (MCA) and local politicians approached jhuggi communities. Initially 'persuaded' in 1997 and later forced and their houses torn down, jhuggi settlers were relocated to Challih Khuh with the promise of affordable housing. They left their squatter settlements in the Wallah Canal area at the eastern edge of the city, where the Wallah Mandi (market) and the small industrial centres offered numerous employment options. The same was true for those who had to leave their settlements in the Durgiana temple and Sitla Mandir neighbourhood near the Walled City, the geographic centre of the city and hub of economic activities.

For the relocation process, the MCA carried out a survey and developed a list of jhuggi-settlers in Amritsar. Since migrant jhuggi communities in the city had been excluded from the municipality's 'slums' list developed in 1983, which has, to date, not been updated, they neither fit into the National Slum Development Programme (NSDP 1996–2006) nor did they benefit from the Valmiki Ambedkar Awas Yojana (VAMBAY-2001), which dealt with the provision of basic amenities in notified slum settlements. Interestingly, most jhuggi settlers of migrant origin also did not qualify for caste-based housing programmes in Punjab. Officially, low-caste people migrating from one state to another are not necessarily entitled to the rights and reservations of the Scheduled Castes (SC) recognised in the new state. This puts migrants such as the jhuggi communities in Jhuggi Mokhampura in a particularly marginal and vulnerable position.

The neglect and exclusion of jhuggi communities in Amritsar from the different reservations and housing and poverty alleviation programmes has lasted decades. Only in 2005, under the JNNURM and BSUP programmes, did the municipality[18] undertake the construction plan of the flats to relocate jhuggi communities. Under the JNNURM, affordable housing projects were rolled out all over India as a co-funding venture between the national government, state governments, and ULBs. In so doing, JNNURM aimed at strengthening municipal governance in accordance with the 74th Constitutional Amendment Act, 1992, supporting local projects that could create 'economically productive, efficient, equitable, and responsive cities' by upgrading infrastructures in cities and providing services under the sub-programme BSUP.

In 2005, because of the launch of BSUP and under the initiative of local politicians, all remaining jhuggi dwellers, represented by their local *pardhans* (community leaders), negotiated the relocation from their temporary settlements to Challih Khuh. Those who refused the resettlement settled along the highway (the 'bypass road') that draws the administrative limit of the Municipal Corporation beyond which the MCA has no jurisdiction. Most of the jhuggi communities though, hoping to benefit from the promised housing, shifted to Challih Khuh. In the absence of new houses until 2008, they clustered in the newly developed temporary Jhuggi settlement in specific areas according to their state of origin: Bihar, Maharashtra, and West Bengal (Fig. 2). In the process of relocation and resettlement, local politicians played a role as mediators between *pardhans* and the municipality authorities. Although municipalities are supposed to be in-charge of provision of low-income housing, in practice, interviews showed that political patronage was influential in facilitating access to the flats provided in the low-income housing scheme to some jhuggi settlers. Since the available flats by 2012 could not be allocated to the increasing number of jhuggi settlers, political connections, particularly in the run-up to the 2013 elections, became a strong asset in securing the allotment of a flat.

ALLOTMENT OF FLATS AND THE ROLE OF PARDHANS

In contrast with previous schemes and missions, the eligibility criteria of potential beneficiaries of low-income flats in Jhuggi Mokhampura were not specified. The MCA directly targeted and listed jhuggi inhabitants for future allotment of flats. In an attempt to render transparent the process of distribution in 2012–13, spurred in no small measure by the upcoming elections, a lottery was conducted[19] and reported in the local media. The elapsed time between the collection of application forms and the lottery draw—nearly five years—complicated the process. Many residents accused municipal officers of having forged the data in application forms, which ultimately made many residents ineligible at the time of the lottery draw.[20] As a result, several flats remained unclaimed. Subsequently, the vacant and newly completed flats could be allotted at the discretion of the municipal corporation officers. In interviews with residents, they reported accusations against the municipality for accepting high payments against allotments of flats in collusion with the *pardhans*.

This resulted in an increase in the initially subsidised prices of the flats. While the market price of flats was estimated to be INR 2.5 lacs, allotees were only required to cover 10 per cent of the cost for those who could prove their scheduled caste origins and 12 per cent for those belonging to any 'general caste'. Some interviewees reported that in order to access Scheduled Caste subsidised prices and further social benefits such as education grants and reservations, they sought fake local SC certificates. So that access to subsidised flats would reach a larger pool of low-income residents, the housing programme was initially designed to facilitate the poorer families by allowing them to make monthly instalments of INR 400; this option, however, was never implemented. Beneficiaries were required to cover the whole amount in a single payment, an extra hindrance in accessing the new housing for many among the jhuggi communities who did not have enough to pay at once.

The role of the three *pardhans*[21] representing the three main jhuggi communities—migrants from Bihar, Maharashtra, and Bengal—goes much beyond acting as brokers between residents and the municipality. It encompasses negotiation with MCA officers and local politicians at the time of resettlement and allocation of flats, collection of identity documents of residents for accessing allotments or SC benefits, negotiation with the municipality for improvement of services, and even social control of the jhuggi settlers. Although *pardhans* present themselves as the most influential members of the jhuggi communities—exercising considerable power and authority over the rest of the community members—they are considered by many as self-designated community leaders. *Pardhans* are neither elected nor selected; they nominate themselves based on their education level (i.e. literacy), their access to local politicians, and their ability to negotiate with government officers.

Several residents have criticised them for seeking personal benefits from their intermediation between the communities and the local administration. Respondents sought to substantiate these claims by bringing the social mobility manifest in the 'prosperous lifestyle' of one of the *pardhans*: 'he "owns" a flat, a shop in the jhuggi settlement from which he earns a living, and a "*pakka*" (stable) house in the consolidated and serviced neighbouring area of Mokhampura, about 300 meters away from Challih Khuh flats' (see also Fig. 2). Another *pardhan* has secured 'one of the most valued flats—on the ground floor which provides easier access to the community-arranged submersible water pump'. These claims, commonly shared by residents, show the increasing distrust of *pardhans* among the communities they are supposed to lead and represent.

As a way of legitimising their position and work to the community members or outsiders—such as NGO members or researchers—*pardhans* have collected and maintain a large number of official documents and residents' identifications over the years.[22] These documents have helped them negotiate with local politicians and urban local bodies and at the same time, helped them maintain social control and exercise power over other residents.

CURRENT ACCESS TO HOUSING AND SERVICES AND THE CITY SPACE AT LARGE

While municipality reports from 2014 stated that the Jhuggi Mokhampura housing scheme had 'successfully provided accommodation and basic services [i.e. water supply, electricity, and sewage] to about eighty families', several visits to the field in 2014–15 and early 2016 reveal a different situation on the ground. About twenty years after the first jhuggi communities shifted to Challih Khuh, the site presented quite a distressing scene. Out of 320 planned flats, only 128 have been constructed and allotted at the time of this research and no more housing units are expected to be constructed in the coming years. Interviews revealed that several of those who were allotted flats did not move into them. They decided to stay in the nearby jhuggi settlements, keeping their allotted flats empty. Many reasons were given for that; the main one being that the flats were too small. With an area of 28 sq. yards (approximately 23.41 m²) and one single room, the living space can hardly accommodate an average-sized family.[23] On the other hand, the lack of water supply in the flats forces residents to carry buckets of water from the community submersible water pump on a daily basis.

It is striking that flats were allotted and handed over to residents in 2012–13 despite the fact that neither the construction of houses nor the provision of services was completed at the time. Interviews conducted among municipal officers demonstrate that the celerity of the allotment and occupation of flats responded to a political decision. On the one hand, it was a move undertaken to help Amritsar's perception as a 'slum-free city' while on the other, the provision of flats would ensure the support of jhuggi communities as a consolidated voting bank in the 2013 elections. This explains the lack of care in the provision of services after the initial burst of activity that went into the allotments of flats. During the several months in which fieldwork was conducted, no major changes in terms of services provision were reported.

Not unlike the incomplete state of the housing scheme, since 2013, several blocks of flats have been abandoned in the middle of the construction process while those already completed exhibit construction of poor quality. As depicted in the cognitive map above (Fig. 2), the settlement is surrounded by 'katcha' (unpaved) roads connecting the housing scheme to the neighbouring localities. Drainage and sewage systems have not been completed; the dysfunctional water tower has become a landmark in the cognitive map of residents. Years-long negotiations between residents and the municipality, mediated by pardhans and local politicians, had produced no improvement in the water supply at the time of this research. Municipality officers denounce the 'kundi' (illegal electricity) connections of residents as the reason for it. Jhuggi residents have linked their private electricity connections to the electrical transformer supplying the water tower motor. This, according to the municipality officials, increases the risk of overloading the electrical transformer. The lack of proper electricity supply to residents—even after they have applied for it and paid the administrative costs to the electrical company (INR 16,000) to access formal electricity connections and meters—is presented by municipal actors as the core of the water supply conflict, while residents directly point at the unwillingness and neglect of the municipality. Local politicians and the current councillor claim to have mediated between the residents and the electricity board to solve the issue of electricity provision but with limited success. The 'action and mobilisation' tactic, suggested by the current councillor as a way to pressurise the electricity board, seems to have been delayed purposefully until the new elections.

Given that the water overhead reservoir remains non-functional and the municipality refuses to turn it on, jhuggi dwellers have installed hand pumps in the settlements, while the flats' residents have contributed to install a community (electrical) submersible water pump. Hand pumps have progressively stopped working due to depletion of the water table and the limited depth of the bore. Hence, water quality is lacking, exposing jhuggi residents to the risk of water-related diseases. Although the arrangement of the community submersible water pump resolves to a certain extent the issue of basic access to water, it exemplifies the withdrawal of municipalities from their duties and the marginalisation of the jhuggi communities.[24]

In the immediate surrounding areas of the blocks, jhuggi houses in the locality have grown further since the allotment of flats, hosting more than 200 families today. In between flats and jhuggi settlements, the public space has largely been transformed into dumpsites that have become the centre of major economic activity of the residents of Jhuggi Mokhampura and the centre of everyday practices of several respondents. Removed from the Walled City and their previous employment opportunities, many of the residents rely solely on waste-picking activities as a way of life. Everyday activities of residents include collection and sorting of garbage, with women operating mostly in the space immediately next to their residences and men in the city space at large. This can be traced in the representation of the cognitive map in Fig. 2 as well.

The cityscapes of the residents of Jhuggi Mokhampura portray a discomforting image (Figs. 3–6). Outside their previous residential area and their garbage collection routes, the rest of the city spaces have become 'invisible' for most of the residents. The maps presented here are only a selection of four residents' mental maps. They highlight larger parts of the city (listed as 'unknown/unvisited areas' in the maps) from which residents of Jhuggi Mokhampura have become alienated. On the one hand, the grey spheres in the maps depicting residents' everyday practices in the city— previously quite diverse within the Walled City area and Wallah Mandi— are now mostly restricted to the area of the settlement and the marginal activities of waste collection. This entails quite limited access to the lived and experienced urban space beyond Jhuggi Mokhampura. On the other hand, the lack of further landmarks (in the maps) in the city beyond their current residential area and the ones collected from their memories of the past (before the resettlement project) implies narrow urban imaginaries of the city. These reduced 'imagined worlds' of the city manifest limited spaces of interaction between those living in Jhuggi Mokhampura and elsewhere in the city, leading to isolation and marginalisation.

Discontent with the living conditions in flats and the location of the housing scheme manifests itself in the often-expressed desires and aspirations of community members to move back to their previous settlements in the city (Fig. 3) or move out elsewhere (Fig. 5). These mobilities, lived, imagined, or aspired, are drafted in the cognitive maps (Figs. 3 to 6). People continue to harbour positive memories of the Durgiana Temple and Sitla Mandir areas (Figs. 3 and 6) in the vicinity of the Walled City for it provided better employment opportunities and better access to central locations in the city.

However, when asked about the possibility of selling the flats, access to transfer, and moving out of Jhuggi Mokhampura, all the respondents reported this to be unfeasible. The allotment letters specify that residents have obtained the 'right to live' in the allotted houses for a period of time limited to 15 years. Under the current conditions of tenure that hinder residents from selling or sub-renting their flats, only a few transfer cases were reported during the interviews. The *pardhans'* control over the community members ensures that flats are neither encroached upon by 'outsiders' nor sub-rented or resold violating the agreement with the municipality. According to the municipality, 'allotment letters are provided for a limited period of lease in order to prevent jhuggi settlers from selling their flats and resettling in slums again'.[25] This can be seen as a control-by-design mechanism that the municipality exercises over the residents through the housing project.

As a result, the future of their homes and livelihoods after the tenure period remains unclear. Many conveyed their fear of being evicted in the future, while others expressed resignation to constant uncertainty and tenure insecurity. The possibility to renegotiate in 'due time' the terms and conditions of their stay with the municipality seems to be the most shared impression among residents. Others see some possibility of renegotiating their tenure when the politicians and bureaucrats return to them to seek their support for the next elections. This supports Gilbert's observation that titling programmes for the urban poor are merely 'winner's strategies in times of elections' which provide a basis for political patronage and dependency of the urban poor on political elites (Gilbert, 2002; Payne et al., 2009) or, in this case, on *pardhans*.

Only a few residents in Jhuggi Mokhampura believe—despite lack of official documents supporting this hope—that once the tenure period elapsed, they would automatically become eligible for formal ownership of their houses. This would entitle residents to sell and transfer the property of

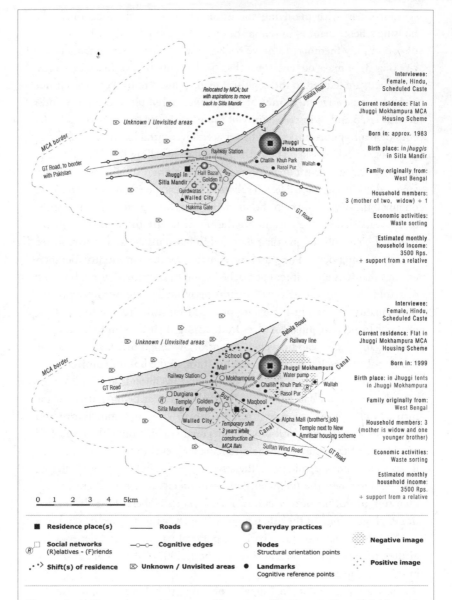

Figures 3–4: City-scale cognitive maps of interviewed residents in Jhuggi Mokhampura © Helena Cermeño

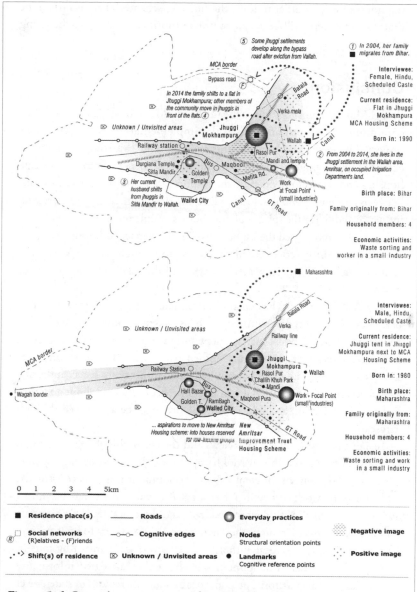

Figures 5–6: City-scale cognitive maps of interviewed residents in Jhuggi Mokhampura
© Helena Cermeño

the houses freely in order to leave the housing scheme. There is little hope that concrete steps will be taken by the authorities to improve the living conditions.

Conclusion

Jhuggi Mokhampura exemplifies the further exclusion of already marginalised communities in Amritsar through the implementation of a resettlement project. Taking an access-versus-rights approach, the case study explored the extent to which migrant jhuggi communities can benefit from low-income housing and services provided by the municipality, and the power relations between residents, *pardhans*, local politicians, and municipality officers who influence and shape the spheres of possibilities. While the provided allotment letters of flats recognised the 'right to live' in the particular housing scheme, they did not, in practice, entail the access to enough living space, basic facilities such as electricity, water, sewage, and drainage, and the city space at large.

The 'access analysis' has been operationalised by looking at everyday practices (e.g. everyday routines such as waste picking/sorting, water collection, cooking, house management and improvement, gathering, etc.), power resources (e.g. documents, information, gender, literacy, income, social status, friendships and kinship, political connections, force, authority, legitimacy, social control) and urban imaginaries of residents about how they situate themselves in, and relate with, the urban space as mapped through 'cityscapes'.

Insights gained from the interviews and the collection of cognitive maps demonstrates that the Jhuggi Mokhampura low-income housing scheme, which was born out of different urban development missions constructed within a framework of neoliberal visions of development, has become a 'calculated informality' field where residents and their local leaders renegotiate on a constant basis to improve their living conditions, access to housing, and basic services with the local authorities. However, as Ananya Roy puts it: 'there is nothing casual or spontaneous about the calculated informality that undergirds the territorial practices of the state; this idiom of state power is structural' (2009: 83). Hence, while this informality, manifested across diverse issues ranging from relocating communities to making housing allotments to the provision of basic services, certainly creates space for negotiations and contestations for the subaltern communities, for the most part, it actually benefits the calculations of the municipality, politicians, and *pardhans* who can conveniently bend or bypass the rules and regulations to their own advantage.

Cityscapes traced for selected residents highlighted not only lived experiences of access and conflict over resources but also imagined dimensions—aspirations, desires, and perceptions of the city. The relocation project seems to have influenced the image of the city held by jhuggi communities in the sense that it has contributed to limit their perception of the city space to the isolated area where they have been resettled. The major part of the city has become 'unknown/unvisited', distant from the realm of their everyday practices and even invisible from the horizon of their existence. Both cityscapes and narrative accounts of actors involved in the housing scheme also make it abundantly clear that the implementation of the relocation project has progressively contributed to the individually constructed and collectively shared negative image of their current home. As a result, the early optimism of interviewed residents to improve their living conditions in the Jhuggi Mokhampura housing scheme has given way to frustration and aspirations of moving out of the Challih Khuh.

Overall, the case study reinforces the idea that urban planning practices are promoting housing solutions that purposely congregate and segregate the urban poor in under-serviced, marginal locations distant from employment opportunities and cut off from the city space at large. Under the emblem of 'legality' and 'development', the Jhuggi Mokhampura housing scheme has been imagined and implemented to congregate, control, and govern the urban poor, and to exclude them from the rest of the city. Hence, already marginalised communities are further segregated from urban life and its promises. The findings presented in this chapter are reflective of how planning is inducing spatial boundary-making and thus generating new kinds of urban spatial exclusion.

NOTES

1. In the different documents and interviews gathered during the research, the housing scheme has been referred to with different names, e.g. Mokhampura, Jhuggi Mokhampura, Challih Khuh (Forty Wells), Rasoolpur Kaller, Indira Nagar-Mokhampura. Notwithstanding the significance of each of these designations and the underlying reasons for the terminology, for the sake of

clarity I will refer to the settlement along the text mostly as 'Jhuggi Mokhampura'. This labelling is borrowed from many of the Aadhaar cards (identification documents) of interviewees that reside in the jhuggi tents next to the housing scheme. The diverse range of names used to refer to this location can be seen from a toponymical perspective as the existence of different perceptions over the place according to different actors. Although it is beyond the scope of this paper to analyse toponymic practices, it is worth mentioning that the discursive act of designing a certain place with a specific name denotes more than merely the description of an already existing location. The act of naming can be seen as an attempt to translate the complexity of socio-spatial processes of a place into a more comprehensible, more 'manageable' order in the form of a text inscription, according to the specific subjective perception of one observer (Medway and Warnaby 2014). Different actors, with different interests and perceptions, can adopt different designations for the same place; hence, toponymic practices in Jhuggi Mokhampura can underline power relations, determining the way names are used to classify, manage, and control the space.

2. The selection of this residential scheme as case study for this chapter is motivated by the particular social status and migration background of the target, or 'beneficiary', group that reflects particular levels of marginalisation.

3. I borrow here Tania Murray Li's reflection on 'the will to improve' of development projects that she refers to as 'benevolent' but also 'stubborn' and 'parasitic'. She uses the term 'benevolent' for there is often a gap between what is intended and what

is finally accomplished. Li refers as well not only to the failures of certain development programs but to the new problems produced by the 'solutions' implemented. She uses 'stubborn' and 'parasitic', for, despite recurrent failures, schemes 'to improve' continue to be implemented, while they find their raison d'être in their own failures and shortcomings (Li 2007).

4. The City Development Plan for Amritsar presents the following vision statement where the 'world class' concept is introduced: 'Amritsar to be an international cultural, historical, pilgrim centre with agro-based food processing destination, having improved "world class: urban infrastructure [and] transport system' (MCA 2006).

5. Examples include Indira Gandhi Awas Yojana (GAY) or the Swarna Jayanti Shahari Rozgar Yojana (SJSRY) launched in 1997 and revamped in 2009 (GOI and MoHUPA 2016).

6. The URIF is derived from the City Challenge Fund (CCF) created in 2003 and inspired by development foreign 'experts' (from USAID and United Kingdom Department for International Development [UKDFID]).

7. In March 2005, 24 states had signed the Memorandum of Agreement for these reforms. In return, they would then receive grants from URIF in proportion to their urban population (Sivaramakrishnan 2011: 10).

8. The trends followed by the centre-sponsored 'missions' such as the JNNURM or the more recently launched 'Smart City Mission' that exemplify a growing influence of urban global paradigms and neoliberal trends, go hand in hand with the evolution of the national housing policies. In the last thirty years, about a dozen different national housing policies have been

developed in India (GOI and MoUD 2015). The National Housing Bank (NHB) was set up in 1988 and in 1990, V. P. Singh's government introduced the National Housing Policy (NHP) with a provision for housing for the poor. In 1998, however, the new National Housing Policy and Habitat Policy (NHP-HP) established guidelines that fostered public–private partnerships, which meant a substantial withdrawal of central and state governments from housing issues. The latest National Urban Housing and Habitat Policy (NUHHP-2007) developed in 2007 devolved part of the responsibilities over housing and infrastructure provision to Urban Local Bodies (ULBs) following the CAA 1992. Under the slogan of 'affordable housing for all' (Sandhu 2013) the NUHHP-2007 establishes general guidelines with focus on housing for the poor, but letting the implementation under the framework of missions such as the JNNURM, the Basic Services to the Urban Poor (BSUP) program—a submission of the JNNURM—and later on the Rajiv Awaas Yojana (RAY) programme, among others. This implies a focus on foreign direct investment (FDI), PPPs, and ultimately the provision of property rights in the logic that residents can then 'navigate the property and finance markets' along the lines of the World Bank economist Hernando De Soto (Mahadevia, 2011). Although a large part of the allocation of the BSUP targeted construction of low-income housing and therefore can be considered an important effort toward low-income housing allocation, the outcome of these constructions have been reported to be difficult to trace in the available reports, e.g. the location of housing units, the state of construction, if allotted or

occupied etc. (Sivaramakrishnan 2011; Sandhu 2013).

9. The JNNURM classifies urban agglomerations on the basis of population: Category 'A' - Super-Metropolitan Cities; Category 'B' - Cities having populations exceeding 10 lacs, but excluding the super-metros; Category 'C' - Cities having populations between 3 to 10 lacs and Category 'D' - Cities having populations between 2 to 3 lacs. Amritsar is listed within the Category 'B' - Cities having populations exceeding 10 lacs (Mahadevia 2006: 3399).

10. These include the Ministry of Urban Development (MoUD) and the Ministry of Urban Employment and Poverty Alleviation (now renamed as the Ministry of Housing and Urban Poverty Alleviation - MoHUPA). Until 2004, the two were part of the same Ministry. Because of the split, the JNNURM was separated into two—significantly overlapping— 'sub-missions'.

11. Besides the two major sub-missions, the programme evolved into four main components: The Urban Infrastructure and Governance (UIG), the Basic Services to the Urban Poor (BSUP), the Urban Infrastructures Development Scheme for Small and Medium Towns (UIDSSMT) and the Integrated Housing and Slum Development Programme (IHSDP). The BSUP and the IHSDP (already very similar, one addresses the cities included in the JNNURM, the IHSDP addresses those not included) had common predecessors: the National Slum Development Programme (NSDP 1996–97) which dealt with the provision of basic amenities to slum dwellers and was discontinued in 2005–06 and the Valmiki Ambedkar Awas Yojana (VAMBAY)—emerged from a previous scheme the Ambedkar Malin Basti Awas

Yojana (AMBAY)—both focused on the marginalised Dalits communities; subsequently, these programmes were subsumed into the BSUP and the IHSDP (GOI and MoHUPA 2007; Sivaramakrishnan 2011).

12. One example is the Pradhan Mantri Awas Yojana - Housing For All') (PMAY-HFA) rolled out in June 2015. The new 'mission' is to be implemented between 2015 and 2022, and aims to provide housing particularly for the 'Economically Weaker Sections' (EWS). Similarly, the GOI has also launched the 'Smart City Mission'. The programme aims to foster 'economic growth and improve the quality of life of people by enabling local area development' in Indian cities selected on the basis of competition (GOI and MoUD 2015).

13. A Jhuggi is a semi-temporary settle-ment in the form of tents and mud constructions.

14. The concept of 'habitus' developed by Bourdieu entails that by living and socialising in a specific social environment, individuals develop a set of internalised beliefs and attitudes that produces recurring patterns of behaviour (Bourdieu 1977).

15. The concept of 'cityscape' is a novel approach that is currently under exploration within the framework of a larger research that compares the cities of Amritsar and Lahore. This theoretical elaboration of cityscapes was first presented by the author in: 'Lahore's Cityscapes: Reimagining the Urban' in THAAP (Trust for History Art and Architecture, Pakistan) 6th International Conference 2015: 'People's History of Pakistan', held on 6–8 November 2015 at THAAP, Lahore, Pakistan, later published in Cermeño and Mielke (2016).

16. In *Modernity at Large*, Appadurai elaborates a framework of five dimensions of 'global cultural flows' referred to as '-scapes', that related to each other and shaped the lived and imagined word of individuals: ethnoscapes, mediascapes, technoscapes, financescapes, and ideoscapes (Appadurai 2005 [1996]: 33).

17. Although the term 'cityscape' can be also found in urban studies' literature, it then mostly refers to the visuality, legibility, and 'imageability' of the *form* of the city or urban landscapes (Lynch 1960; Lindner 2006).

18. In theory, the MCA has the mandate to develop housing schemes and services for the poor in Amritsar within its municipal limits, as well as to sanction privately developed colonies, while the Town Planning Office (TPO) is merely in-charge of sanctioning land use changes according to the current Master Plan 2010–31. In practice, Jhuggi Mokhampura is the only low-income housing scheme managed and implemented by the Municipal Corporation since more than two decades. Although the Municipal Corporation is the main actor responsible of the construction of low-income housing schemes, the Amritsar Improvement Trust (AIT)—an institution unaccountable to urban local bodies—has overtaken this mandate and has, over the years, developed several low-income and EWS-reserved flats in the city.

19. Based on the list of jhuggi residents produced by the municipality, MCA officers filled application forms on site with community members. The adopted gender-based approach entailed that only female members were entitled to apply for the allotment of flats. This process was reported by residents

to be problematic for a number of reasons. Some families for instance were not listed initially in the document produced by the municipality; some were not present in the area at the time applications were filled by municipality officers; others had moved later to Challih Khuh; or there were no female members in the households. This was the case for many migrant men whose wives had stayed back in their state of origin and therefore could not be eligible for the application process.

20. Out of around 80 applicants, 60 were allotted flats in the lottery draw, among which 15 per cent reported administrative problems for which allotees became non-eligible.

21. The current *pardhans* have been leading the communities since shortly after they moved to the Challih Khuh area. Before them, other *pardhans* negotiated the first relocation from the Durgiana temple and Vallah Canal to Forty-Wells between 1997 and 2005 with the municipality. Once established in the new location, a few individuals progressively developed links with local politicians and became the new *pardhans*.

22. These included documents from each family in order to 'help' residents with different administrative procedures: obtaining Aadhaar (identification) cards, voting cards, flat allotment letters, payment bills, and electricity meters. They have also kept records of newspapers clippings about the settlement, lists of residents (as vote bank for local politicians) and letters sent to the municipal officers and politicians stating community complaints and requests.

23. The average size of an Indian household is 4.8 family members according to the India National Family Health Survey (NFHS-3) 2005–06, released by the Government of India on 11 October 2007.

24. A community member has been appointed by residents to turn the engine on and off according to an agreed schedule, to take care of the maintenance of the pump, and to collect contributions from residents for reparations. Residents, mostly women and children, queue three times per day at specific scheduled times to collect water in buckets to carry up to their flats.

25. Interview with municipal corporation officer, 2015.

REFERENCES

Amoo-Adare, Epifania, 'Teaching to Transgress: Crossroads Perspective and Adventures in (?)-Disciplinarity', in K. Mielke and A. K. Hornidge (eds.), *Area Studies at the Crossroads: Knowledge Production after the Mobility Turn*, New York: Palgrave Macmillan, 2017, pp. 269–86.

Anderson, Benedict, *Imagined communities: Reflections on the Origin and Spread of Nationalism*, London: Verso, 2006.

Appadurai, Arjun, *Modernity at Large: Cultural Dimensions of Globalization*, Minneapolis and London: University of Minnesota Press, 2005.

————, 'The Right to Participate in the Work of the Imagination. Interview by Arjen Mulder', in J. Brouwer and A. Mulder (eds.), *TransUrbanism*, Rotterdam: Architecture Institute (NAI) Publishers, 2002.

Banerjee, Banashree, 'Security of Tenure in Indian Cities', in A. Durand-Lasserve and L. Royston (eds.), *Holding Their Ground: Secure Land Tenure for the Urban Poor in Developing Countries*, London: Routledge, 2002, pp. 37–58.

Banerjee-Guha, Swapna, 'Neoliberalising the 'Urban': New Geographies of Power and Injustice in Indian Cities', *Economic and Political Weekly*, 44, 22 (2009), pp. 95–107.

Bourdieu, Pierre, *Sociologie Générale: Cours au Collège de France 1981–1983*, (vol. 1), Paris: Raisons d'agir, Seuil, 2015.

————, 'Habitus', in: J. Hillier and E. Rooksby, (eds.), *Habitus: A Sense of Place*, Aldershot: Ashgate, 2002, pp. 27–36.

————, *Raisons Pratiques: Sur la Theorie de l'action*, Paris: Editions du Seuil, 1994.

————, *Outline of a Theory of Practice*, Cambridge and New York: Cambridge University Press, 1977.

————, and Loïc J. D. Wacquant, *An Invitation to Reflexive Sociology*, Chicago: University of Chicago Press, 1992.

Cermeño, Helena and Katja Mielke, 'Cityscapes of Lahore: Reimagining the Urban', in P. Vandal (ed.), *Thaap Journal 2016: People's history of Pakistan*, Lahore: Trust for History, Arts and Architecture, Pakistan (THAAP), 2016, pp. 110–39.

Eichholz, Michael, Kristof van Assche, Lisa Oberkircher, and Anna-Katharina Hornidge, 'Trading Capitals? Bourdieu, Land and Water in Rural Uzbekistan', *Journal of Environmental Planning and Management*, 56, 6 (2013), pp. 868–92.

Gilbert, Alan, 'On the Mystery of Capital and the Myths of Hernando de Soto: What Difference Does Legal Title Make?', *International Development Planning Review*, 24, 1 (2002), pp. 1–19.

Government of India (GOI) and Ministry of Home Affairs (MoHA), *Census of India*, 2011, last accessed 10 January 2016 <www.censusindia.gov.in>.

Government of India (GOI) and Ministry of Housing and Urban Poverty Alleviation (MoHUPA), *Towards More Inclusive Cities, Report*, 2016, last accessed 15 August 2016 <www.mhupa.gov.in/writereaddata/1266.pdf>.

————, *Pradhan Mantri Awas Yojana The Joint Secretary (Housing for All), Scheme Guidelines 2015*, 2015, last accessed 15 August 2016 <www.pmaymis.gov.in>.

————, *National Urban Housing and Habitat Policy 2007*, 2007.

Government of India (GOI) and Ministry of Urban Development (MoUD), *Smart Cities, Mission Statement and Guidelines*, 2015, last accessed 15 August 2016 <www.smartcities.gov.in>.

Jessop, Bob, 'Liberalism, Neoliberalism, and Urban Governance: A State–Theoretical Perspective', *Antipode*, 34, 3 (2002), pp. 452–72.

Kessides, Christine, *Cities in Transition: World Bank Urban and Local Government Strategy*, Washington, DC: The World Bank, 2000.

Li, Tania, *The Will to Improve: Governmentality, Development, and the Practice of Politics*, Durham: Duke University Press, 2007.

Lindner, Christoph, *Urban Space and Cityscapes: Perspectives from Modern and Contemporary Culture*, London and New York: Routledge, 2006.

Lynch, Kevin, *The Image of the City*, Cambridge: MIT press, 1960.

Mahadevia, Darshini, 'Tenure Security and Urban Social Protection in India', *Centre for Social Protection Research Report*, 5 (2011).

_____, Rutul Joshi, and Rutool Sharma, 'Integrating the Urban Poor in Planning and Governance Systems, India', Working Paper, *Centre for Urban Equity*, 2009.

_____, 'NURM and the Poor in Globalising Mega Cities', *Economic and Political Weekly*, 41, 31 (2006), pp. 3399–401.

Medway, Dominic, and Gary Warnaby, 'Whats in a Name. Place Branding and Toponymic Commodification', *Place Branding and Toponymic Commodification. Environment & Planning*, 46, 1 (2014), pp. 153–67.

Mielke, Katja, *Constructing Afghanistan? Rewriting Rural Afghans' Lebenswelten into Recent Development and State-Making Processes: An Analysis of Local Governance and Social Order*, Doctoral Dissertation, Center for Development Research (ZEFa), Bonn: University of Bonn, 2015, p. 396.

Mignolo, Walter D., 'Introduction: Coloniality of Power and De-colonial Thinking', *Cultural studies*, 21, 2–3 (2007), pp. 155–67.

Mitchell, Timothy, 'How Neoliberalism Makes its World', in: P. Mirowski and D. Plehwe (eds.), *The Road from Mont Pèlerin: The Making of the Neoliberal Thought Collective*, Cambridge: Harvard University Press, 2009, pp. 386–416.

Municipal Corporation Amritsar (MCA), *City Development Plan 2006–2025*, 2006.

Nuijten, Monique, 'Power in Practice: A Force Field Approach to Power in Natural Resource Management', *Journal of Transdisciplinary Environmental Studies*, 4, 2 (2005), pp. 3–14.

_____, *Power, Community and the State: The Political Anthropology of Organisation in Mexico*, London: Pluto Press, 2003.

Payne, Geoffrey, Alain Durand-Lasserve and Carole Rakodi, 'The Limits of Land Titling and Home Ownership', *Environment and Urbanization*, 21, 2 (2009), pp. 443–62.

Punjab Urban Planning and Development Authority (PUDA), *Amritsar Draft Master Plan 2010–2035*, 2010.

Ribot, Jesse C. and Nancy L. Peluso, 'A Theory of Access', *Rural sociology*, 68, 2 (2003), pp. 153–81.

Roy, Ananya, 'Why India Cannot Plan Its Cities: Informality, Insurgence and the Idiom of Urbanization', *Planning Theory*, 8, 1 (2009), pp. 76–87.

Sandhu, Kiran, 'Formal Housing Finance Outreach and the Urban Poor in India', *International Journal of Housing Markets and Analysis*, 6, 3 (2013), pp. 269–83.

————, 'Access to Land by the Urban Poor in Amritsar City, India; Grim Realities and Blurred Hopes', in University of Architecture in Venice (IUAV) (ed.), *Proceedings of N-Aerus 6th Annual Conference; Promoting social exclusion in urban areas: policies and practice, held in Lund, Sweden on September 16–17, 2005*, Venice: Department of Urban and Regional Planning, 2006, pp. 110–20.

————, and Gurpreet Singh, 'Impact of Neo-Urban Paraphernalia on Amritsar City: Of Transformations and Transgressions', *Sri Lanka Journal of Real Estate*, 1, 4 (2011).

Sandhu, Ranvinder S. and Manoj K. Teoria, *The State of Cities in North-Western India: A Case of Selected JNNURM Cities (Study Focus City: Amritsar)*, Amritsar: Centre for Research in Rural and Industrial Development (CRRID), 2013.

Scott, James C., *Seeing like a State: How Certain Schemes to Improve the Human Condition have Failed*, New Haven and London: Yale University Press, 1998.

Sikor, Thomas, and Christian Lund, 'Access and Property: A Question of Power and Authority', in T. Sikor and C. Lund (eds.), *The Politics of Possession: Property, Authority, and Access to Natural Resources*, Malden, Oxford and Chichester: Wiley and Blackwell, 2010, pp. 1–22.

Sivaramakrishnan, Kallidaikurichi C., *Re-visioning Indian Cities: The Urban Renewal Mission*, New Delhi: SAGE Publications, 2011.

de Soto, Hernando, *The Mystery of Capital: Why Capitalism Triumphs in the West and Fails Everywhere Else*, New York: Basic Books, 2000.

Trust of India, *Punjab: Sukhbir Singh Badal Approves Plan to Transform Amritsar into a World Class City*, 2014, last accessed 18 June 2014 <www.news18.com/news/india/sukhbir-singh-badal-approves-revised-amritsar-master-plan-616110.html>.

Uphoff, Norman, 'Distinguishing Power, Authority and Legitimacy: Taking Max Weber at His Word by Using Resources-Exchange Analysis', *Polity*, 22, 2 (1989), pp. 295–322.

4

Bolstering Security by Erecting Barriers and Restricting Access: The Case of Karachi[1]

Noman Ahmed

Introduction

Karachi, the most populous city of Pakistan, has faced the most turbulent times recently for a plethora of reasons. Sudden and repeated breakdown of public safety and the security situation is a central matter that has become a major concern for all who live in the city. Multiple terrorist attacks during the past two decades have taken their toll on the city. These attacks targeted military installations, places of worship, marketplaces, government buildings, residential quarters, buses and public transport vehicles, major streets and intersections, and a wide variety of commercial locations. Thousands of people have lost their lives while many more have been severely or partially wounded. These attacks have damaged assets and property of the people and government.

Shock, fear, psychological disorders, and anger are some of the common conditions that continue to affect millions of residents in the city. Lawless elements have strengthened their stronghold in the city, especially along peripheral and low-income neighbourhoods, due to weakening norms of urban governance and gradual decline in the maintenance of public safety. The residents of different neighbourhoods developed various measures to respond to rising street crimes, extortion, kidnappings for ransom, target killings, arson attacks, and other forms of anti-social activities. Ordinary people have resorted to initiatives to safeguard their residences, places of worship, public spaces, workplaces, and other categories of spaces themselves.

Installation of physical barriers on streets, thoroughfares, alleys, public assembly grounds, and other such spaces are a major visible outcome. These interventions have changed the status of conventional public, semi-public, and semi-private spaces in the functional and jurisdictional sense.

Other power-holders of the city have taken parallel measures. The organised resident groups of the city have barricaded and walled their houses and streets, and have hired private security guards for added protection. Many political parties have constructed fortifications around their headquarters, homes, and offices of prominent leaders after closing access roads for their protection, with armed guards and police patrolling the area. Police and military authorities have also adopted similar measures for protecting their offices and installations.

This chapter outlines the impact of terrorism in general and street crimes in particular on the profile of public and private spaces in Karachi and its repercussions on the urban fabric of the city. It examines the impacts of violent conflicts over the control and contestation of public spaces in Karachi. It also focuses specifically on the effects of public and private actors to enhance safety and security through the use of physical barriers as a form of conflict infrastructure. The core substance of this chapter is based upon a study conducted by the author during 2013–14 in association with the International Institute of Environment and Development (IIED). The present chapter also takes into consideration changes that have occurred during 2015 and after.

Karachi: A Conflict Profile

Karachi, the business capital of Pakistan and also the largest metropolis of the country, is facing serious security concerns. The city was once famously known as the 'city of lights' because of its long hours of active urban life and multi-cultural activities. It now seems to have lost that degree of vibrancy and social liberty. Karachi has seen recurring outbreaks of violence which have claimed thousands of lives. Data collected in Pakistan through different sources suggests that, of the 11,990 civilians who lost their lives due to bombs, suicide, and other fatal attacks in the country from 2006 to 2014, Karachi's share was nearly 50 per cent.[2] And whereby its business and employment opportunities motivate people from all over the country to flock to the city and try their luck, the growing crime rates of the city create rising fear among its residents. The situation looks no different when one observes the trend of other crimes. Be it car snatching and theft or abduction for ransom, all show an upward rise. According to press reports,[3] there were 19,983 cases of mobile phone snatching and 1,949 cars and 18,000 cases of motor bikes being stolen or snatched in 2015. Additionally, huge caches of arms and ammunition were recovered during the various operations by the police and rangers during the same year.

The Government of Pakistan, under the leadership of then Prime Minister Nawaz Sharif, launched a full-scale operation to restore law and order in Karachi in 2013. Rangers, police, intelligence, and other security agencies joined the operation—administratively led by the Sindh Chief Minster. Mixed perceptions prevailed about the effectiveness of this operation. The rangers, supported by the federal government and military leadership, took some daring initiatives like arrests of senior leaders, raids on the headquarters of political parties, etc. Ordinary citizens continued to experience the imposing presence of Rangers and police personnel on the streets and neighbourhoods, especially the areas that were politically more sensitive. Little headway could be made in curbing the network of terror financing. Experts believe that the informed nature of transactions, utmost difficulty in accessing verifiable evidence, and logistic limitations pose a key hurdle. If post-operation governance is not made a part of the core agenda of planning and implementation, then benefits achieved through the operation will be very difficult to sustain. Comprehensive police reform too, remains a basic pre-requisite for lasting peace in the city.

It is worth remembering that many crimes go unreported for fear of victimisation and extortion by the local police. Beyond the economic standpoint, Karachi is perceived by many as a key node in terrorism across Pakistan and the region. It has been viewed as one of the locations for militant recruitment, fundraising, and collaboration. Despite the operation against those labelled 'terrorists', the situation is far from satisfactory.

De-weaponising Karachi is a useful idea. The problem is that Karachi is a location where weapons can be brought without much restraint. The core issue in implementing any serious de-weaponisation programme is the collective will and consensus of political and administrative stakeholders. While lukewarm support is generally observed in respect to improving law and order conditions of the city, political parties and their key leaders and members are generally averse to the idea of de-weaponisation. Most of them view the possession, ownership, and use of weapons as a means of protecting political influence and the informally acquired ability to coerce opponents.

The violence, based mainly on sectarian and political grounds, in many ways reflect the state of security in Pakistan's urban centres. The government has taken several steps in resolving the precarious state of affairs with respect to the safety and security of common people in the city. The situation in Karachi is being reviewed on an urgent basis as a national security issue that impacts the conduct of the business of the state.

Despite efforts and claims made by law enforcement agencies, the citizens began adopting measures on their own to safeguard their residences, business and commercial spaces, and streets and compounds. The following section describes these efforts.

Theories and Discussion

This chapter generally looks at the multiple—but perhaps not all—reasons of conflict, violence, crime and terror, and how these have, over a period of time, impacted and manifested in the physical outlook of Karachi city. On similar lines, Mike Davis in the *Planet of Slums* (2007) explores the trend towards gated communities. He also explores how this phenomenon of gated communities has affected the lives of the marginalised. Moreover, he alludes that because of this, social relations have become fragmented as people are confined to their own neighbourhoods. In his other work, titled *City of Quartz* (2014), he conceptualises the city in terms of inequality and exclusion. He indicates how the gates and security around buildings, especially the elitist cocoons that are created as the result of these safety measures, 'ruthlessly detach' them from street life. Thus, the writer attempts to rediscover public spaces and tie these together into a comprehensive system of living and experiencing.

On similar lines, Theresa Caldeira (2010) studies the impacts of fear, crime, and segregation in the dynamics of built environment. Her study revolves around the urban changes in São Paulo with a comparative analysis of Los Angeles. She indicates that the recent trend towards high walls, closed circuit televisions, and armed guards is a response to the increase in crime and fear of violence. This fear, she points out, exists in all social classes. She then discusses how people from all walks of life choose to isolate themselves because of this fear.

Moreover, Landman (2002: 151) also indicates that modern-day residential apartments are now designed, while keeping this fear in mind, as a solution against crime by creating a city within a city. Pow (2009: 91–2), while criticising the ideological grounds of gated communities, argues that although the presence of a barrier does not make a community completely excluded and safe, it might have a psychological effect, providing a kind of satisfaction that would encourage people to surround themselves with walls, gates, and barriers.

Although there is a growing amount of literature on the processes of boundary-making and social exclusion in cities, this chapter takes a slightly different route to analyse the situation. While acknowledging the above-mentioned analysis, this chapter attempts to unpack the process of conflict and crime mitigation over a particular period of time in Karachi. Moreover, this chapter takes a step towards discussing the physical manifestation of these mitigation processes in the spatial layout of the city. By doing this, this chapter posits that there is a need for repositioning oneself while studying and analysing such phenomena and processes of security and safety. It also points to the chances of other theories emerging through an analysis of the recent trends related to processes of securitisation.

Elements of Design and Safety

DETERRENCE METHODS

Cities around the world are increasingly constructing security infrastructures as a response to various types of conflict (intra-city, regional, and inter-national), violence, inter-ethnic fear, contests over territory, and as attempts to control immigration (Pullan 2013). Karachi is no exception. Many people and institutions have adopted deterrence methods as the first line of defence, specifically to curtail criminal acts and acts of terrorism. The goal of deterrence methods is to convince potential attackers that a successful attack is unlikely due to strong defences. The initial layer of security for a campus, building, office, or other physical space uses crime prevention through environmental design to deter threats. Surveillance systems are often used to detect weapons (e.g. metal detectors) and intrusions (e.g. alarm systems), monitor and record intruders (e.g. video recording systems), and trigger incident responses (e.g. by security guards and the police) (Talbot and Jakeman 2009). Some of the most common examples are also the most basic: warning signs or window stickers, fences, vehicle barriers, vehicle height-restrictors, restricted access points, security lighting, and trenches.

Physical Barriers[2]

Physical barriers such as fences, walls, and vehicle barriers act as the outermost layer of security. They serve to prevent, or at least delay, attacks, and also act as a psychological deterrent by defining the perimeter of the facility and making intrusions seem more difficult. Tall fencing, topped with barbed wire, razor wire, or metal spikes, are often placed on the perimeter of a property, generally with some type of signage that warns people not to attempt to enter. A police officer (who wished to remain anonymous), during a discussion, mentioned that containers and physical barriers are temporary barriers put in place to cordon off areas to avoid clashes and to remove any possibility of skirmishes. He further specified that for events such as rallies, processions, and protest sit-ins, direct coordination is formed with party leaders and main organisers, and security is provided according to their demands. Many times, the interests of two political parties are provided for, while anticipating any need for additional security in case of clashes between the two. Streets and areas are blocked which are understood to be main threat zones and are seen as vulnerable to attacks. In some cases, areas are also sealed, and a route for the main rally is decided and noted. Care is taken that no outsider or unrelated person is able to enter the demarcated area.

The inconvenience to other citizens—those who are not part of these gatherings—is a second priority. The main focus is the security of the people who are part of the event. He further mentioned that street barriers are helpful to the extent that they stop the movement of cars and mainly motorcycles, which are the main mode of transport for criminals on the street. If a person complains about the blockades on the streets or violation of his right of passage, according to the officer, their opinions are heard and action is taken according to the merit of their argument.

A senior security officer, during a discussion, mentioned that many administrators do not even have rudimentary knowledge of security. They think that by putting up a sand bag or concrete blocks, one is secure. Nobody asks security experts for advice. There are 350 private security companies in Pakistan and there is only one company that offers a complete training course for the guards. When the operation began in September 2013, the rangers acted to remove physical barriers, many of which were believed to be controlled by political parties. The residents thought that the situation would improve with robust vigilance of law enforcement agencies. In many parts of the city, this was not so. People began re-installing barriers on their own. Gulshan-e-Iqbal, North Nazimabad, and many other neighbourhoods experienced this phenomenon. These are the representative residential neighbourhoods, which have now transformed into mixed land use (i.e. incorporation of commercial activities along the residential profile of the area), and where the emergence of barriers and other devices were found at an earlier stage.

Another major form of deterrence that has been incorporated into the design of facilities is natural surveillance, whereby architects seek to build spaces that are more open and visible to security personnel and authorised users, so that intruders/attackers are unable to perform unauthorised activity without being seen. An example would be decreasing the amount of dense, tall vegetation in the landscaping so that potential attackers cannot conceal themselves within it, or placing critical resources in areas where intruders would have to cross over a wide, open space to reach them (making it likely that someone would notice them).

Closed-circuit television (CCTV) is a commonly used technology in monitoring public and private spaces. It is a security system providing live coverage and recording of the sensitive area in institutions, offices, factories, shopping malls, etc. The purpose of the CCTV system is to protect assets against theft and manage staff and resources. It is not only intended to serve as a deterrent for criminals but can also provide forensic evidence in complicated cases.

A senior journalist, while talking about the conflict-ridden area of Lyari, stated that it was just the strong political backing that criminal groups have; otherwise, he said, it is not difficult for the police or Rangers to arrest them. He said that their network is stronger than the police network. They make their own bombs and get the latest bullets. Therefore, CCTV technology is not effective enough in keeping this area safe.

In situations where political influence is being exercised through the use of force, several mechanisms are applied by contesting stakeholders. Barriers, wall-chalking, party flags, banners, loud speakers, and wall posters are used to display alleged control over the territory by a particular political party or group. The opponents, depending upon the intention and political strength, either observe in silence or retaliate with violence. Usually, the conflicts subside after the contesting parties reach some sort of consensus.

Residents and political parties can be equal stakeholders to show their willingness to deploy such barriers wherever and whenever they feel insecure. However, residents who object to the creation of barriers resort to the intervention of courts of law. They file cases to adjust or completely remove the barriers. However, the verdicts normally follow a mixed approach. Such cases are always divided on specific merits.

The police and other law enforcement agencies now use cargo containers to protect the territory from any impending attack. Important processions, movement of politicians and government functionaries, political rallies and protests, demonstrations, residences of 'important' people, and vital installations are cordoned off by police using containers. The right of pedestrian and vehicular movement is completely denied. Ashura processions, the International Defence Services, Exhibition and Seminar (IDEAS) Fair during 1–4 December 2014, and rallies by various political parties were protected by the enhanced use of containers. Sometimes trucks, buses, and trailers are also parked in order to block streets.

CAUSES AND CONSEQUENCES OF SECURITY THREATS AND THE DEVELOPMENT OF BARRIERS

Street barriers are installed due to fear and anxiety in the public regarding the increasing cases of street snatching and bomb blasts. This has led to ends of the streets being blocked by barriers, turning it into a corner for dumping construction debris and garbage. Another form of barriers are the concrete blocks and barbed wires installed due to the general threat to life, especially of political leaders, and threats to national security, leading to the emergence of muted footpaths causing hindrance for pedestrians. Sectarian violence is yet another cause of people opting for street barriers and gates, minimising open spaces. Moreover, concrete blocks, spikes, sand bags, and barbed wires are also installed around the boundary walls of security agencies because they are always under the terrorism threat. This has minimised green belts in the city. Also, there are gates installed on the streets of areas populated by specific religious and/or minority groups. This leads the community to socialise within itself and become isolated from the rest of the city's activities. Then there are non-physical barriers like flags, wall-chalking etc., as discussed before, for a political group to mark their territory and to declare their control over it.

Forced Cul-de-sacs

These are modified versions of streets which now depict a dead-end status. These streets were initially planned, developed, and functioned as 'normal' streets with usual accessibility. At present, they are either accessible from one end or are closed off from both the sides. Entry is permitted only after checking by security guards who monitor the street.

Access to common residential streets has been controlled by installation of lever arms, which may or may not be monitored by security guards and *chowkidars*. In some cases, iron gates are installed, some of which are closed permanently while guards operate others. Forced cul-de-sacs are generally observed in the following categories:

- Residential neighbourhoods
- Streets around religious gathering spaces
- Streets around residences of high-profile people
- Marketplaces

The arm lever barriers, in various locations, showed a mixed status of repairs and upkeep. Some were rusting away while others were painted regularly in bright white and red stripes so as to be visible from a distance as a warning for people. Many of these barriers feature signs and notices declaring when the barriers will be operational and when they will be closed. They also instruct those who approach to seek permission from the stationed security guards. Metal grill gates about eight feet high are also installed in some areas. One side of the gate remains open for cars and people to pass through. In some instances, separate, smaller pedestrian entrances are also made with these gates. These gates are sometimes reinforced with arm lever barriers installed a few feet behind them. In some unusual cases, walls have also been built around residential areas and streets to provide protection against people who are perceived to cause security problems for the residents.

CASE STUDY ANALYSIS

The following section outlines case studies of particular neighbourhoods where security measures have been put in place.

Gulshan-e-Iqbal, Block 9

Gulshan-e-Iqbal is a middle- to upper-income planned neighbourhood in the eastern part of Karachi. The residents generally belong to mixed religious, sectarian, and ethnic backgrounds. Due to security concerns, most of the streets and lanes of this neighbourhood have installed metal, concrete, or combination barriers. In some cases, the residents have even constructed opaque metal gates on the streets, which are operated by a supervising chowkidar or armed guard.[3] The residents pool together funds to undertake such construction and to pay the guards their monthly salary. As a consequence of this development, only cars of the residents or their permitted guests are allowed to enter. Similarly, only those pedestrians are granted access who are known to the guards or verified by lane residents. The streets and lanes, which are public spaces and are meant for access to all, now become semi-private spaces for the residents alone. The municipal administration, law enforcement agencies, and other government bodies seem to have informally accepted the existence of this new spatial arrangement. It is important to note that this adjustment of space is practically spread out in almost all the neighbourhoods of the city.

This area which is adjacent to a major public park and a nearby *katchi abadi* (squatter settlement) is said to be strongly afflicted by petty theft and street crimes. As a response to countless mobile phone and motorcycle snatching incidents, the residents, with permission from the local police authorities, have taken it upon themselves to install various kinds of barriers.

Arm lever barriers, grilled gates, and even walls that were meant to close off access on a permanent basis, were seen. Walls were created at the end of the street which met a narrow road behind the Hakeem Sayed playground; that road has on many occasions been the spot where passers-by were robbed of their cell phones and belongings. During conversations with the residents, they reported an improvement in safety and security.

It is interesting to note that these barriers and gates were removed after the Rangers-led Operation began in October 2013. However, as the street crimes did not stop, people re-installed these gates.

Mehfil-e-Shah-e-Khurasan Numaish, Near M. A. Jinnah Road

The central religious processions by Shia Muslims in Karachi begin from Mehfil-e-Shah-e-Khurasan. It is a focal place of worship which attracts hundreds of thousands of worshippers, especially during the Muharram/Ashura period. After congregating here and performing necessary rituals, the procession then moves to M. A. Jinnah Road, a central thoroughfare in Karachi's business district, and proceeds some three kilometres to reach Hussainian Iranian Imambargah (a major place of worship for Shia Muslims) in Kharadar, further south.

The Khurasan Imambargah lies in a residential neighbourhood which was developed during the 1930s. Like other places of Shia worship, this location faces serious threats from various extremist militant outfits. The administration has blocked all the lanes and streets that lead to Khurasan. Metal and concrete barriers are installed, obstructing the movement of all vehicles. No one can enter the precinct without a body search and identity clearance. During Muharram and other important days, the police places empty cargo containers in addition to barriers, to visually and physically seal the Khurasan Imambargah. It may be noted that the procession zone of these rituals is declared as a no-vehicle area to facilitate the worshippers. However, access for the residents of the neighbourhoods remains an acute problem for most of the year due to expanding and intensifying religious activities.

Ancholi, Federal 'B' Area

This neighbourhood has become a predominantly Shia Muslim settlement due to various reasons. Initially, this neighbourhood had an imambargah and reasonable presence of Shia Muslims. But during the last ten years, attacks on Shias and threat to their life and property have increased considerably. As a result, the Shia community prefers to relocate in neighbourhoods where they are in majority and possess the ability to control security arrangements. Therefore, Ancholi in Federal B Area has become a desirable location where many middle-income members of the community have now bought or rented houses. The streets, entry points, exits, and neighbourhood boundaries are very strictly guarded with the help of private security guards and assistance from the police. All the streets, lanes, and the boundary of the imambargah are fortified with barriers, checkpoint gates, and *chowkis* (watch posts). Measures such as barriers, check points, and surveillance cameras are used to prevent any unknown outsiders from entering. Despite these stringent precautions, targeted attacks by rival sectarian groups and their accomplices continue to take place. The barriers and surveillance provide some relief and sense of security to the ordinary citizens. However, their vulnerability increases when they leave the area for work or social trips to other parts of the city.

The containers placed at the intersection of the main road and the secondary street immediately indicate the sensitivity of the area. For quick placement, empty containers are stacked on the sidewalks. They are put on the road whenever it has to be blocked. A policeman stands next to the blue cargo containers marked 'POLICE'. Each street has been closed by gates, which only open for area residents after verification. Recently, the residents collected money to increase the strength of guards for increased security. Further into the heart of Ancholi is an imambargah around which streets have been permanently closed and are no longer used. Five to six policemen guard the house where two members were killed in sectarian attacks. There are arm lever barriers in the inner streets apart from the gates that block the main streets. The residents said that these have been the only places to keep out unwanted parking in front of houses. Shopkeepers say that the barriers have affected their business as they restrict movement of people and do not allow the main pedestrian traffic inside. Pushcart vendors and hawkers also complain that they are no longer allowed to operate in these areas.[4]

The fact that the city closes down at a single call for protests is because ordinary citizens fear revenge and reprisals. Records provide evidence that people who refused to respond to calls for forced closure or any similar order issued by political parties were killed.

Conclusion

From the various findings, analysis of information, and viewpoints of those concerned, it has become adequately clear that the barriers installed in various parts of the city will not be removed any time soon. As it is a sensitive issue, state institutions and civil society organisations have not been able to evolve and develop any alternative model of ensuring the safety and security of ordinary citizens.

An abnormal living environment is being created because of the constant fear and resultant restrictions on access and movement. Such an environment discourages free social interaction and ordinary passage of pedestrians and vehicles. It is, however, important to note that the barriers and obstructions were initially treated as temporary interventions. Presently, most of the people perceive it as a permanent addition to spatial management and regulation.

A veteran transportation planner said that there has been a mushrooming of these physical barriers in Karachi, and all they do is provide psychological security, not actual security. The unpronounced development and extension of barricaded locations has given birth to a new range of spaces. The city now possesses many thoroughfares which comprise active carriageways but passive and non-accessible footpaths. This is visible in the parking of vehicles, treating the closed street as a private parking lot, stacking any excess items on the road space in front of houses, and even creating fresh dumping points. In the absence of any regulatory check from civic authorities or law enforcement agencies, these arrangements are likely to take on a permanent status in the spatial layout of the city. Informed discussion and dialogue is necessary to examine these changes and evolve a working consensus between diverse citizens and state institutions.

Introduction of physical obstructions that need less volume and space could be one alternative. Creation of buffer spaces and tunnel routes for pedestrians could be the other possible solution. Controlled pedestrian ways could be designed and developed at suitable thresholds to enable people to pass through without obstruction. The installation of barriers seems to have benefitted some groups. The area residents now derive a certain sense of safety and security, with reduced possibility of motorcycles and cars entering into barricaded locations. The residents have also benefited from greater liberty in using street space often as an extension to private space. The law enforcement agencies consider barriers as tools that have reduced their expanded responsibility of maintaining safety and security inside neighbourhoods. Therefore, they informally approve of the construction of barriers, provided it is done with consensus of all the residents. Private security companies have benefitted directly as more and more contracts are awarded for deployment of guards at barrier posts. Many unemployed, semi-educated youth have been able to find low-paying jobs as watchmen along the barriers, managed by neighbourhood resident committees. Vulnerable communities, especially religious minorities, consider barriers and barricaded environments as enhanced security.

The pushcart vendors, hawkers, and petty service providers are directly affected. Their access has been greatly curtailed especially in neighbourhoods belonging to minority communities. Vehicles such as taxis and auto-rickshaws are also denied access. General motorists, who would like to pass through internal lanes to shorten the routes to their destination, find it impossible to do so. The traffic volume on main roads and streets has generally increased due to this state of affairs, which further discourages pedestrian activity.

The definition of public space, its access, rights of various citizens to benefit from it, and the restriction on many others to be restrained from accessing and benefitting from it, needs to be deliberated. The evolution of new categories of spaces, such as extended thresholds of residences in barricaded neighbourhoods, also require a detailed review. There is also no discussion on how long these measures will actually last. Barriers were initially perceived as a temporary arrangement to deal with the issues of law and order. It is now evident that they have been accepted for an extended time. There seems to be no discussion amongst civic institutions about the time frame for which barriers will be allowed. Furthermore, there are many neighbourhoods, especially comprising low-income communities, that wish to install barriers. However, due to the influence of politically influential groups or police personnel, they are not able to do so. Institutional arrangements and involvement are needed to address their concerns and fear regarding their security and safety. Regarding this, a political worker during a discussion alluded that it is the state's responsibility to provide security and equal rights to every citizen and the state has failed to fulfil its duties. The complete system has been privatised now.

Orangi, Korangi, Landhi, Baldia, and Lyari are large-scale settlements. However, due to their relatively lower economic status, these areas are in many ways marginalised by the city administration. Due to this perceived remoteness, the inability of the city administration to properly manage urban affairs, the existence of criminal groups, and the collusion between crime syndicates and local armed groups, it is difficult to properly govern these settlements. The control and contestation of space in such a context is usually more intangible. As the study has shown, wall-chalking, graffiti, flags, and banners occasionally show—in physical terms—otherwise invisible territorial limits of various politically motivated armed groups.

It is obvious that not much change is expected in the style of local and provincial politics, the focus and capacity of local institutions, and the intentions of law enforcement agencies. The majority of urban citizens, however, remain the silent and captive affectees of this unique control syndrome. Emancipation and relief can only be achieved by socially mobilised reform initiatives. The work of organisations such as the Orangi Pilot Project and the Citizens-Police Liaison Committee can be bolstered. There are visible indications that ordinary residents are against the militant outfits and their activities. If mobilised and provided with proper social guidance, their role could be effective in developing a potent resistance against the armed gangs and terror outfits and could lead to eventually de-securitising and reintegrating an increasingly fragmented city.

NOTES

1. The author gratefully acknowledges the valuable input of Sana Tajuddin, architect and independent consultant, in editing this chapter. The author also acknowledges the support of the International Institute of Environment and Development, London, UK, for extending partial financial assistance in the conduct of this research and publication of an expanded monograph.

2. Discussion with a police officer.

3. Chowkidars are usually the contractless, informal service providers to the residents of any apartments to look after the gate of the building and other maintenance chores. However, security guards are hired and provided to the residents or for the security of other public and private properties by security companies. These companies have a customised contract with them.

4. Founded in 1989–90, the Citizens-Police Liaison Committee (CPLC) is a non-political statutory institution setup by the then Governor of Sindh. Its key purpose was to streamline the link of citizens with police. The CPLC maintains record of the crimes that are reported in Karachi and it also prepares an inventory of the cases that were registered during any specific period.

REFERENCES

Caldeira, Teresa P. R., *City of Walls: Crime, Segregation, and Citizenship in Sao Paulo*, Berkeley, California: University of California Press, 2010.

Choon-Piew, Pow, '"Good" and "Real" Places: A Geographical-Moral Critique of Territorial Place-Making', Geografiska Annaler, Series B: *Human Geography*, 91, 2 (2009), pp. 91–105.

Davis, Mike, *Planet of Slums*, Verso Books, 2007.

————, *City of Quartz: Excavating the Future in Los Angeles*, Verso Books, 2014.

Landman, Karina, 'Gated Communities in South Africa: The Challenge for Spatial Planning and Land Use Management', *Town Planning Review*, 75, 2 (2004), pp. 151–72.

5

Mafia Domination or Victim of Neoliberalism? Contextualising the Woes of Karachi's Transport Sector

Kabeer Dawani and Asad Sayeed

Introduction

Karachi's existing public transport infrastructure falls exceedingly short of the demands of the city. While its population has almost doubled over the last two decades, totalling approximately 16 million to date,[1] the total number of buses has remained almost stagnant—in fact, the number has nominally declined. Today, Karachi is one of the few megacities in the world without a planned system of mass transit.

The gravity of the problem can be illustrated through a few statistics. In 2011, only 0.85 per cent of the vehicles in Karachi were buses, compared to cars and motorbikes, which constitute 87.8 per cent of the total vehicles in the city (Hasan and Raza 2015). However, of the more than 24 million trips generated in the city each day, 60 per cent are undertaken through the existing infrastructure of buses and rickshaws (Ibid.). Moreover, there are 45 passengers per seat for every bus in Karachi, making the bus seat-to-passenger ratio one of the highest in the world (World Bank 2016). In comparison, in Mumbai, this ratio is eight passengers for every seat (Ibid.). All these statistics illustrate a demand far exceeding the existing capacity of public transport in Karachi.

The prevailing explanation, including that commonly cited in the news media, for why the city's public transport infrastructure has not grown to

101

match the needs of the city is because of the presence of a 'transport mafia' which dominates and controls this sector.[2] While a mafia may have controlled Karachi's transport sector in the past, and there may be a presence of mafias or mafia-like arrangements in other areas of service delivery in the city, this chapter attempts to demonstrate that, as of 2015, when the data for this paper was collected, there was no transport mafia remaining in Karachi. Instead, the decline in Karachi's transport can be explained by the lack of state capacity and the failure of neoliberal economic policies to meet the mass transit demands of the city. Moreover, the resulting informal transport is sub-optimal, and this chapter argues that the state needs to start providing this service again on a large scale.

The rest of this chapter is organised as follows. Section 1 tracks the historical evolution of public transport in Karachi. Section 2 discusses the emergence of a transport mafia in the city in the context of the geo-political environment prevalent at the time. Section 3 analyses the economic and political dynamics that led to the withering away of the mafia. Section 4 discusses the causes of decline of mass transit in the city over the last three decades, which include a lack of state capacity and the onset of neoliberal modes of urban development. Section 5 discusses informal and market driven forms of mass transit and argues that these are sub-optimal for a city like Karachi, while section 6 highlights the problems associated with informal transport. Finally, Section 7 contextualises the poor service delivery within Karachi's broader political economy, before the chapter concludes with some recommendations for a possible way forward towards developing an efficient and equitable mass transit system for Karachi.

Section 1: Transport over the Years

Immediately following Partition (1947), transport in Karachi was dominated by the public sector. A tramway was established towards the end of the nineteenth century, which expanded to cover most of the city by 1947. Soon after Partition, public buses were started to provide transport to the new settlements that had been established as a result of mass migration from India. There were some private buses as well, but their routes were regulated by the state.

Over the next decade, demand for transport rose as a result of the city's population nearly tripling and the concurrent growth in Karachi's inhabited area.[3] As a consequence, the government at the time increased the number of cars for the tramway by almost 400 per cent, as well as increasing the number of buses (see Table 1). Private bus owners also responded to this surge in demand by increasing the number of buses.

During the 1950s and early 1960s, the state disbanded some transport operating bodies while creating new ones due to a combination of financial reasons and changes in policy by successive governments at the time. During the process, some of the public buses were sold to private entrepreneurs; hence, as Table 1 shows, the number of private buses eclipsed state-owned buses in 1964. Nevertheless, state involvement remained prominent, as that year the Karachi Circular Railway (KCR) was set up. This was an important addition to the transport infrastructure in Karachi to help meet the rising demand from the city's growing population.

Until this point, the state was at the forefront in the provision of transport in Karachi.[4] This was to change in the 1970s. Although private buses had been operating in the city, they had been strictly regulated by the state. In 1971, however, the 'Free Transport Policy' was introduced, which liberalised the process of obtaining route permits (Hasan and Raza 2015). Now, anyone with the financial capacity to purchase a bus could also acquire a route permit. As Table 1 shows, this resulted in a surge in privately owned buses as well as the introduction and spread of the minibus,[5] whose number jumped to 1,800 in just three years.

In addition to the liberalisation of route permits, further recession of the state during this time was also marked by the closure of the tramway in 1974. The reason for the tram being shut down was because the Karachi Master Plan 1975–85 had planned a mass transit system whose primary corridor overlapped with that of the tram (Hasan and Raza 2015). Over the next decade and a half, the private sector took over transport in Karachi, with the number of buses and minibuses rising significantly without a proportionate increase in public sector buses. By 1988, the number of trips of the KCR had also declined.[6]

A decade later, the private sector had virtually monopolised transport in Karachi. The KCR was shut down in 1999, and the Karachi Transport Corporation's (a public sector body) buses had stopped operating a few years earlier. The primary reason for the state shutting down these services was because they were operating at significant financial losses (Hasan and Raza 2015).

However, for multiple reasons, private transport has been inadequate in catering to the city's transport needs. From 1999 to 2013, the number of private buses declined because their high operational costs meant that the business was a loss-making enterprise. Even though the number of minibuses has increased slightly, this has not kept up with the much more significant rise in Karachi's population.[7]

Consequently, this shortfall has been filled with the introduction of Qingqis (pronounced *chingchis*),[8] which first emerged in the city in 2002 (Sayeed, Husain, and Raza 2016). Over the last 15 years, their number has increased to 50,000. This is a completely informal form of transport that is not regulated by the state or given official permits to operate. They are also not organised by a particular ethnic group, unlike buses and minibuses, which are mostly run by Pakhtuns. However, they fill the vacuum that lack of mass transit has created in the city and have proved to be a popular alternative to the other, more inadequate forms of public transport because they are considered to be both convenient and affordable.[9]

Table 1: Mass Transit in Karachi Over the Years

Year	Tramway (No. of cars)	Karachi Circular Railway (No. of trips daily)	Buses		Mini-buses	*Chingchis*
			Public	Private		
1948	37	-	20	35	-	-
1957	157	-	344	259	-	-
1964	157	Initiated	317	583	-	-
1974	Shut Down	104	891	1,000	1,800	-
1988	-	93	1,050	1,450	5,500	-
1999	-	Shut Down	200	4,000	8,000	-
2013	-	2	160	1,000	9,000	50,000

Source: Sayeed, Husain and Raza (2016: 25)

Section 2: Origins of the Transport Mafia

The existence of a transport mafia first came to the fore following a road accident in April 1985. A minibus driver, while racing with a competitor, drove into a group of students, killing one female student named Bushra Zaidi (Gayer 2014: 45). This incident sparked ethnic riots between the Muhajirs—the name given to Urdu-speaking migrants from India, which was the community Zaidi belonged to—and the Pakhtuns, which was the alleged[10] ethnicity of the minibus driver.[11] Following the incident and the violent reaction, the view that a Pakhtun transport mafia existed gained credence. In this section, we explore the possible development of a mafia within the broader historical context of the informalisation of transport in Karachi.

DEFINING THE MAFIA

To be able to assess the existence of a mafia, however, we must first formally define it. In the literature, the word 'mafia' has been used to refer to groups that performed very different functions. For instance, in Sicily, where the original mafia developed as a result of weak property rights, Gambetta (1993: 1) defines it as an 'economic enterprise, an industry which produces, promotes, and sells private protection.' However, within Sicily the mafia evolved tremendously over time to perform different functions, such as vote buying and enforcement of illegal cartels in public procurement, and then illegal activities such as prostitution and gambling.

Varese (2001: 4), however, attempts to come up with a broader definition, defining a mafia as a 'particular type of organised crime that specialises in one particular commodity.' Thus, when applied to Gambetta's definition, this would mean that the Sicilian Mafia specialised in the provision of private protection. However, it is important to note that while Varese calls it organised crime, Gambetta refers to it as an economic enterprise. Characteristics of a mafia include offering protection to legal and illegal transactions, with the latter not being a necessary condition.

Drawing on this literature along with the popular depiction of the transport mafia in Karachi in the late 1980s, we define a mafia as a group that, by virtue of its control over an activity, appropriates rent and distributes it amongst its members, while having (legal and extra-legal) powers of enforcement and protection.

Karachi's Transport Sector in the 1980s

As the private sector's domination increased in the provision of public transport in Karachi during the 1980s, Pakistan was embroiled in the Soviet–Afghan war between 1979 and 1989. One adverse effect of being involved in this war was that it made Karachi a hub for arms and drugs, which resulted in the 'emergence of major crime syndicates' (Gayer 2014: 44). As the main seaport, Karachi was used to supply arms to Afghanistan for the war, while heroin was produced and transported from Afghanistan to Karachi to be exported elsewhere. Revenue from the latter in particular was then reinvested into the transport and real estate sectors by the Pakhtuns (including Afghan refugees), who were the primary beneficiaries of the illicit drug trade (Ibid.).

By the early 1980s, the transport sector had become a virtual Pakhtun monopoly. This was because, following the 1965 election, Ayub Khan, the president at the time, had patronised the Pakhtuns by giving them priority when allocating bus routes (Gayer 2014). It was, therefore, convenient for the 'drug-barons', who were also predominantly Pakhtun, to invest in this sector (Gayer 2014: 44).

The structure of the transport sector changed a few years before the money from these criminal syndicates entered, and this would prove to have a significant influence in Karachi by enabling the emergence of the transport mafia. Arif Hasan (1986), writing in *The Herald*, outlines how this change took place. Initially, the bus owner (also called the 'transporter')—who held the route permit—operated his own vehicles on the route through hired bus operators. However, at some point during the late 1970s, the operational model changed. From hiring operators, the bus owners switched to giving out informal loans on extremely onerous terms to the operators to buy buses and run them on the route. 'With the switchover from hired operators to prospective owners operating this transport, the Karachi minibus mafia was born' (Hasan 1986). The terms of this informal loan were important in enabling this mafia, as the power dynamic between the two parties was disproportionately in favour of the lender. Until all the debt was paid off, the legal owner of the bus was the lender, and even if one payment was missed, the lender would take the bus away, leaving the borrower with nothing. For the borrower, this was thus an extremely vulnerable position to be in and enabled the lender to exercise a significant degree of control over them.

At this point, however, this mafia-like structure did not have the political power to systematically extract rents from this sector. This would change with the influx of the arms and drug money from the Afghan War in the 1980s. The ability of the transporter to give loans increased manifold, and consequently the number of minibuses also increased exponentially. According to Hasan (1986), between 1979 and 1986, Rs 1.5 billion was given as loans for almost 5,000 minibuses, compared to only Rs 90 million between 1973 and 1979 for roughly 600 minibuses.

Hence, the new structure of the sector and the money from this illicit trade resulted in a shift of political and economic power to the hands of the transporters, which in turn determined the relationship they had with the state. They were able to facilitate the bus operators in obtaining driving licenses and generally protected them from law-enforcement agencies. Moreover, the concurrent development of a land mafia—where the profits from the arms and drug trade were invested in real estate—meant that the state lost control over some Pakhtun settlements (Hasan 1986). These changes in the city meant that the 'rules of coexistence between Karachi's ethnic groups were brutally uprooted' (Gayer 2014: 44), and resulted in violence and contestation over the city's resources (Sayeed et al. 2016). The control of the city's public transport system was one aspect of this.

Section 3: Is There a Transport Mafia Today?

While there is some evidence to support the presence of a mafia that controlled Karachi's transport sector throughout the 1980s and perhaps part of the 1990s, our research shows that no such mafia existed as of 2015 in this sector.

Ownership of buses in Karachi in 2015 was highly dispersed; the existing 1,000 buses are owned by 650–700 different individuals, with a similar ratio amongst minibus owners.[12] Moreover, there is minimal collective action[13] among the owners, despite their ethnic homogeneity.[14] In addition, Sayeed et al. (2016: 26) show that the sector is highly unprofitable due to high vehicle costs and a need to keep prices affordable for the majority of the public, which has been the primary reason for underinvestment in transport in Karachi. Therefore, given its lack of profitability, there are no significant rents to be extracted in this sector. This is why public intra-city transport, in most parts of the world, is considered a public good and subsidised by the state. Finally, there are no discernible linkages between Pakhtuns in the transport sector, who had historically dominated this sector, or any political party either, which could help in collective action, protection, or the enforcement of contracts.

Thus, it is clear that there is no one 'group' that controls this sector, there are no substantial rents to be earned, and neither are there any means for enforcement or protection. Therefore, it is factually incorrect to continue to cite this as the reason for the decline in Karachi's public transport. Instead, we need to identify other factors that have led to this failure in service delivery.

Section 4: Explaining the Decline in Mass Transit

There are two primary reasons for the large gap between the supply and demand of transport in Karachi: first, the inability of the state to operate public transport and second, failure of the market to efficiently and equitably meet the demand for public transport in the city.

LACK OF STATE CAPACITY

In the first instance, a lack of state capacity led to the informalisation of transport. As was outlined earlier, the state adequately provided public transport in Karachi at the time of Partition and in the decade after. Problems started arising in the late 1960s and early 1970s, however, because the transport organisations formulated by the state were operating at a loss. Hence, the tramway closed down in 1974. Over the next two decades, the state was unable to revamp the financial structure of the sector. This resulted in the privatisation or shutting down of the state-owned Karachi Transport Corporation and the Karachi Circular Railway in the late-1990s, both of which were operating at significant losses.[15]

The state was thus unable to run public transport in Karachi and did not have the capacity to reform its operations to make state-owned mass transit fiscally feasible. It left the provision of mass transit in Karachi to private entrepreneurs. While this process began in the 1970s due to capacity and fiscal constraints, over the next two decades, consigning the transport sector to the vagaries of the market mechanism was further legitimised by the prevalent global consensus on neoliberalism.

FAILURE OF NEOLIBERALISM

In the aftermath of the state's withdrawal from public transport in Karachi, however, was the failure of neoliberal policies to meet Karachi's transport requirements. In other words, private transporters operating in a free market were unable to fulfil the city's demand. In fact, instead of growing in number, the total number of buses and minibuses has stayed roughly stagnant over the years. The primary reasons for this are a non-conducive incentive structure and ineffective regulation.

In interviews with bus owners, we discovered that the rate of return on buses has decreased over time. Furthermore, banks refuse to provide credit for investment in this sector because it is not recognised as an industry by the Chamber of Commerce. Added to this is the greater operational risk arising from transport being a 'victim' of instability in Karachi (Sayeed et al. 2016: 28). Together, these have resulted in significant underinvestment in the sector. In fact, Irshad Bukhari, the President of the Karachi Transport Ittehad (KTI), which is the city's transport association, said that most people try to make some money quickly and then exit this sector. The underinvestment is depicted by the fact that the average bus model is more than 35 years old, while the average minibus model is 15 years old. Bukhari explained this phenomenon, 'This is because there is no money in this business and so no one is willing to invest in newer models, and neither do banks provide credit for this.'[16]

The violence and lack of incentives have contributed to the dissipation of surplus from this sector, and also explain why the 'mafia' withdrew from it sometime during the 1990s. The ineffectiveness of the state to address these market failures through regulation has further contributed to public transport shortage in Karachi. As a market response, other informal forms of public transport have come up in recent years.

Section 5: New Forms of Mass Transit

In the absence of private buses and minibuses meeting the needs of Karachi's citizens, there have been two market responses, in the shape of motorbikes and Qingqis. Both are more cost-effective and convenient for commuters than buses and minibuses.

Since 2004, the number of motorbikes has increased exponentially, such that Hasan and Raza (2011) argue that this is now a form of mass transit. From 1990 to 2004, motorbikes only increased from 450,000 to 500,000. However, over the next six years they doubled, increasing to 1 million in 2010 (Ibid.). In 2015, there was another huge jump, with the total rising to 1.85 million (Raza 2016). This means that there are 116 motorbikes for every 1,000 persons in Karachi. This is an extremely high number and shows the popularity of this vehicle.

There are two primary reasons for why motorbikes are such a popular choice among individuals and families in Karachi (Hasan and Raza 2011). First, they are cheaper than public transport, apart from the initial investment required. With the spread of options to purchase motorbikes on relatively easy instalments, the latter problem has also been diminished. Second, motorbikes are much more efficient and convenient for families when compared to public transport, which is inefficient and time consuming, particularly during peak hours, as they would have to change buses or fit into overcrowded ones. In this regard, motorbikes have the advantage of being able to carry a family of four at once and transport them directly to their destination much quicker. Hasan and Raza (2011) note that motorbikes can reduce commuting times by 50 per cent.

The number of Qingqis, although lesser in absolute terms, has seen a similarly astronomical increase in just fifteen years, rising to 65,000 in 2015.[17] They are operated on the same format as a bus: they have a fixed route between two points, and transport passengers at a fixed fare anywhere along that route. These vehicles are popular because they are suitable for short distances, connect passengers to areas outside of regular bus routes, and are relatively safer from muggings.[18] They are also especially favoured by women because it increases their mobility, as they run on shorter distances, and the vehicle design, with a lower height, is more amenable to them getting on and off quickly (in buses this is much more difficult because the drivers only stop the vehicle fleetingly). Moreover, women also face less harassment on Qingqis than they would on buses (Hasan and Raza 2015).

Section 6: Problems with Informal Mass Transit

There are several reasons that render market-driven and hence informal forms of mass transit prevalent in Karachi sub-optimal.[19] First, the shift to smaller vehicles mentioned earlier means that per unit cost of transport is higher than those of buses, trams, or trains, both in terms of operational and capital costs. Moreover, motorcycles and Qingqis are hazardous for passengers and create a traffic menace for regular motorised traffic, which includes buses and minibuses as well as cars.

Second, because of the informal nature of the industry, bus owners can neither access formal sector banks for credit nor the formal insurance market. Transport has not been declared an industry and therefore it is unable to access bank credit. According to the President of KTI, Irshad Bukhari, they applied twice for industry status with the Federation of Pakistan Chambers of Commerce and Industry (FPCCI) but were rejected on both occasions. Probable reasons for this occurrence are because of dispersed ownership in the sector, low levels of profitability, no interest on the part of the formal corporate sector to invest, and above all the law and order situation in the city, which poses a higher risk to buses and minibuses (Sayeed et al.: 2016). As a result, there is severe underinvestment in buses and mini buses. Both buses and mini buses are very old and lack of credit is one of the main reasons for the number of vehicles declining in the city.[20] The inability to access the formal insurance market has meant that vehicle owners have had to informally insure their vehicles at a high premium, and benefits do not cover the replacement cost of the vehicle.[21]

Third, the contractual arrangement between vehicle owners and operators is based on a residual payment system. This system requires drivers to pay a specific amount to owners on a daily basis after excluding fuel costs (and payments to the police) and the rest is divided between the driver and the conductor. This creates a perverse incentive structure to work long hours (and hence self-exploit) as well as overcrowd buses. Both these conditions are hazardous for transport workers as well as commuters. For instance, drivers, since they are effectively on daily wages, cannot really afford a day off. One newspaper quotes a driver saying, 'I have a hole in my kidney … I lose Rs 500 a day if I don't go to work' (Maher 2014). Moreover, it is equally harmful for commuters to travel in buses that are overcrowded and driven by transporters who have often been working for 12 hours. One female passenger is quoted as saying, 'Sometimes so many people get on the bus that the men start pushing their way into the women's section … we find no place to sit and there is nobody to assist us' (Hasnain 2016).

Fourth, with the demise of the public sector and informalisation of the transport sector in the city, there is no union or other forms of occupation collective action for workers in the sector. This has further intensified self-exploitation of workers, which in turn has created negative externalities for the commuting public.

Section 7: Explaining Weak Service Delivery in Karachi

The transport sector is symptomatic of lack of service delivery and bad governance in the city as a whole. Many other public services—such as provision of water, sanitation, and solid waste management—are also severely neglected within the city. This lack of effective local governance is underpinned by the ethnicisation of political organisations and violence that has marred the city for the last three decades.

The Muttahida Qaumi Movement (MQM)[22] was the first entity to politically mobilise a large segment of the Urdu-speaking population of the city in the early 1980s.[23] Thereafter the Sindhi, Baloch, and Pakhtun segments of the population have similarly organised politically along ethnic lines.[24] At one level, this ethnicisation of politics is reflected in national and provincial elections held in the city since 1988. Along with the ethnicisation of politics, Karachi has witnessed the gradual ethnicisation of business, trade, and residential associations.[25] Furthermore, neoliberal economic policies of de-regulation and privatisation have weakened trade unions. As such, collective action along class, occupational, and geographical axes has gradually declined within the city.

Ethnicisation of political and civic organisations in the city has also impacted the ability of the state to efficiently and impartially deliver services in various ways. Because of the ethnic basis of political organisations, victors in electoral competitions are often accused of discrimination in the provision of public services to rival ethnic groups. Electoral victors have also been accused of ethnicising the bureaucratic arms of service delivery departments. The effectiveness as well as credibility of the local state as an impartial provider of services has thus been severely compromised.

The local state has been further compromised by the ensuing violence that has accompanied ethnic political organisation in the city. As mentioned earlier, Karachi experienced an influx of arms during the First Afghan War, and the trend has continued because of flawed policies of the higher levels (provincial and federal) of state taking sides in ethnic conflict in the city.[26] This has meant that perpetrators of violence from one group are often given impunity as the state cracks down on its rivals.

The partisan role of the state in violent conflict across ethno-political lines implies that the local state has lost its (legitimate) monopoly on violence. This erosion of the writ of the state appears to underpin its lack of effective governance in general and in the provision of public services in particular, which includes the provision of public transport.

Conclusion: Signs of Change

This paper has attempted to demonstrate that contrary to popular perception, Karachi's transport sector is no longer dominated by a mafia. Instead, as things stand now, the sector represents a classic case of market failure where low returns to investment have resulted in underinvestment and under provision of an essential public service. As we demonstrate in this chapter, one important reason for this failure is the neoliberal model adopted by the state, which denies the provision of public goods such as affordable transport in favour of private ventures. As such, it was losses to the exchequer from the public provisioning of the KCR and public buses that prompted the withdrawal of the state from this sector.

However, with the introduction of the metro bus service in the federal capital, Islamabad, and in Rawalpindi and Lahore, the trend regarding the public goods nature of urban mass transit in Pakistan may be changing. As such, the revival of the KCR and state investment in the proposed Karachi Rapid Bus Transit System (BRT) is on the cards again.[27] It appears that financing for part of the project has been resolved. Besides financing, the only hurdle in completing these projects will be removing encroachments to allow for construction and credible resettlement plans for those affected by these developments. Karachi's volatile political economy may also prove to be an obstacle. An affordable and effective public transport system can only become a reality when the Pakistani state shifts the focus of urban development to socio-economic equity rather than simply to the maintenance of law and order and the attainment of short-term profits.

NOTES

1. We assume a population of 16 million (UN DESA 2014). Since there has been no census data released since 1998, various numbers are cited for the total population of Karachi. This is one of the few estimates that uses a systematic methodology. It should be noted, however, that a census was conducted between March and May 2017, but the data has not been released at the time of writing this paper.

2. See, for example, Dunya News (2012) and AFP (2012).

3. There was a 161 per cent increase in Karachi's population between 1941 and 1951, which is when the censuses were conducted (Hasan 1999). This translates to an average annual growth rate of 11.5 per cent. In the 1950s, there was another significant rise, with an 80 per cent increase in population, which is equivalent to a 6.05 per cent growth per year on average (ibid.).

4. There was a slight decrease in the number of private buses between 1957 and 1964, but this was temporary as the number would increase in the subsequent years.

5. Compared to buses, mini buses are smaller and cheaper, therefore requiring lower investment. They have a capacity of 25 people, while buses can seat up to 40.

6. See Section 4 for an explanation of why the state stepped back from the transport sector.

7. Growth in minibuses for this period was about 13 per cent, while the population has grown by an estimated 60 per cent for the same period.

8. These are small motor-rickshaws that can seat 4–12 people, depending on the type. They have the engine and front of a motor bike but the back of a rickshaw.

The name of the vehicle comes from a Chinese company, called Qingqi, which produced the first variant of the vehicle. The adapted name, *chingchi*, is now used to refer to similar vehicles which are usually manufactured locally in Pakistan.

9. An attempt was made to ban *chingchis* in August 2015 because these are essentially illegal vehicles, running on the roads as unregistered vehicles and without any route permits issued by the government's transport department. In fact, in the Sindh government's list of vehicle categories, there is no recognition of a vehicle such as the *chingchi*. Nevertheless, this ban was then overturned by the Supreme Court of Pakistan in January 2016 on the condition that the *chingchi* association works with the government to come up with a design of the vehicle that is safe and is registered before plying the roads of the province.

10. The ethnicity of the driver is still contested; some claim he was Punjabi-speaking while others say he was Kashmiri (Imtiaz and Ahmed 2012).

11. This incident happened around the same time as the formation of the MQM, which, as we explain later, was the beginning of ethnicisation of politics in Karachi.

12. Interview with Irshad Bukhari, President of Karachi Transport Ittehad, on 21 March 2015.

13. There is some occupational collective action. Due to no avenues of formal insurance for buses—because they are often targeted during violent strikes in Karachi, they have a high risk—the owners have come together to create an informal insurance mechanism. Sayeed et al. (2016: 26) outline the working of this informal insurance in detail.

14. The owners are still predominantly Pakhtuns. An interview with Khurram Gulzar, former Deputy Inspector General Traffic, on 16 March 2015 and with the Karachi Transport Ittehad on 21 March 2015 revealed this fact.

15. The Karachi Transport Corporation was operating at a yearly loss of Rs 120 million in 1996, while the Circular Railway was losing Rs 6 million per year in 1998, by which time its number of trips had also declined tremendously (Sohail 2000).

16. Interview with Irshad Bukhari, President of Karachi Transport Ittehad, on 21 March 2015.

17. Interview with Safdar Shah, President of All Karachi Chingchi Rickshaw Welfare Association.

18. In interviews with minibus drivers and owners, we found that muggings in buses were common. The way robbers would carry these out is that two of them would climb aboard a bus, one of them would hold the driver hostage at gunpoint and tell him to keep driving without stopping, while the other would collect valuables from the passengers (mobile phones, cash, jewelry, etc.). After stealing all they could, they would then tell the driver to drop them off and drive away. In *chingchis*, this does not happen, or is much less likely, because these are much smaller and more open or visible vehicles. They are also less valuable targets simply because they have fewer people on board (6 people on average compared to 25 on a mini bus).

19. For details on the impact of informality on bus operations, see Sayeed, et al. (2016: 25–8).

20. The average model of buses is of 1980 and mini buses from the mid-1990s.

21. The umbrella owners association in the city—Karachi Transport Ittehad

(KTI)—insures vehicles. The maximum benefit that owners can receive is Rs 600,000 which is significantly lower than the replacement cost of vehicles in the case of total loss. See Sayeed, et al. (2016: 25) for more details on this.

22. The MQM was previously known as the 'Mohajir Qaumi Movement' and represented the Urdu-speaking migrants who came to Pakistan after Partition. The political party changed its name in 1997 to the more inclusive Muttahida Qaumi Movement (MQM) but remained strongly associated with the Urdu-speaking community.

23. There was ethnic political mobilisation earlier also. Most notably in 1964 and 1972 by the Pakhtuns and Mohajirs respectively but they were episodic events that did not lead to the formation of political parties. See Gayer (2014) for further details.

24. This is manifested in voting patterns in Karachi over the last two decades. The Sindhi and Baloch population has voted for the PPP and the Pakhtun segment of the population for ANP and PTI. See Gazdar (2011) and Sayeed, et al. (2016) for further details.

25. Earlier, it was ideological divides— mainly Islamic, centre, right, or left—prevalent in political parties that influenced local or occupational level collective action in the city. This pattern changed once politics in the city took on an ethnic colour. See Sayeed, et al. (2016) for further details.

26. Several 'operations' have been launched against one ethnic group and later the same ethnic group has been given a virtual carte blanche to rule the city. See Sayeed, et al. (2016: 8) for a description of this phenomenon.

27. The BRT comprises of five different lines, but work on only two lines had started by mid-2017. The first,

Green Line, is funded by the federal government with technical assistance from the Asian Development Bank and this cuts across the north-south axis of the city. The second, the Orange Line, is funded by the Government of Sindh and cuts across the east-west axis of the city.

REFERENCES

AFP, 'Sindh Minister Yields to Transport Mafia', *Geo News*, 5 November 2012 <https://www.geo.tv/latest/82167-sindh-minister-yields-to-transport-mafia>.

Dunya News, 'Karachi 'Transport Mafia' Refuse to Reduce Transport Fares', 2 February 2012 <http://dunyanews.tv/en/Pakistan/258980-Karachi-transport-mafia-refuse-to-reduce-transpo>.

Gambetta, Diego, *The Sicilian Mafia: The Business of Private Protection*, Cambridge, MA: Harvard University Press, 1993.

Gazdar, Haris, 'Karachi's Violence: Duality and Negotiation', SPO Discussion Paper Series No. 10, *Strengthening Participatory Organization*, Karachi, 2011 <http://researchcollective.org/Documents/Karachi_Violence_Duality_and_Negotiation.pdf>.

Hasan, Arif, *Understanding Karachi: Planning and Reform for the Future*, Karachi: City Press, 1999.

_____ and Mansoor Raza, 'Karachi: The Transport Crisis', Unpublished draft, 2015 <http://arifhasan.org/reports/karachi-the-transport-crisis>.

_____, 'Motorbike Mass Transit', Unpublished draft, 2011 <http://arifhasan.org/wp-content/uploads/2012/10/motorbikemasstransit-AH-138.pdf>.

Hasnain, Subuk, 'Mass Movement: Karachi's Public Transport Woes', *The Herald*, March 2016 <http://herald.dawn.com/news/1153420>.

Imtiaz, Saba, and Noman Ahmed, 'Bushra Zaidi, the Woman who Changed Karachi Forever', *The Express Tribune*, Karachi, 8 March 2012, <http://tribune.com.pk/story/346933/march-8-bushra-zaidi-the-woman-who-changed-karachi-forever-by-dying>.

Maher, Mahim, 'Timekeeping and Transport: The Minute Men of Karachi', *The Express Tribune*, 22 May 2014 <https://tribune.com.pk/story/711471/timekeeping-and-transport-the-minute-men-of-karachi>.

Raza, Mansoor, 'Exploring Karachi's Transport Problems: A Diversity of Stakeholder Perspectives', Working Paper, *International Institute for Environment and Development*, London, 2016.

Sayeed, Asad, Khurram Husain, and Salim Raza, 'Informality in Karachi's Land, Manufacturing and Transport Sectors: Implications for Stability', Peaceworks No. 114, *United States Institute of Peace*, Washington DC, 2016 <http://www.usip.org/sites/default/files/PW114-Informality-in-Karachis-Land-Manufacturing-and-Transport-Sectors.pdf>.

Sohail, M. (ed.), 'Urban Public Transport and Sustainable Livelihoods for the Poor, A Case Study: Karachi, Pakistan', *Water, Engineering and Development Centre*, Loughborough University, UK, 2000.

Varese, Federico, *The Russian Mafia: Private Protection in a New Market Economy*, New York: Oxford University Press, 2001.

World Bank, 'Karachi City Diagnostic: City Sustainability, Inclusion and Service Delivery', Discussion Draft, Karachi, 2016.

6

In the Time of Toxic Air: Environmental Contestations, Collaborations, and Justice in Delhi

Rohit Negi and Prerna Srigyan

Introduction

Urban regions of South Asia, and the Global South more generally, are in the midst of transformation with profound environmental consequences (Rademacher and Sivaramakrishnan 2013). Driven by a policy agenda that is skewed towards economic growth at all costs, urbanisation has taken a decidedly toxic turn in the region. Large-scale changes in land cover, pollution of various kinds, and the proliferation of untreated waste and wastewater contribute to making regional cities progressively unlivable. We term this linking of urbanisation and perverse environmental change in South Asian cities, of which Delhi is an exemplar, 'toxic urbanism'.

In Delhi, this unpleasant, poisonous, and risky form of urbanisation has in turn brought the question of ecology to the forefront of public discourse, and with it, urban policy and governance. There is an ongoing and vibrant debate on the causes and effects of various manifestations of toxic urbanism to which a multiplicity of agents contribute. To be sure, the debate is marked by contestations and distrust, but also, creative collaborations and marked reflexivity. Using a historical perspective, we place the debate on air that occurred during the late 1990s and early 2000s in conversation with its emergent avatar since 2014, identifying continuities and dissonances in the terms of the debate as well as the agents and stakes involved.

Based on participant observation of events around air in Delhi in 2015–16, interviews with a cross-section of involved individuals and groups, and

118

an analysis of technical reports, court orders, and media coverage, our paper shows how new collectives around air have emerged beyond the established environmental advocates, how the question of expertise remains salient even though the production and dissemination of data is more democratised than before, and, finally, that inequalities continue to shape the landscape of social media-driven knowledge regimes and the evolving market-driven possibilities of conditioned air.

Air has been a point of discussion in Delhi since at least the early twentieth century though with time, the way it has been talked about has undergone a series of important shifts. In addition to government laboratories, the measurement of air's components now takes place via hundreds of low-cost, hand-held devices that many residents possess. Apart from state policymakers and the courts, the debate now includes the print and television media, social media, and everyday interactions across the city's various demographics. Alongside the older citizen science initiatives, new collectives composed of diverse publics now participate in the production of expertise related to the air. Prodded by environmental activists and collectives, the judiciary initiated a series of interventions in the late 1990s. Many of these, like the conversion of the auto-rickshaw fleet to compressed natural gas (CNG) and the closure and relocation of hundreds of so-called 'hazardous' industries, were vehemently opposed by those directly affected and by the city's social justice movement.

As the immediate impacts of these orders wore away and air became visibly cleaner, critical scholarship seemed to turn its attention away from the matter. In the interim, a novel articulation began to take shape within a context wrought by the sharp economic downturn following the global crisis, the emergence of the anti-corruption movement, and local environmental collectives that had rethought their strategies after the criticism they faced from social activists. As a result, the debate on air has undergone a major reconfiguration, and contemporary vocabularies of cause and remediation are strikingly different. Rather than public transport and industry, private automobiles and the city's 'unfortunate' geography—straddled between the desert and the mountains—are being held responsible, while interventions have included a vehicle rationing system (locally known as 'odd-even'), the removal of dust from roads, and temporary closure of power plants adjacent to the city. It is now common to find questions of justice woven into the environmental discourse: much of the ongoing discussion has been about limiting the use of cars, and the elite and upwardly mobile urban residents are now being squarely blamed for endangering the health of the public at large.

If, as scholars have convincingly argued (e.g. Ghertner 2015), urban policy in millennial Delhi worked through an aspirational prism of making it 'world-class' through the production of large infrastructures, emphasis on individualised mobility, and an aesthetic that tended to make the poor superfluous and invisible, then the larger economic crisis *and* Delhi's toxic air have effectively punctured these dreams. In recent discourse, Delhi is retrieved from an abstract global (urban) space to its immediate geography, powerful symbols of development are recast as leading to a progressively unlivable city, and the supposed vectors of Delhi's world-class pursuits— its middle classes—now shoulder the blame owing to their conspicuous consumption. In this scenario, philosopher Albert Pope's following question seems remarkably prescient. He asks if 'a set of ontological rights—such as breathing—actually challenge or even displace economic hegemony?' (quoted in Graham 2015: 200). In Delhi, it can be argued that air has emerged as a potent critique of the neoliberal project, and mainstream ecological thinking is today in opposition to, rather than culpable in, this project, as was previously the case (Negi 2010).

Toxic Urbanism

Since the early 1990s, and in the pursuit of capitalism qua development (Wainwright 2008), states across the world have unleashed a political economic agenda that pivots around growth at all costs. Critics have shown that processes linked to this pursuit, while increasing the overall size of the economy, have generated enormous inequalities together with deleterious environmental impacts (Held and Young 2011). It has also been argued that neoliberal economic growth has been especially concentrated in certain metropolises that are considered to be potential growth poles and to that extent have been the locus of state policy via the production of what Kevin Cox calls 'the good geography' (2016), that is, appropriate capital-friendly regimes and infrastructural investments. These efforts have assumed greater importance in the globalised world since cities now compete over investment and resources and must continually (re)package themselves given the shifting geographies of the international division of labour. In the process, while certain urban regions, like coastal China, have received significant flows of capital, others, including those on the North American Rustbelt, have witnessed the withdrawal of economic activities and the erosion of social welfare. These imperatives and competitive calculations have been salient to urban policy across the world, including in South Asia.

Delhi is one of the regional epicentres of the neoliberal project in India. State resources have poured into the city in the form of large-scale infrastructural projects, and changes in regulatory regimes pertaining to land, labour, and the environment have been enacted to make the city 'attractive' to capital (Ghertner 2015). Indeed, by the mid-2000s, Delhi and its satellites like Gurgaon and Noida had become important nodes of capitalist activity following investments in the information technology, real estate, and financial sectors. At certain moments during the neoliberal era, it seemed within reason that Delhi was on the way to a post-industrial future and would join the ranks of the so-called 'world cities'—networked urban nodes exchanging capital and materials far in excess of other comparable cities and regions. These visions of the impending future, akin to what Walter Benjamin called 'wish images', were dialectically linked to the spaces like malls, the metro, and recreational areas produced in their pursuit (Srivastava 2009).

We do not wish to fully recount this history, but bring it up to make the point that the numerical and statistical metrics typically used to judge the effectiveness of neoliberal pursuits are only partially useful to critical scholars, who must also turn attention to their materiality. In India, the environmental legacies of the so-called 'India Shining' era are plainly visible contemporarily. Where a post-industrial future was imminent, the property boom cut into natural habitats and commons (D'Souza and Nagendra 2011), unceasing construction created several backward (mining) and forward (dust and debris) hazards (Padel and Das 2010), the unceasing consumption of processed goods produced mountains of waste (Schindler, Demaria and Pandit 2012), and a shift in urban transportation towards private automobiles generated poisonous emissions that have been worsened by the combination of poor quality fuel and inefficient engines (Badami 2005). Urban areas across the breadth of the country are beset with these and other concerns, which seem to worsen by the day. They are together producing a material and lived form of urbanism that is ecologically fraught at its core. What we call 'toxic urbanism' then is not simply located at specific points, but is a general condition with varied expressions and experiences.

Our use of 'toxic' has three specific imbrications that provide insight into the contemporary urban process in South Asia, each coinciding with a specific meaning of the term. The first is its common usage to signify a 'poisonous' phenomenon. This use implies objectivity: an entity is either poisonous or it is not depending on accepted metrics. This signification further refers to the world of facts and classificatory regimes through which environmental concerns are understood and talked about. The second meaning is as something 'unpleasant', pointing to subjective content and a relationship with the domain of sensory experiences. Finally, the third aspect draws on the use of the term in financial discourse to signify high risk, most commonly to describe loans with little probability of recovery. As a tradition of work in environmental humanities tells us (e.g. Beck 1992), risk prefigures a specific imaginary of the world by projecting trends and anxieties onto the future. Toxic urbanism then is poisonous, unpleasant, and risky, just as it is objective, subjective, and an indication of the city to come. These concerns have become increasingly critical in discussions related to India's urban futures. There is an ongoing debate at the sites of knowledge-production, distribution, and action involving collectives that continue to think through and respond to the questions posed by toxic urbanism. It brings together elements of urban planning, scientific expertise, environmental activism, the judiciary, and the local state.

Prior to the neoliberal shifts, Delhi and its immediate hinterland—clubbed together as the National Capital Region (NCR)—was in significant part an administrative and industrial centre, bringing together workers from several different states in the small and large manufacturing facilities (Nigam 2001). Given the lack of administrative will and technological capacity to account for the environmental consequences of these activities, efforts have been historically underwhelming (Greenstone and Hanna 2014). Unsurprisingly, the NCR has long been seen as a pollution hotspot. Until recently, however, pollution was largely viewed through a point source geography in popular and scientific imaginaries. That is, it could be precisely located and corrected through appropriate technological interventions.

It was only in the late 1980s that faith in techno-scientific fixes began to waver in the wake of, first, the Bhopal gas disaster of 1984 that caused thousands of deaths and other deleterious health impacts, and second, the nuclear disaster in Chernobyl in 1986. These incidents significantly undermined the population's confidence in the mostly-public systems tasked with understanding, communicating, and managing risks (Fortun 2004). The urban environmental justice movement too emerged as a response to disasters like Bhopal (Fortun 2001) and perceived hazards like the siting of point sources like power plants and waste disposal facilities in otherwise disenfranchised neighbourhoods. In other contexts, Rachel Brahinsky (2014) and Sharad Chari (2013), for instance, write about the long history of environmental injustice but also spirited activism that shape people's relationship with toxicity in San Francisco and Durban respectively. The next two sections bring a similar perspective to bear on the air discourse in Delhi.

Comparisons and Contestations

According to Hajer (1997), environmental discourses do not have an unmediated relationship with objective empirical truth but rely on negotiated points of agreement or alignment between different actors, which may emerge in a contextual and contingent manner but are very often explained retrospectively as value-neutral science. In Delhi's story, the Supreme Court's decisions from the late 1990s to early 2000s have drawn heavily on the purportedly objective power of the Delhi Master Plan (DMP)-2001 on the one hand and of unmediated scientific expertise on the other. However, a historically-nuanced view of the matter reveals that contestations over knowledge, expertise, and best practices have always stalked these formulations. The air issue, in particular, has combined ideas related to planning and pollution, each of which presents a compelling vantage point from where the constitution of 'valid' knowledge as well as its contested nature may be studied.

In the early twentieth century, as the Indian Industrial Commission of 1916 noted, Delhi had few mechanised industries, and stagnation persisted till the 1930s, when the Second World War offered opportunities for newer industrial establishments. Around this time, industrialists, under the Association for the Development of *Swadeshi* (Indigenous) Industries and the Association of the Factory Owners and Industrialists of Delhi, demanded that a new industrial area be demarcated at the city's fringes since the older industrial areas around Old Delhi were congested and were saddled with poor provision of electricity, water, and sewage (Sharan 2014: 169–70). This was echoed by A. P. Hume of the Delhi Improvement Trust in his *Report on the Relief of Congestion in Delhi*, which argued that establishment of an 'industrial colony' would not only decongest industries in Delhi, but also relieve population pressure through migration of a large labour force outside Delhi (Hume 1936).

However, questions soon followed regarding the lack of precise information about the location of such an area and the noxious nature of industries. Some Trust officials were concerned that if vacant areas near the city neighbourhoods of Karol Bagh and Rohtak Road were notified, it would lead to the concentration of industries near Old Delhi rather than the colonial capital of New Delhi. Eventually, Hume proposed that Najafgarh in west Delhi be demarcated, owing to railway and road connectivity, with the Najafgarh drain serving as a source of water supply and an outlet for sewage (Sharan 2014: 173). Soon, uncertainty about the number and type (light or heavy) of industries gave way to debates between the Delhi Improvement Trust and the Delhi Municipal Committee, both pointing out either legal or administrative restraints to demarcate the area. In the end, as the *Report of the Delhi Improvement Trust Enquiry Committee* (Ministry of Health, Government of India 1951) stated two decades later, this transfer never happened, with post-Independence industrial activity heavily concentrated in non- and semi-permanent structures scattered across the city (Sharan 2014: 186).

Due to the adjacency of housing and industries, congestion and pollution became primary concerns of planners of post-Independence Delhi. City planning was supposed to be the panacea, but questions about the nature of both industries and workers persisted. Two strands of thought emerged in response: the Geddesian framework of social scientific survey, which emphasised precise information about a region and its population leading to a plan with a public education programme about planning, and the more centralised idea of zoning which had emerged in response to perplexities of nuisance laws in growing metropolitan cities elsewhere (Sharan 2014: 188). Proponents of zoning won this debate by highlighting successes of zoning in the USA and the importance of sovereign power to discipline a growing population. In practice, authorities conducted scientific surveys only to estimate the number, size, and type of industries, whereas nuisances (noise, smoke, odours) were to be judged through personal inspection by the planners. Thus, the Delhi Master Plan of 1962, which zoned Delhi, was a product of two contested forms of knowledge: 'personal inspection' to judge the scale of nuisance and the compatibility of industries with the city's zonal plans, and surveys to estimate their size. This produced two categories: polluting (hazardous/noxious/obnoxious) and non-conforming industries (industries not conforming to the new Master Plan), which did not always overlap. Moreover, many noxious industries were in fact household industries with small operational scale and could not be considered as manufacturing units under the zoning regulations (Shafi 1965).

These contestations over polluting industries were reconvened in 1984, when the lawyer, M. C. Mehta, filed a petition in the Supreme Court of India lamenting that Delhi, which was 'once beautiful', had been severely polluted and was sitting on a 'volcano without knowing when it would erupt'.[1] The Supreme Court turned to the Master Plan of 1962 for guidance, concluding that Delhi's continued unregulated industrial growth was a failure of its implementation. This elided the contradictory nature of the plan per se, as suggested above, and had the effect of setting the precedence for drawing on the master plan as a legal instrument. Meanwhile, a second Master Plan for 2001 was drafted, which again stated that 'hazardous/noxious/heavy/large industries were not permitted to operate in Delhi ... these categories are to be relocated'.[2]

A survey carried out by the Delhi Pollution Control Committee (DPCC) in 1995–6 showed that one lac industries were non-conforming.[3] A group of experts was then set up by the SC to determine polluting industries listed under the Master Plan of Delhi-2001, which recommended that 33 activities be classified as polluting.[4] These two surveys superseded a third one carried out by the state government, which the Supreme Court said was based on perception-based research, and therefore, was 'neither scientific, nor precise nor reliable'. In September 1999, when in response to M. C. Mehta versus Union of India and Others,[5] the court ordered the relocation of 98,000 non-conforming industries, the conflation between polluting and non-conforming became apparent. The sensory and material category of nuisance was made to share space with a purely aesthetic-classificatory notion of conformity with zoning. Both were now marked as incongruent with the modernising city. In this manner, the relocation of polluting industries as an air pollution control measure effectively closed many more units because of the conflation.

Contestations later emerged in the air pollution issue around emission standards and fuel quality in the 1990s, this time brought into prominence by the Centre of Science and Environment (CSE), a scientifically-driven organisation that advocates for environmental justice. It spearheaded a movement against poor emission standards, diesel, and fuel adulteration, publishing provocative reports such as *Slow Murder: The Deadly Story of Vehicular Pollution in India* (Roychowdhury 1996) and *Engines of the Devil* (Agarwal 1999) on deteriorating air quality associated with an increasing number of diesel vehicles. Standards were in question on three aspects: Indian vs European driving cycles,[6] warm start vs cold start,[7] and on catalytic converters.[8] After deliberations by three different technical committees, emission standards were diluted based on warm start and did not mention driving cycles. The use of catalytic converters to meet revised 2000 emissions standards required diesel with low-sulphur content. This sparked a debate on fuel quality because this was the time the court created the Environmental Pollution Control Authority (EPCA), of which CSE was and continues to be an important participant, and was championing the conversion of the entire fleet of public transport in Delhi to natural gas, as discussed in depth below. It backed this stand by referring to global expertise: in 1998, the California Air Resources Board (CARB) had identified Particulate Matter (PM) from diesel as a Toxic Air Contaminant (TAC) and indicted it as the major contributor to potential cancer risk after a ten-year review process (CARB 2000: 11). Another report by the US Department of Energy asserted that CNG was significantly safer and less polluting than diesel (US DoE 2000; CSE 2001).

Despite such global expertise that the EPCA built its case on, at least three sources contradicted its claims: one study said that CNG emitted nanoparticles (Agarwal 2000); TERI released a study claiming that ultra-low sulphur diesel was a better option; and an Indian Institute of Technology-Delhi professor argued that CNG could lead to more oxides of nitrogen and carbon monoxide compared to low-sulphur diesel. These meant that the EPCA had to revise CNG's value in anti-pollution imaginaries: over time, it morphed from a 'clean fuel' to an 'environmentally acceptable' one in the agency's communications. As Sharan notes (2006: 232), the SC had hoped that the EPCA would help to bring about a scientific consensus regarding fuel quality. Witnessing these contradictions, however, led to the SC changing its own stand on air-related matters. Given the overall risk that was widely acknowledged but also the uncertain nature of available data, the Court decided to build its opinions on the so-called 'precautionary principle', which implies erring on the side of caution while waiting for a scientific consensus to emerge.

After a decade, scientific knowledge appears more uncertain and contested today than ever before, especially in the wake of new representational technologies. The central government came up with a first-ever nationwide 'National Air Quality Index' (NAQI) on 17 September 2014—a 'one colour-one number' index where health advisories could be issued based on a scale from 'good' to 'hazardous' depending on concentration of a series of pollutants notified as such by Central Pollution Control Board (CPCB): particulates (PM10, PM2.5), gases (oxides of nitrogen-NOx, ozone-O_3, carbon monoxide-CO, sulfur dioxide-SO_2, ammonia-NH_3), and lead (Pb). This tool was immediately picked up by both print and online social media as newspapers began to publish figures with a single number to denote hazardous air and Facebook groups were formed to discuss air quality. However, Greenpeace criticises the NAQI system for not being comprehensive, updated, and participatory enough (Greenpeace, 2016), while others question its scientific validity. According to an environmental scientist at a major public university, 'the AQI is only advisory, not scientific. We work with data and want to be confident about what we say ... But advice is different from science'.[9] This is despite the fact that the AQI was developed by the Indian Institute of Technology (IIT) at Kharagpur, West Bengal, one of most respected institutions in the country.

The simple idea—i.e. colour coding—behind the AQI makes it apt for comparisons across urban areas part of heterogeneous geographical regions leading to a recognition that other cities in India are as affected by air pollution as Delhi, if not more. It has, for instance, enabled comparisons— even heated competition, if newspapers are to be believed—between Beijing and Delhi, two megacities with similar indices. Many reports are even in awe of Beijing, lauding the city's strict implementation of action plans (*Hindustan Times* 2016; *Business Standard* 2016). However, a scientist from DPCC we spoke with suggested that particularities of each context trumped equalising logics when he stated that, '[Beijing] has nearest sea port at 60 km ... I have at 600 km away. Is this taken into account? They have a very high mountain nearby. And we don't ... here geography is different'. The supposed uniqueness of Delhi helps the scientist to position its air as lacking critical valves that makes it worse than Beijing. At the same time, Delhi and Beijing do have certain processes in common: creeping toxic urbanism, in the form of growing consumerist cultures that privilege personal mobility, tends to make their ecological presents and futures commensurable, if not interwoven. These realisations are part of many current texts. The Clean Air Initiative-Asia's document, for instance, says the following:

> PM10 is a critical pollutant for most Asian cities ... several developed countries have established PM2.5 guidelines (for WHO) and standards (for US and European Union [EU]) ... Asian countries are slowly moving towards developing PM2.5 as well ... still a long way to go (CAI-Asia 2010).

Comparisons are not only textualised, they are also performed at various air pollution-related events. At a CSE public meeting titled 'Clean Air Conclave', an expert from Beijing gave a presentation on lessons to be learnt from Beijing's air pollution problems: similar problems, she said, merited similar solutions. At another talk by an international air management consultant and a former CEO of CARB, California's air was made comparable with Delhi's through the targeting of diesel as a transnational villain, with appeals to adopt certain globally consistent technological fixes. Such calls tend to produce an abstract space where metrics, expertise, and gadgets move freely between contexts. This is made possible by internationally mobile experts, who resemble 'a knowledge worker operating ... as a private consultant or as a specialist ... defining truths about, providing information on, and implementing techniques that facilitate governmental programs' (McCann 2008: 4).

Like pollution-abatement technologies, the abstract transnational space supports the proliferation of products designed to condition air, to produce a supposedly clean, leak-free, smoke-free environment for those who can afford it. At the Clean Air Fair organised by the group Help Delhi Breathe, NirvanaBeing, an importer of expensive Vogmasks (priced at INR 2,000 onwards), claimed to filter 99 per cent of breathable particles. An air-purifier by Atlanta Healthcare (for INR 45,000) promised completely sanitised air after going through a nine-step filtration system. Competing hand-held monitors to measure ambient air quality were also prominently displayed and attracted the curiosity of visitors. Yet both the DPCC and the Central Pollution Control Board (CPCB) argue that unless monitors are US-EPA verified and average out data to control for complex dynamics of ambient air, they only display data without a baseline and without controlling for climate and therefore cannot be called 'scientific' no matter their claims (*Times of India* 2014). Still, these and other products seek to create sanitised urban environments that are within the reach of a few, being neither sustainable nor equitable, despite them claiming to be social enterprises and despite their owners thinking of themselves as activists rather than merely entrepreneurs.

In the 1990s, environmental advocates represented by the SC, EPCA, and CSE saw a clear target: industries and diesel were to be moved out of the city. These advocates pointed out that public health could not be compromised even if it meant that industrial workers and transporters lost their livelihoods. Stricter implementation of the master plan(s) by the state, they argued, should have taken care of this problem earlier. Further, scientists (often from outside India) were relied upon for technical knowledge, which was imparted to the public through popular mediums. With the more recent focus on diffused and invisible particulate matter, it is harder to pinpoint the source of pollution, and focus on monitoring and surveillance along with demands for data-driven advocacy has centred the discourse on prognosis. In *Risk Society*, Ulrich Beck (1992) argues that post-industrial societies are, more than ever, being structured by risks of various kinds, including human-mediated ones. When the risk society encounters uncertain hazards, it seeks to legitimise and control them, accompanied by the anxiety that they are really beyond the grasp of institutions. In the specifically regional conditions under which toxic urbanism proceeds, questions of class, privilege, and environmental justice—as have been highlighted in the case of Delhi— also come to inform the debate. All of this has led to mutual learning: activists are beginning to engage with the objective elements of pollutants and the mutations of biologies that they engender, while at the same time, expertise has come to see the geography of the city and its inhabitants not as externalities but as essential agents co-producing urban futures.

Collaborations and Learning

As discussions on Delhi's poisonous air reached the city's living rooms via unprecedented media attention in January 2016, a nascent collective of different individuals ('Help Delhi Breathe') joined established advocacy groups to organise a public event in the heart of the city to, as their Facebook event page expressed it, 'make some noise' and pressure the government to take appropriate measures. On the day of the event, Jantar Mantar—

the officially mandated protest site in the city—reverberated with music, testimonies, and impassioned pleas to 'clean up the city's air'. Key individuals from Help Delhi Breathe shared the stage with representatives from the city's ubiquitous and influential Residents Welfare Associations (RWAs) and environmental groups like Greenpeace and CSE, while the media was also present in force, relaying live images on the various news channels. To someone trained in the critical social sciences with a sense of Delhi's environmental politics, the setting would be easily tagged as another instance of 'bourgeois environmentalism' (Baviskar 2003, Véron 2006).

Almost all the participants at Jantar Mantar, including a smattering of expats wearing anti-pollution masks, were from Delhi's elite sections; everyone who spoke at the event did so in English, and technical concepts such as the AQI and PM formed the backbone of the various interventions. A certain hypocrisy could also be observed given that those speaking out on air pollution were arguably disproportionately responsible for it through their use of personal cars while also being somewhat buffered from it by air conditioners and purifiers. And yet, this would be a partial, if not incorrect, view of the story of activism and advocacy around Delhi's air. Though many of the protagonists—the members of civil society, the local state, and the judiciary—remain salient, the terms of the discourse and the field of possibilities have shifted greatly since the early 2000s towards what we call reflexive advocacy. We thus recount the story of activism around air in Delhi in recent decades.

In response to activists approaching it on air-related matters, in 1995, the SC constituted the EPCA for the NCR under the Environment Protection Act of 1986, which published reports that led to a constitutional bench deciding on 31 March 2001, that the entire bus fleet of Delhi should be converted to CNG, a 'clean fuel'. From this order until 1 December 2002, when the last diesel bus was flagged out of Delhi, Delhi's air was hotly contested: governments in power and in opposition accused each other of 'playing politics', scientists from industry and from environmental or academic organisations argued over how emission standards should be set (European vs Indian road conditions, warm start or cold start, usefulness of catalytic convertors) leading to the constitution of three 'high-level' committees and the eventual dilution of standards.

Though the Court offered six years' wages to compensate those affected by closure and relocation of industries, thousands of workers were not on the rolls, being casual, migrant, subcontracted labourers (Martinez-Alier 2002: 17). The indifference of the judiciary and civil society towards workers, who would continue to suffer health effects, and their living spaces, which were never classified as 'residential' by the Master Plan, was also glaring. Further, no mention was made of how pollution would be regulated in areas where industries were to be located. Instead, the worker-industry assemblage, seen as one polluting and undesirable whole, was to be moved out of the city. Similarly, Sunalini Kumar (2004) noted in a study that most auto-rickshaw drivers did not own their vehicles, and those who did had bought them on loans. After the conversion order to CNG, they sold their vehicles to contractors to meet the high costs of retro-fitting with CNG engines. The previous owner-drivers became contract drivers.

It is apparent that both these decisions led to seriously unequal outcomes for Delhi's marginalised residents, and were critiqued as 'bourgeois environmentalism' by scholars and alternative publications, wherein the middle class-state-judiciary nexus dictated terms of urban governance and civic participation (*Frontline* 2000; Baviskar 2003; 2006). Other scholars have complicated the picture: whereas Mawdsley (2004) argues that the term 'middle class' in urban Indian contexts is loaded with multiple meanings and demographies, Negi (2010) argues that this points towards a 'neoliberal turn' in urban governance, where industrial landscapes were moved out of Delhi to make way for tertiary sector services, such as retail and entertainment, and was in line with 'development' of a wider NCR region.

Much has happened since 2002: Delhi hosted the 2010 Commonwealth Games, during which concerns about air quality being nulled by increasing number of vehicles were raised by CSE and other civil society organisations, leading to the installation of air quality monitors and displays at sporting venues which showed that air quality had indeed become dismal once again. Then, in 2015, the World Health Organization (WHO) labelled Delhi the 'world's most polluted city', and the US Embassy reportedly bought 1,800 air purifiers before President Obama's visit for Republic Day functions in January 2015 (*The Indian Express* 2015).

In response, the Aam Aadmi Party (AAP, literally meaning the 'common man's party'), which has held power since February 2015, organised a massive volunteer drive to implement its 'odd-even' scheme (odd and even numbered cars to ply on alternate days, with exceptions granted to female drivers), requesting people to follow through mass advertising by radio, TV, and even personalised phone calls and text messages. Meanwhile, the SC, along with the National Green Tribunal (NGT, constituted so that scientific and judicial experts can resolve environmental disputes together) has contributed to the discussion and passed orders accordingly, rather than leading the supposed charge against pollution. CSE continues to remain an influential actor, organising public meetings to discuss air pollution and policies to reduce it, many of which we observed closely.

However, some of the most vocal and active groups are the newly formed collectives comprising expatriates (who claim to have experienced better air quality elsewhere in the world), engineering and medical professionals, representatives from Residents' Welfare Associations, and 'air entrepreneurs', or individuals who have initiated air-related startups involving air quality monitors, purifiers, and masks. One such group, Help Delhi Breathe, has organised multiple public events around the issue of air, including the one we opened this section with. A few weeks earlier, the group had conducted a camp at a city school, where volunteer health practitioners offered the audience the chance to estimate their lung capacity. In this manner, the collective invited city residents to join the debate on air through a biological route: objective knowledge of one's body is here positioned as an entry point to political participation—a form of what Adriana Petryna calls 'biological citizenship' (2004). These entrepreneur-activists work hard to keep the issue burning in public view via online campaigns and public events. While this may be considered part of an initiative to promote discussion on the matter, it may also be argued that the greater the alarm regarding air quality, the more apps are downloaded, and masks and purifiers purchased by concerned residents. One of the more prominent air-entrepreneurs, for instance, went to court asking for a popular half-marathon to be postponed on account of the hazardous air. The petition was rejected, but the effort was widely reported in the media, keeping air alive in the public consciousness—even though empirically the previous month's smog had cleared—while also evidently adding to the 'activist' credentials of the concerned individual.

We discern important differences from the previous discourse, mainly in how the actors' articulations about air and about each other have shifted and the strategies through which these articulations are woven together or disentangled. First, we find that the actors involved in the previous moment—the SC, CSE, and the local government (AAP)—have engaged with critiques of bourgeois environmentalism and now visibly use the rhetoric and symbolism associated with social justice and participatory governance. In the 1990s, the Supreme Court had positioned itself as the protector of peoples' public health, portraying almost everyone else as self-interested. When confronted by issues of technical complexity during the struggle for better emission standards and fuel quality, it had worked through the EPCA, a high-level committee comprised of experts who published reports that the SC acted upon. Now, even as it issues high-impact orders such as evolution of Euro-V standards and clearing a national action plan on air, it directs the NGT on many issues concerning air pollution. Consider its statement's during a hearing: 'Despite Expert Members … in the interest of justice, we adopt the approach which is more consultative and provide a leverage for deliberations with the stake holders and the Authorities.'[10]

The CSE's position is similarly deliberative, and acknowledges that air is a complex phenomenon with constantly shifting science. Apart from other sources, for instance, the CSE has lately begun highlighting the deleterious effects of atmospheric ozone, mirroring scientific developments in the US. In a recent article, it also re-evaluates its own expertise-driven position, stating that 'there is a class system at work—which works its ways into mindsets of planners and engineers' and that indeed, Delhi has consistently pushed away its pollution where someone else lives, with the conversion to CNG affecting the lives of auto-rickshaw drivers (*Down to Earth* 2016). Still, actions of the 1990s have helped the CSE position itself as a regional actor that now participates in global discourses around sustainable mobility in cities (in India, Southeast Asia, and East Africa), hoping to impart lessons from Delhi's experiences and learn some of its own, as was evident in a meeting it had organised in Delhi where participants included air pollution experts from far-off places like England and China.

Further, one of the most emphatic contributions has been from the state itself. The Arvind Kejriwal-led AAP government has been involved with 'grassroots' mobilisation from its emergence, working with trade and auto-rickshaw unions. At a public meeting organised by Help Delhi Breathe, one of its representatives explicitly stated that Delhi is not and cannot be a world-class city for a long time, and that their efforts are to improve decentralised governance rather than engage in discourses around making Delhi a post-industrial utopia. During its odd-even scheme, it even offered an apology to the public for inconvenience, requesting them to nevertheless 'participate' in the scheme. The government also formed the Delhi Dialogue

Commission, comprising AAP members and representatives from civil society, to identify best solutions and practices to manage air pollution, partnering with the University of Chicago's Urban Labs to organise an open competition to crowdsource ideas to deal with air pollution in the city.

Despite appeals to air as a common concern, class continues to underpin much of the debate. An article in *The New Yorker* viscerally portrays two children suffering from chronic breathing problems: one of them lives in a one-room house in a poor neighbourhood and is unable to afford any of the protection measures on the market; the other lives in an elegant apartment, surrounded by air purifiers. In the end, the parents decide to move out of Delhi, a choice unavailable to the first child (Barry 2016). This picture makes it obvious that data-driven consumerism is out of reach for most of Delhi's residents due to its technical complexity, the language of communication, and the prohibitive cost of the various technologies.

In sum, it is evident that the state, judiciary, and civil society organisations have adopted a more deliberative and reflexive approach in their articulations of air pollution. This has both produced and facilitated the expansion of the spaces where air pollution is discussed in Delhi. In the 1990s, deliberations mostly occurred in courtrooms through high-level committees, driven by scientific information that was not easily available to the public. As the CSE says, 'In 1996, Delhi didn't know what it breathed. In 2016, it does … public awareness is sharper than 20 years ago' (*Down to Earth* 2016). Contrast this with the CSE's earlier statements in its above-cited reports, where it constantly reminded readers that technical complexity around air impedes wider public participation.

Over time, the enlargement of air's publics has been mediated by data and their representations. The increased salience of the AQI has already been discussed. The Central Pollution Control Board communicates air quality through an interactive online portal and makes annual and monthly reports of air quality of various cities and states, while the Delhi Pollution Control Committee does the same for its ten monitoring stations in Delhi. Another state-supported air monitoring network (required to sample air for all NAAQS-notified pollutants[11]) is the Indian Institute of Tropical Meteorology (IITM)'s System of Air Quality and Weather Forecasting and Research (SAFAR). Both CPCB and SAFAR have their own mobile applications, or apps: Sameer (meaning wind in Hindi), and SAFAR-Air, respectively. Apart from these, we counted at least twenty different mobile applications for India alone by different publishers. Though most of these source their data from either CPCB's or SAFAR's networks (such as Greenpeace's 'Clean Air Nation' and Air Alert), some of them (like Airveda and BreathEasy) connect to both the state's monitoring networks and their own independent air quality monitors. They go further than just communicating data, issuing advisories and measures to manage exposure to polluted air (one recommends installation of air purifiers; another asks to consider indoor plants).

In fact, interactive interfaces along with availability of easily accessible data online make it possible for not only civil society organisations and news agencies to share the most recent air quality data, they also interpellate an informed individual armed with data who takes charge to protect her family. As Delhi's air worsened in the immediate aftermath of Diwali in November 2016, an unprecedented number of masks, monitors, and purifiers were being bought by concerned residents. We were told that one manufacturer of masks could no longer keep up with the increased demand, even as new startups like Treeco entered the market with assembled air purifiers which cost almost half of similar gadgets sold by well-known multinationals. On the Facebook page devoted to the city's air, a feverish discussion ensued: several interventions vented at the government's lack of action; some looked inwards at the irresponsible behaviour of those who celebrated Diwali by bursting crackers, while others asked—or answered—queries related to the relative merits of the various air-related products in the market. To be sure, knowledge and action intersect here to produce a consumer aware of potential risks and possible individual solutions. However, many of these 'armed' individuals are also entering the wider discussion, and thus enlarging the public sphere within which issues and actions are being debated in Delhi.

Conclusion

The rapid transformation of South Asian cities in the last three decades is well understood in terms of population change as well as its social, economic, and political dimensions. More recently, the environmental imbrications of urbanisation in the region have begun to be problematised. From loss of habitats to mountains of untreated waste, environmental concerns have steadily crept into popular discussions and policy spaces. In particular, what we call 'toxic urbanism'—a poisonous, unpleasant, and risky form of urban change—increasingly defines residents' everyday lives and experiences, though adjacency to toxicity is differentiated along lines of class, caste, and other forces. Lately, and not only, but particularly in Delhi, toxic air has been represented, discussed, and acted upon by diverse agents in multiple ways. Predominant forms of energy—coal and fossil fuel—and poorly implemented regulatory controls over industrial emissions, contribute to South Asian urban regions emerging as global air pollution hotspots. Delhi is an especially instructive vantage point here, given that the debate around air in the city is of a historical and deeply political nature.

Air's visibility has in turn led to the retooling of individual actions, collective organising, and urban governance. Far from being the inert backdrop on which social-ecological processes are popularly perceived to take place, air itself has assumed political agency (Negi 2017): governments enforce rationing of road space, experts debate emission norms, families who can afford them invest in air purifiers, and many individuals contend with impairment of lung function. As these concerns begin to impinge upon other urban regions, it is productive to seriously consider Delhi's case, with its shifting emphasis, representations, and political logics.

The air debate has unfolded in the present era defined by environmental indeterminacy and more or less thoughtful responses to uncertainty. Whereas the judiciary operates on the precautionary principle and the state tries to implement popular policies, civil society organisations and journalists often find it difficult to translate complex scientific data for easy public access. This mediation often puts them into contrary positions with many scientists, especially when the latter focus on precise knowledge while the former are compelled to write in a simpler fashion, which expresses the urgency of the situation. At the same time, we find that there is an effort to overcome these gaps by all the actors involved, which precipitates new networks. For example, AAP has tried to institutionalise collaboration with different actors by forming the Delhi Dialogue Commission, which has ties with the CSE and universities outside India. There are also nascent collectives such as Help Delhi Breathe through whom a host of new actors enter the scene, including expatriates and air entrepreneurs. Not only have the various agents moved towards deliberative and reflexive approaches, data-driven representations of air also seem to blur boundaries between the articulations of state, civil society, and the 'public', as these actors come together under aforementioned collectives. The media often shifts gears to campaign mode, long-time campaigners sit on government advisory committees, government representatives attend and contribute to activist meetings, while entrepreneurs have turned into activists. Attention to air thus raises critical questions related to the nature and forms of environmental politics under conditions of toxic urbanism: Who exactly is responsible? How is accountability to work?

A comparative analysis of Delhi's discourse on air in the late 1990s–early 2000s, and from 2014 onwards, shows that it has been integral to shaping the city's landscapes, public provisions, and governance. We have examined how networks of actors formed around urban air during the two critical moments, and whom they included and excluded. To be sure, the air debate has been frequently marked by contestations and distrust. Plans for the city since the 1930s have been loaded against the aspirations of the poor, who have found themselves blamed for the worsening environmental conditions, even though they bear heavy costs given that they inhabit vulnerable neighbourhoods with grossly inadequate infrastructures. Even the court-ordered industrial relocation conflated pollution and planning violations by bundling the two and leading to widespread closure of units and subsequent losses of livelihoods. These cases clearly demonstrate why those invested in social justice in Delhi have been suspicious of urban environmentalism, which they consider to be an extension of bourgeois attempts to remake the city in its image.

Yet we find that actors present in both moments—the local government, judiciary, and civil society organisations—have shifted towards environmental justice positions, responding to the previous critiques of environmentalism, which saw in it attempts to transform Delhi into a 'world-class city' at the cost of purportedly asynchronous elements like small- and medium-sized industries. Further, there is a difference in how these networks formed, enrolled other actors, and substantiated themselves. In the 1990s, most of the discourse was produced in the courtrooms and via established environmental advocacy groups, wherein the state was admonished for not following the SC's orders. Now, the AAP-led local government articulates participatory urban governance and refuses to either label Delhi as a 'world-class city', or that it harbours any ambition to become one. By targeting vehicular pollution through its odd-even plans and more recent construction of cycling tracks (flyovers), it has turned the tables on Delhi's car-owning elite. These are important shifts with the potential to alter the basic foundations of the neoliberal urban agenda, which was based on expanding consumption and individual mobility. Contradictorily, however, neoliberal logics increasingly mediate the representation and conditioning of air by gadgets like air monitors and purifiers respectively. Even as governance moves towards a public conception of air, these interventions rescale air from a shared entity to an individual or household-scaled phenomenon, producing a differentiated geography of risk. It is critical then to appreciate the progressive shifts while also recognising the problematic continuities that exist within urban environmentalism.

NOTES

1. SC, M. C. Mehta vs Government of India and Others, WP 4677, 1985.
2. SC, M. C. Mehta vs Union of India and Others, WP 4677, on 10 May 1996; 1996 AIR 1977.
3. SC WP 4677, DLT 345SC, p. 5.
4. SC WP 4677, DLT 345SC, p. 17.
5. SC WP 4677, DLT 345SC.
6. The India driving cycle simulation, which considers deceleration, idling, and skewed acceleration emits more pollutants compared to the European driving cycle, which is based on better road conditions and consequently produces lesser emissions.
7. Engines give more emissions when started from cold as opposed to when they are already warm.
8. Catalytic converters contain lead or palladium as catalysts, which are made

ineffective when the fuel contains sulphur. Meeting the newer norms required vehicles to install catalytic convertors, which in turn, demanded diesel with low sulphur content.
9. Personal communication.
10. NGT original application No. 21 of 2014; Vardhaman Kaushik vs Union of India and Ors 28/11/2014.
11. National Ambient Air Quality Standards, or NAAQS notifies 12 pollutants to be monitored with different time intervals that depend on pollutants' characteristics. For example, SO_2, $PM10$, and $PM2.5$ have both annual and 24-hour standards, but ozone and carbon monoxide have an 8-hour standard, whereas benzene, arsenic, and nickel have only annual standards specified.

REFERENCES

Agarwal, Anil, *Engines of the Devil*, Delhi: Centre for Science & Environment, 1999.
'Air at public places badly polluted', The Times of India <https://timesofindia. indiatimes.com/home/environment/pollution/Air-at-public-places-badly-polluted/articleshow/45465646.cms> last accessed 29 August 2019.
'Analysing the National Air Quality Index Platform', Greenpeace, 2016 <https:// www.greenpeace.org/archive-india/en/Blog/Campaign_blogs/analysing-the-effectiveness-of-the-national-a/blog/56069/>, accessed 7 September 2019.

Badami, Madhav G., 'Transport and Urban Air Pollution in India', *Environmental Management*, 36, 2 (2005), pp. 195–204.

Baviskar, Amita, 'Demolishing Delhi: World Class City in the Making', *Mute*, 2, 3 (2006) <http://www.metamute.org/editorial/articles/demolishing-delhi-world-class-city-making>.

_____, 'Between Violence and Desire: Space, Power, and Identity in the Making of Metropolitan Delhi', *International Social Science Journal*, 55, 175 (2003), pp. 89–98.

Beck, Ulrich, 'From Industrial Society to the Risk Society: Questions of Survival, Social Structure and Ecological Enlightenment', *Theory, Culture & Society*, 9, 1 (1992), pp. 97–123.

'Beijing Air Has Improved Rapidly, New Delhi could learn: Expert', *Hindustan Times* <https://www.hindustantimes.com/world-news/beijing-air-has-improved-rapidly-new-delhi-could-learn/story-Ow8yY7nT7KpCWfe9XDuhJK.html>.

Brahinsky, Rachel, 'Race and the Making of Southeast San Francisco: Towards a Theory of Race-class', *Antipode*, 46, 5 (2014), pp. 1258–76.

California Air Resources Board, *Risk Reduction Plan to Reduce Particulate Matter Emissions from Diesel-Fueled Engines and Vehicles*, Sacramento: California Environmental Protection Agency, 2000.

Chari Sharad, 'Detritus in Durban: Polluted Environs and the Biopolitics of Refusal', in: L.A. Stoler, (ed.), *Imperial Debris: On Ruins and Ruination*, Durham: Duke University Press, 2013.

Cox, Kevin R., *The Politics of Urban and Regional Development and the American Exception*, Syracuse: Syracuse University Press, 2016.

'Delhi's Air Pollution: What China Got Right and Where We Fall Behind', *Business Standard* <https://www.business-standard.com/article/economy-policy/delhi-s-air-pollution-what-china-got-right-and-where-we-fall-behind-116112100175_1.html>, accessed 29 August 2019.

D'Souza, Rohan, and Harini Nagendra, 'Changes in Public Commons as a Consequence of Urbanisation: the Agara Lake in Bangalore, India', *Environmental Management*, 47, 5 (2011), pp. 840–50.

Fortun, Kim, *Advocacy after Bhopal: Environmentalism, Disaster, New Global Orders*, Chicago: University of Chicago Press, 2001.

_____, 'From Bhopal to the Informating of Environmentalism: Risk Communication in Historical Perspective', *Osiris*, 19 (2001), pp. 283–96.

Ghertner, D. Asher, *Rule by Aesthetics: World-class City Making in Delhi*, Oxford: Oxford University Press, 2015.

Graham, Stephen, 'Life Support: The Political Ecology of Urban Air', *City*, 19, 2 (2015), pp. 192–215.

Greenstone, Michael, and Rema Hanna, 'Environmental Regulations, Air and Water Pollution and Infant Mortality in India', *The American Economic Review*, 104, 10 (2014), pp. 3038–72.

Hajer, Maarten A., *The Politics of Environmental Discourse*, Oxford: Oxford University Press, 1997.

Held, David, and Kevin Young, 'Crisis in Parallel Worlds: The Governance of Global Risks in Finance, Security and the Environment', in C. Calhoun and G. Derluguian, (eds.), *The Deepening Crisis: Governance Challenges after Neoliberalism*, New York: NYU Press, 2011.

'High on Gas', Down to Earth <https://www.downtoearth.org.in/blog/high-on-gas-18547>, accessed 29 August 2019.

Hume, A. P., *Report on the Relief of Congestion in Delhi*, 1, pp. 50–1, Shimla: Government of India Press, 1936.

Kumar, Sunalini, 'Clean Air, Dirty Logic? Environmental Activism, Citizenship, and the Public Sphere in Delhi', in R. Desai and R. Sanyal (eds.), *Urbanising Citizenship: Contested Spaces in Indian Cities*, Thousand Oaks, California: SAGE, 2004.

Martinez-Alier, Joan, 'The Environmentalism of the Poor', paper presented for conference 'The Political Economy of Sustainable Development: Environmental Conflict, Participation and Movement', South Africa: University of Witwatersrand, 2002.

Mawdsley, Emma, 'India's Middle Classes and the Environment', *Development and Change*, 35, 1 (2004), pp. 79–103.

McCann, Eugene J., 'Expertise, Truth, and Urban Policy Mobilities: Global Circuits of Knowledge in the Development of Vancouver, Canada's 'Four Pillar' Drug Strategy', *Environment and Planning*, 40, 4 (2008), pp. 885–904.

Ministry of Health, *Report of the Delhi Trust Improvement Enquiry Committee*, Government of India, 1951.

Negi, Rohit, 'Neoliberalism, Environmentalism, and Urban Politics in Delhi', in W. Ahmed, A. Kundu and R. Peet (eds.), *India's New Economic Policy: A Critical Analysis*, Routledge, 2010.

Nigam, Aditya, 'Dislocating Delhi: A City in the 1990s', in *Sarai Reader 1: The Public Domain*, Sarai: the New Media Initiative, CSDS, 2001, pp. 40–6.

Padel, Felix, and Samarendra Das, 'Cultural Genocide and the Rhetoric of Sustainable Mining in East India', *Contemporary South Asia*, 18, 3 (2010), pp. 333–41.

Parish, R., *Natural Gas Buses: Separating Myth from Fact*, U.S. Department of Energy, 2000.

'Particulate Matter (PM) standards in Asia', CAI-Asia <https://cleanairasia.org/wp-content/uploads/portal/files/documents/2_Particulate_Matter_PM_Standards_in_Asia_Fact_Sheet_26_Aug_2010_0.pdf>, accessed 29 August 2019.

Petryna, Adriana, 'Biological Citizenship: The Science and Politics of Chernobyl-Exposed Populations', *Osiris*, 19, 2004, pp. 250–65.

Rademacher, Anne, and K. Sivaramakrishnan, *Ecologies of Urbanism in India: Metropolitan Civility and Sustainability*, Hong Kong: Hong Kong University Press, 2013.

Schindler, Seth, Federico Demaria and Shashi B Pandit, 'Delhi's Waste Conflict', *Economic and Political Weekly*, 47, 42 (2012), pp. 18–21.

Shafi, S. S., 'Non-conforming Industrial Uses and the Role of 'Flatted Factories' in Urban Renewal', *Journal of the Institute of Town Planners of India*, 42 and 43 (1965), pp. 140–4.

Sharan, Awadhendra, *In the City, Out of Place: Nuisance, Pollution, and Dwelling in Delhi, c. 1850–2000*, Oxford: Oxford University Press, 2014.

Sharma, Anju, and Anumita Roychowdhury, *Slow Murder: The Deadly Story of Vehicular Pollution in India*, Delhi: Centre for Science and Environment, 1996.

Srivastava, Sanjay, 'Urban Spaces, Disney-divinity and Moral Middle Classes in Delhi', *Economic and Political Weekly*, 44, 26/27 (2009), pp. 338–45.

'The Lethal Zones', *Frontline*, <https://frontline.thehindu.com/static/html/fl1725/17250140.htm>, accessed 29 August 2019.

'Two Children, One Rich, One Poor, Gasping for Air in Delhi's Smog', *The New Yorker* <https://www.nytimes.com/2016/11/23/world/asia/india-delhi-pollution.html>, last accessed 29 August 2019.

'US Embassy Purchased over 1,800 Air Purifiers before President Obama's India visit', *The Indian Express* <https://indianexpress.com/article/technology/technology-others/us-embassy-purchased-over-1800-air-purifiers-before-president-obamas-india-visit/>, accessed 29 August 2019.

Véron, René, 'Remaking Urban Environments: The Political Ecology of Air Pollution in Delhi', *Environment and Planning A*, 38, 11 (2006), pp. 2093–109.

Wainwright, Joel, *Decolonizing Development: Colonial Power and the Maya*, Maiden: Blackwell, 2008.

7

Electoral Politics in
Delhi's Informal Settlements:
Contestation, Negotiation, and Exclusion

Shahana Sheikh, Sonal Sharma, and Subhadra Banda

Introduction

This chapter[1] highlights the nature of contestations and the negotiations around election time in India's capital city, Delhi. We draw upon fieldwork conducted prior to two elections: the Delhi State Assembly elections in 2013 and the Indian Parliamentary elections in 2014. Our emphasis is on electoral promises relating to basic services such as water and sanitation, as well as reformist measures such as regularisation and rehabilitation of informal settlements. Manifestation of contestations are highlighted from election campaign documents (such as manifestos and posters) and speeches during public meetings and processions of three major political parties—the Bharatiya Janata Party (BJP), the Indian National Congress (INC), and the Aam Aadmi Party (AAP)—that contested these elections.

The 2013 Delhi State Assembly elections were significant for two reasons. First, the INC had a majority in the state legislature for fifteen years prior to this (1998–2013). Throughout this period, Sheila Dixit was the Chief Minister of Delhi, which made her the longest serving female Chief Minister of any state. Second, this was the first election where AAP—which originated as a result of the nationwide anti-corruption movement—entered electoral politics.[2]

Since 1992, there have been six elections for legislators to the Delhi State Assembly, with the first one in 1993 and the most recent one in 2015. Of the twenty years from 1993 to 2013, the BJP formed the Delhi Government only for the first five years. From 1998 to 2013, the INC formed a majority government in the Delhi State Assembly, while the BJP was the political party with the second highest number of legislators during this time. The two most recent elections for the Delhi State Assembly took place in December 2013 and in February 2015. During the December 2013 Delhi State Assembly elections, for the first time, a new political party—the AAP—contested elections. We will discuss details about the electoral promises of the AAP later in this paper, but it is notable that much of their narrative in the run-up to these elections was about reducing corruption and about decreasing the dominance of the two national political parties—the BJP and the INC—in the Delhi Government, in an effort to 'give power back to the people'.

The 2013 election resulted in a hung assembly since no political party had legislators more than 50 per cent (35 of the total 70) of the Delhi State Assembly constituencies (ACs). AAP won 28 of the 70 legislative seats and formed a minority government in the end of December 2013 with support from the INC legislators. However, within a short time span of 49 days, the Chief Minister of this government, Arvind Kejriwal, resigned, which led the Delhi State assembly to go into 'suspended animation'. Effectively, Delhi came under 'President's Rule' i.e. the Lieutenant-Governor of Delhi became the head of government in Delhi during this time. During this President's Rule, the 2014 Parliamentary elections were held too. Ultimately, Delhi's Legislative Assembly was dissolved in November 2014, and the next election for the Delhi State Assembly was held in February 2015.

This chapter is situated in the context of a larger body of literature on India which connects urban informality, party politics, and service delivery. Using survey and ethnographic data, Jha, et al. (2007) explain the dynamics of slum leadership and the significant role played by *pradhans* (leaders), especially their education and political affiliations, in gaining access to basic services in Delhi's slums. Das and Walton (2015: S44) closely analyse political leadership in one informal settlement in Delhi and another in NOIDA,[3] and argue that leaders in these localities emerge as part of the process of 'learning how to engage institutional processes of law and bureaucracy' to achieve housing and basic services' infrastructure. Drawing on evidence from the slums in the cities of Jaipur and Bhopal, Auerbach (2016: 3) finds that the greater the density of party networks in slums, the higher is the competition among party workers, which in turn leads to greater accountability in local patron-client relations with positive impacts on slum development.

Our work aims to add to this literature by focusing exclusively on an analysis of the interactions between political parties and residents of informal settlements in the months and weeks prior to elections in six settlements in Delhi. Further, the case of Delhi, as most of the other global south cities, shows that the practices of informality are not confined to only the urban poor (Roy and AlSayyad 2004; Baviskar and Sundar 2008). In this article, we approach informality through the administrative definitions specific to Delhi which render a large variety of housing as unplanned, and thereby 'informal', compared to a lot less common 'formal' or planned housing. The practices of informality, however in a different degree and form, are observed in the 'planned' settlements also. For instance, in planned housing constructed by the Delhi Development Authority (DDA), residents often reconstruct their houses in such a way that it amounts to violation of the plan.

This chapter presents a case of politics of informality by examining the unplanned settlements and the specific forms of informal practices which define them in relation to each other and the 'planned settlements'. Drawing on Roy and AlSayyad (2004), we see informality as the 'organising urban logic' (ibid: 5), as they have argued: 'if formality operates through the fixing of value, including the mapping of spatial value, then informality operates through the constant negotiability of value and unmapping of space.' The three categories of unplanned settlements we analyse here offer insights into how electoral politics turns into a sight where informality is negotiated and transformed.

To contextualise our research, we first describe the levels of government that operate in Delhi and the different official classifications of Delhi's settlements. Section 3 of this chapter presents our findings on electoral promises, the election 'machinery', and the modes of campaigning it carried out in Delhi's informal settlements. Finally, Section 4 will conclude the chapter. We argue that the electoral politics in Delhi's informal settlements presents an irony. On the one hand, election campaigns greatly penetrate these settlements through party organisation and modes of campaigning. And, electoral promises reflect this. However, when the same electoral promises are made time and again, with only incremental improvements on the ground during the time in between elections, voters from informal settlements become cynical with regards to attaining an improved quality of life, thereby further consolidating exclusion of these groups from the 'planned' city.

Context and Background

Three levels of government exist and operate in Delhi at the local, state, and central (or union) levels. This is not different from other Indian cities; however, since Delhi is the capital city, there is considerable influence of the central (or union) level of government, i.e. the Government of India, in its governance. At the local or municipal level, about 95 per cent of Delhi's area is in the jurisdiction of three Delhi Municipal Corporations (DMCs): North, East, and South.[4] A chief responsibility of the DMCs is to manage Delhi's solid waste. Since 1992, Delhi has had a state-level government called the Government of National Capital Territory of Delhi (or GNCTD). The GNCTD[5] is similar to any other state level government as it carries out functions such as transport, revenue administration, power generation, and health and family welfare. Basic service provision in Delhi is largely the purview of the GNCTD, including water and sewage related infrastructure which is handled by the Delhi *Jal* (Water) Board (DJB), and slum-related activities, which are to be carried out by the Delhi Urban Shelter Improvement Board (DUSIB).

Unlike other state governments, the GNCTD is not responsible for Delhi's physical planning, development of land, or law and order; instead, these responsibilities are vested with the Union Government. The Lieutenant Governor (or LG) of Delhi heads these governance functions by leading executive bodies which carry out functions of land use planning, police, and public order—consequently, Delhi has 'limited statehood'. Specifically, physical planning and development of land and housing are performed by the DDA, which has monopoly over land use planning and construction of 'planned' housing in the city and is accountable to the Union Government's Ministry of Urban Development. This is an exception; the development authorities of other Indian cities are accountable to the corresponding state governments. Overall, policy making and policy implementation for Delhi's settlements is largely under the purview of the state government and India's national government; hence, focusing on elections for these two levels of government is appropriate (Sheikh and Mandelkern 2014).[6]

Settlements which house Delhi's population are divided into eight categories, of which 'planned colonies' is one, estimated to house less than a quarter of Delhi's population in 2000 (GNCTD 2009: 169). Planned colonies are built on land in Delhi's 'development area', comply with planning norms, and are fully serviced with network infrastructure when constructed. The remaining seven settlement types are, according to the categorisation, 'unplanned'. We refer to these as 'informal' settlements, and they include slum designated areas (SDAs), jhuggi jhopri clusters (JJCs), resettlement colonies, unauthorised colonies, regularised-unauthorised colonies, rural villages, and urban villages.[7]

SDAs are areas in Delhi which have been notified as 'slums',[8] guaranteeing them due process[9] in case of demolition and/or eviction, and a certain level of basic services. Although these settlements, located on public land,[10] have received basic services incrementally, they have also experienced demolition and eviction without due process.[11] In comparison to all other settlement types, a JJC resident has the least secure tenure. JJCs are scattered across the city and often have densely constructed houses, rising two or three storeys high. SDAs and JJCs in Delhi have experienced rehabilitation during which their residents were evicted and relocated to plots in resettlement colonies, most often at Delhi's periphery. Due to three waves of eviction and rehabilitation, resettlement colonies have been established. These colonies are concentrated in Delhi's west, north-west, and north-east regions. Another category of settlements is unauthorised colonies. They are categorised as 'unauthorised'[12] because they have been built on land demarcated for a non-residential—most often agricultural—land use. These colonies typically have clearly demarcated plots with criss-crossing roads and lanes, and houses constructed a few storeys high. These colonies are perceived as largely housing Delhi's 'middle class' residents (Lemanski and Lama-Rewal 2013).

Of the seven 'unplanned' settlement-types, our focus was on three types: jhuggi jhopri clusters, resettlement colonies, and unauthorised colonies, which we referred to as the 'excluded settlements'.[13] We chose to focus on these three types of settlements because their residents are most vulnerable in terms of security of their tenure, and with regard to basic services, these settlement-types are the most under-served. According to current population estimates, settlements which are included in these three categories accommodate nearly half of Delhi's population.

While it is often assumed that all the adults in these settlements are registered voters, it is usually not the case. We were informed that whether a resident is an 'owner'[14] or a tenant (or 'renter') in an informal settlement often decides the ease with which he or she can register as a voter. The process for registering as a voter and obtaining a voter ID card requires an applicant to submit a 'proof of residence'.[15] However, a new or recent tenant in an informal settlement most often does not have such a proof. Voter ID is often the first kind of identity card that a new or recent tenant applies for. In such a situation, many of these new tenants (or 'renters') submit an electricity bill or water bill, which mentions the residential address and the name of the house owner and a letter from their house 'owner' stating that the person is living in a rented accommodation at that residential address.

We heard a range of narratives regarding this. While in some informal settlements the owners were willing to give the required letter to assist the renter in getting registered as a voter, in other cases, owners either resisted issuing such a letter or were completely unwilling. This unwillingness, according to the narratives of owners, has its roots in the insecure land tenure that residents in informal settlements face; they feared that renters may use such a letter against them or claim ownership and/or be unwilling to vacate their room or floor using the letter as proof. Although there is no official estimate of the number of voters in these settlements, electoral promises and active election campaigning prior to elections reveal the importance of voters residing in these settlements to political parties.

Findings

Walking through Delhi's jhuggi jhopri clusters, unauthorised colonies, and resettlement colonies prior to the elections, one can observe several political party posters, pamphlets, and flags. Often, party offices for the contestants of the upcoming elections are noticeable and sometimes residents and/or local political party workers offer their houses for election-related meetings and work. During this time, it is not uncommon to see auto-rickshaws with loudspeakers passing through the narrow alleys of JJCs, playing appeals to vote for a particular candidate. Such announcements typically urge the voters to 'press the button' for a specific party symbol (*chunaav-chinh*), because often the prospective voters are not literate and, therefore, a symbol is a better sign of identification than the name of the party or the candidate. This mode of campaigning is more effective in unauthorised colonies and JJCs due to their relatively small plot sizes and densely-built nature; the streets are often crowded with people conducting daily activities which would usually take place within the walled confines of home in a middle-class settlement—such as washing clothes, gathering around a local tap/water tanker, women sitting in groups outside their homes on cots, and men playing cards in whatever open spaces are available. Hence, in contrast to planned colonies, these settlements offer fertile grounds for election campaigning.

MANIFESTOS AND ELECTORAL PROMISES

Prior to the Delhi State Assembly elections 2013 (hereafter referred to as the 2013 Delhi elections), the three main political parties contesting the election—BJP, INC, and AAP—all prepared and released city-level manifestos.[16] AAP was the only political party which developed constituency-level manifestos. Most representatives of the BJP and INC emphasised that their party had developed only one city-wide manifesto and there were no manifestos at the constituency level; however, some candidates distributed pamphlets/booklets which had a list of their achievements and their vision/plans for their constituency. While BJP and INC party workers said that they did not know the process for preparing their city-level manifestos, AAP workers explained to us an extensive process. This process involved holding several meetings in various settlements in the form of *nukkad* (road junction) meetings to ask residents about the problems they would want their prospective MLA to address. AAP's party workers (who identified themselves as 'volunteers' and not party workers) explained that these inputs were collated across each assembly constituency and then the information was used to prepare the constituency-level manifestos and the city-level manifesto.

Land/Tenure/Housing

A close look at the city-level manifestos reveals that there was a striking similarity between the electoral promises made by these three main political parties for informal settlements and delivery of basic services. These focused on tackling the issue of tenure insecurity for their residents through 'regularising' or 'rehabilitating' informal settlements, implying that secure access to land and/or housing ought not to be limited to the higher income groups in the city.

For residents of unauthorised colonies, the BJP and the AAP both promised to 'regularise' unauthorised colonies and to provide them with better facilities. The AAP manifesto even set a deadline for the regularisation procedure while promising that 'unauthorised colonies would be regularised within one year'. The INC manifesto explained that, while in power, among its various achievements was the 'regularisation' of 895 unauthorised colonies and 'development works' in 1,500 of them. Our research demonstrated that the colonies which the INC claimed to have 'regularised' were only found to be 'eligible for regularisation' and there was little data to explain the status of progress of works in unauthorised colonies (Sheikh and Banda 2014a). However, in its manifesto, the INC promised that in its effort to make Delhi a 'global city', it would ensure 'improvement of civic services and augmentation of infrastructure' in 'regularised unauthorised colonies', remaining silent on its plan for the colonies which continued to remain unauthorised.

In the context of jhuggi jhopri clusters, both the BJP and the AAP promised to carry out 'in-situ rehabilitation' of the settlements as well as to provide these settlements with basic services including water and sanitation. However, the way in which these promises were articulated in the manifestos differed. The BJP's promise simply said: 'in-situ construction of multi-storied houses for Jhuggi dwellers', implying that this would be a blanket solution for all those living in jhuggis, whereas AAP's manifesto was much more specific. The AAP, in its manifesto, explained that it would first carry out a survey of all families living in Delhi's slums to create a comprehensive list, and then 'as far as possible, most of the slum-dwellers will be provided plots or flats in the same location as the existing slum'; it did say that if this was not possible then rehabilitation would be carried out at the closest possible location. AAP's manifesto also emphasised that, 'until rehabilitation is completed, the slums will not be demolished under any circumstance,'[17] and it detailed the steps which would be taken to ensure provision of basic services in slums.

The AAP also published a one-page pamphlet which specifically targeted voters living in JJCs, and this pamphlet was widely distributed in these settlements. The pamphlet was titled: '*Hum jhuggiyan bilkul nahin tootne dengey—jhuggi walon ko pakke makaan dengey*' ('We will absolutely not let jhuggis be demolished—we will give houses to jhuggi dwellers'). Apart from mentioning the AAP's promises on rehabilitation of JJCs and service provision to them, this pamphlet even pointed out inaction by other political parties, and accused the Indian National Congress (which was the ruling party in Delhi for three continuous terms, i.e. 15 years) of taking advantage of compulsions of residents of JJCs. It said:

Kisi bhi party *ne jhuggi walon ki samasya par dhyaan nahin diya. Aaj tak* Congress *ne jhuggi walon ko apne* vote bank *ki tarah istemaal kiya. Lekin kya* Congress *ne unki dasha sudhaarne ke liye kuch kiya hai? Ulta unki majboori ka faayda uthaya.*

(No party has paid attention to the problems of JJC residents. Congress has used the residents of JJCs as its votebank. But has Congress done anything to improve their predicament? On the contrary, it has taken advantage of their helplessness.)

Further, an AAP representative at a local office in the Patel Nagar assembly constituency expressed, 'If there is a plan to displace them [residents], then AAP will first make arrangements for their rehabilitation in a nearby area. If such a provision cannot be made, the people of these JJCs will not be removed.'[18] Interaction with another AAP representative during a *padyatra*[19] near a JJC revealed that rehabilitation was a key election issue, and he confidently said that upon being elected, the AAP's leaders would prioritise and 'first of all work for the rehabilitation of JJ clusters.'[20] This implies that not only was the electoral promise for JJC residents communicated as part of written manifestos and pamphlets, it was also very much part of the vocal promises that were orally communicated through many local representatives of the AAP.

The manifesto of the Indian National Congress made three points with regard to residents of JJCs:

1) In-situ development to be preferred mode for JJ Clusters;
2) Convergence of all related programmes to make Delhi a slum-free city;
3) Construction of over 400,000 EWS [Economically Weaker Sections] flats under JNNURM [Jawaharlal Nehru National Urban Renewal Mission] for rehabilitating the JJ Cluster Households.[21]

It is worth noting that a similar set of promises, though more detailed, had also been made by the INC in its manifesto for the 2008 Delhi State Assembly election.

Basic Services

While the 'reformist' measures of regularisation and rehabilitation of informal settlements appeared prominently in the manifestos, during our interactions, several political party workers in the field emphasised that more than any other election issue, the 2013 Delhi State Assembly election was being fought on the issue of water. AAP's candidate, contesting from the Sangam Vihar assembly constituency, which includes many blocks of Sangam Vihar—the majority of which are unauthorised colonies and where residents were receiving water via the DJB tankers only once in 15 or 20 days—expressed, 'Our main agenda is water. There is a water distribution problem.'[22] AAP's 'volunteers', as well as party leaders, alleged that there was a 'water mafia' operating as a 'business' across Delhi with the support of the BJP and the INC and this ensured that those residing in informal settlements paid a high price for water.[23] Similarly, an AAP volunteer in Savda Ghevra—a resettlement colony—noted that drinking water was the biggest problem in the area ever since he started living there. He asserted their demand for a water pipeline to the settlement.

The prominence of water as a political issue was very clear in the AAP's manifesto: 'Water is the biggest concern of the *aam aadmi* in Delhi' (emphasis in the original). AAP's electoral promise of 700 litres of free water for every household per month was one which tried to address the issue of unequal access (in terms of quantity and price) of water in Delhi. This promise was spoken about at great lengths during the campaign in informal settlements—during *padyatras*, *jan sabhas*, and in pamphlets and stickers which the AAP distributed. However, the campaign was mostly silent on how they would ensure this provision in several JJCs, unauthorised colonies, and resettlement colonies where households did not have access to piped water, let alone water meters.

The issue of lack of toilets and poorly functioning sewerage systems was also highlighted in the manifestos of the AAP and the BJP. Both the parties promised to improve sewer systems, as well as to build 'public toilets' or 'public conveniences'. However, the level of detail in the promises differed. AAP's manifesto said that it 'will look at the issues related to the sewage system in Delhi from a new perspective and will aim to bring the entire population of the city, irrespective of the nature of legality of settlement type, within the reach of the system in an economical way.' It also enumerated specific steps such as installation of sewage meters and new sewage treatment plants. While the BJP merely said that, 'The sewage system shall be made efficient, environment friendly, and modern by use of updated technology.'[24]

Water supply was also an important issue that was heavily contested in many areas in Delhi which do not receive enough good quality water through formal networks. For instance, many unplanned settlements receive water through water tankers, which could often be irregular in their frequency, particularly during summer. Water tankers are a particularly important source of water for resettlement colonies and JJCs, while the unauthorised colonies depend more on bore-wells. The issue of bore-wells and water tankers became a mainstream issue particularly after the AAP actively showed that the corrupt practices and involvement of water mafias made the water supply inadequate in Delhi. In Sangam Vihar, the AAP candidate had talked about how the control of private players over bore-wells was a key issue and that during the 49-days' rule of the party, the AAP government carried out 'regularisation' of these bore-wells.

While Delhi continued to be in 'suspended animation' of its State Assembly, the campaigning for the 2014 Indian Parliamentary elections began. These elections were for the national level of government, which by definition would imply that the election issues and the electoral promises would be distinct as the jurisdiction of the MLAs and MPs differ. However, at a local level, we observed there to be much overlap in the electoral promises between those mentioned prior to the 2013 Delhi State Assembly elections and those mentioned prior to the 2014 Indian Parliamentary elections. During conversations with residents, while some party workers made a distinction between 'national' issues and 'local' issues, others believed the difference was minor. As one of the party's volunteers during the 2014 election campaign observed, 'In every election, people think about local problem[s] and facility. So, this election also depends on local issues, not on national issues. [The] PM candidate look[s] at national issues but the local candidate fights election on local issues.'[25]

The three parties released national manifestos that were distinct from the city-wide manifestos released prior to the 2013 Delhi State assembly elections. The electoral promises prior to the 2014 elections focused on matters including employment, 'black money', corruption, social security, inflation, judicial reforms, and 'public participation', among many others. Following suit from their initiative of constituency-level manifestos in 2013, the AAP's candidates in Delhi strove to prepare parliamentary constituency-level manifestos. These constituency-level manifestos included electoral promises on housing, land tenure security, and services including water, sanitation, and electricity. Some AAP volunteers explained that the earlier prepared assembly constituency-level manifestos were helpful in preparing the parliamentary constituency-level manifesto. When we inquired about this overlap, most AAP volunteers concurred that the issues which concerned Delhi's voters had not changed in the span of a few months.

The INC's national manifesto spoke of inclusion of 'right to homestead or housing' as one of the 'minimum socio-economic rights'. Prior to the 2014 Parliamentary elections, we observed that an INC candidate, who was also the incumbent MP for the New Delhi Parliamentary constituency, made the 'in-situ rehabilitation' of JJCs one of his main election promises while campaigning in JJCs in central Delhi. During his interactions with voters and in his campaign pamphlets, he cited the example of the in-situ rehabilitation project, which was in-progress at Kathputli colony JJC, and which he had been pivotal in initiating as the then Minister of Housing and Urban Poverty Alleviation. He explained that: *'Jis jagah jhuggi hain wahaan bahu manzil building banaayee jayengi aur jhuggi vaasiyon ko ghar diye jaayengey ... 36 gaz ka flat waheen diya jaaye.'*[26] ('Multi-storeyed buildings will be constructed where jhuggis are, and flats will be given to jhuggi residents—36 sq. yard flats will be given right there.') He further emphasised that all would be done to make the scheme inclusive, *'sab kuch karayengey—kissi ko chhorain ge nahin.'* ('We will do everything—no one will be left out.') The last statement especially tried to tackle the widespread reality of the exclusionary eligibility[27] criteria of rehabilitation projects in Delhi.

The centrality of some local, basic services issues even in the elections at the national level is what re-emphasises that the centre and state both have immense control over the local, and therefore feature them prominently in their election campaigns. However, this may also have been driven by the unique circumstance of 'suspended animation' of Delhi's State Assembly during the 2014 parliamentary elections.

PARTY ORGANISATION PRIOR TO ELECTIONS

In elections, success is not dependent on *what* parties promise, but a large part of the success depends on *how* those promises are communicated to the voters. We found significant differences across parties in terms of how they organised their party cadres to work on the ground for their campaign. Here, we give a glimpse of the parties' campaign strategies in informal settlements based on our observations and interactions with the local party leaders. Political party workers were active in various informal settlements during the period of election campaigning. In many cases, special party offices were set up in these settlements during this time. Many party workers were residents of the settlements or of the neighbouring settlements in which they campaigned, but this was not always the case.

The BJP's candidates relied, to a large extent, on campaigning carried out by office bearers and members of their *mandals*.[28] In Delhi, a *mandal* exists for each municipal ward area, and hence each assembly constituency has four BJP *mandals* in it. We were told by BJP party workers that this structure is in place all year round and not specifically constituted prior to elections. However, in the run-up to the elections, responsibilities (such as door-to-door campaigning, distribution of pamphlets, organising *jan sabhas*) were clearly distributed among the party workers in each *mandal*. Further, for each polling booth in a municipal ward area (which coincides with the area for the *mandal*), there is a *samiti* (committee) and one person who is 'in-charge', who is called the 'booth *prabandhak*'. In Delhi, for every polling booth, the electoral roll lists can have anywhere between 800 and 1,200 voters. A *mandal adhyaksha* (president) explained to us that the party workers who are in each *samiti* strive to know all the voters who belong to the electoral roll for the polling booth they are responsible for. During our interactions with party workers from the BJP, we came across a few of these workers who had come from neighbouring states in the weeks preceding the election. While some said these 'outsiders' were only 'observers',[29] others explained that they were also actively involved in campaign activities.

The difference between party workers, volunteers, and residents, however, was blurred in the case of AAP. Most of AAP's party workers repeatedly emphasised that they were 'AAP volunteers' and that their party had a horizontal structure—distinguishing themselves from other political parties. Various representatives of AAP whom we spoke to emphasised that there was no formal structure in the party—some further stating there was 'no hierarchy'. They explained that a 'temporary' structure was in place in the run-up to the 2013 Delhi State Assembly elections. This included a campaign manager, and in some cases assistant campaign managers, zonal *prabharis* or in-charges, booth *prabharis*, local *prabharis*, and volunteers. The campaign manager planned campaign activities for the constituency and reported to the AAP's Delhi Election Head Office. An AAP representative who introduced himself as an assistant campaign manager and a zonal in-charge for the Savda Ghevra Resettlement Colony explained to us that, 'Most of these positions are not official because we don't want a situation where some people feel like they have been left behind ... Though the positions are unofficial ... but the responsibilities of each person are very clear'[30] This and various instances of AAP's volunteers emphasising the flat structure of the political party are telling; some explained that though they were volunteers, parties such as the BJP and the INC paid their party workers. AAP's volunteer base was largely local in the run up to the 2013 Delhi elections; there were also many volunteers who were 'outsiders'—either belonging to other parts of Delhi or those who had come from other parts of India specifically to campaign for the AAP. By March/April 2014, weeks prior to the 2014 parliamentary elections, the AAP had formalised the organisational structure of its party with five levels of organisation: the primary, block, district, state, and national level.

The INC workers acknowledged that they did not have a perennially existing structure of party workers who they could call upon anytime of the year. Instead, they explained that their party workers came together in the weeks prior to elections. In terms of visibility of their offices and campaign activities, we observed them only becoming active in the last two weeks before the elections.

Apart from political party workers, intermediaries including the residents' welfare associations and *pradhans,* who are local community leaders in informal settlements, assumed greater importance in the run-up to elections. These intermediaries had close interactions with party workers—some openly campaigning for and supporting certain candidates. During our fieldwork in several blocks of Sangam Vihar, Delhi's largest agglomeration of unauthorised colonies, more than two months prior to elections, RWA office bearers maintained that they did not align with any political party. However, in the weeks preceding the elections, they claimed that they could influence voters in their constituency and chose to align with a particular candidate and their political party, who they thought could translate their electoral promises (especially those concerning service delivery) into action. This support was not always publicly known.

We observed a wide variation across RWAs of various blocks in the way they engaged in campaigning prior to elections. For instance, the office bearers of one of the RWAs actively supported and campaigned for the BJP candidate while collaborating efforts with members of the local BJP *mandals* in their constituency, prior to both the 2013 Delhi State Assembly Elections and the 2014 Indian Parliamentary Elections. They even attempted to appeal to voters on a regional basis, specifically trying to reach out to voters who originally belonged to '*Purvanchal*',[31] and encouraged them to vote for the BJP. However, office bearers of another RWA did not openly declare who they were supporting; instead, they strategically planned who to vote for with office bearers of RWAs of neighbouring blocks to ensure that their vote did not split.

On the other hand, at a JJC in west Delhi, the RWA campaigned for AAP in 'hiding', organising their meetings at night and making phone calls to encourage people to vote for the AAP candidate. They explained that they did so because they feared that party workers of the BJP and the INC might find them campaigning for AAP openly during the day, which could have consequences for them. After the elections, an office bearer of this RWA explained, 'We were supporting AAP secretly because [the incumbent MLA] is a goon […] We feared that if he knew that we were supporting AAP then he would stop all services in the *basti*.'

In a JJC in south Delhi, we found that the *pradhan* was a local office bearer of INC. We noted over the course of time that the *pradhan's* ability to get certain work done, such as ordering water tankers, was linked with the political connections he maintained with the local MLA. Thus, mobilising people to vote for the party was a part of the arrangement from which he drew the informal power to mediate between the state and the residents. After the local MLA lost the elections, and then, in the general elections the INC lost the parliamentary seat (which the settlement is part of) to the BJP, the *pradhan* was asked not to distribute water anymore, and the charge was handed over to another resident in the settlement who was allegedly a BJP supporter. In the *pradhan's* words: '*wo sochte hain k ye* Congress *ka hai*; *ye kaise gadi lagayega*' ('They think that he [*pradhan*] is from Congress; how can we let him manage the water tankers').

Modes of Election Campaigning

Our interactions with residents and political party workers revealed that prior to the 2013 Delhi State Assembly elections, a range of campaign strategies were carried out by the three parties. These included door-to-door campaigning, *padyatras*, public meetings (or *jan sabhas*), and rallies.

AAP's door-to-door campaign started the earliest—in some cases more than two months prior to the elections—and was the most intense. During this, AAP representatives went door to door, visiting voters and talking to them about the fundamental ideas of AAP, introducing the candidate for their constituency, as well as asking for contributions to the party—even if households were only able to contribute token amounts. In all the settlements where we carried out fieldwork, residents spoke of AAP's door-to-door campaign, and in certain cases they explained that there had been up till three rounds of such campaigning by AAP representatives. AAP representatives also emphasised that in several cases the candidate who was standing for election personally campaigned door-to-door.

In contrast, BJP's door-to-door campaign, according to the narratives of its own party workers, was less intense and carried out mostly by party workers with little involvement of the candidates themselves. In the words of a BJP party worker who was the campaign in-charge for the candidate for the Patel Nagar AC, 'Based on their conversation with the people, they [BJP's party workers] also make a judgment on whether their vote will go to BJP, Congress, or others. Then, they make a note against their name: B for BJP, C for Congress and N for neutral or others.'[32] We heard similar narratives by BJP party workers in other ACs, and this implied that the door-to-door campaign was specifically aimed at assessing whether a resident would vote for the BJP or the INC.

In addition to door-to-door campaigning, party workers and candidates emphasised the use of phone calls and SMSs for campaigning, not only to encourage voters to vote for their party or candidate, but also to inform voters about campaign events. During our fieldwork prior to the 2013 Delhi State Assembly elections, the BJP candidate, who was also the incumbent MLA, expressed the following: 'SMS campaigning is a good way to communicate with people. They feel it is a matter of pride; for example, if they get an SMS or a call from me then they will tell people that I got a call or an SMS from the MLA … These people are downtrodden, hence an SMS or call matters to them.'[33] Campaigning efforts intensified in the week before each election. A BJP party worker described the week before the election day to be like a *'katl ki raat'* (a metaphor used for decisive moments/events) implying how the campaigning becomes really intense right before polling and every party invests all its resources to make a final attempt to woo voters. He said that during that period, *'Zyadda* campaigning *hogi … koi* booth *na reh jaye'* ('There will be a lot of campaigning … no booth should be left').[34]

In the days preceding Election Day, we also observed 'bike rallies', which were described by some BJP and INC party workers to us as a *'shakti pradarshan'* ('demonstration of power'). These rallies started with a point where more than a hundred bikes and scooters assembled. In addition, there would be cars including large ones—such as open Jeeps and Tata Scorpios—one of which would have the candidate seated inside, and many loud speakers. This kind of rally involved going through the arterial roads in and around informal settlements with much sloganeering, distribution of pamphlets, and waving of party flags. The idea, as we understood, was to demonstrate to the voters the support that the party and its candidate had and to try and influence the undecided voters. We observed these rallies being carried out by all three main political parties in areas where we carried out fieldwork. However, AAP's volunteers alleged that those attending the bike rallies for the BJP and INC were being paid to do so by the party; they claimed, in the words of one volunteer, 'no one has accepted even five *paise* for attending this rally … We have all come here because we want to see change.'[35]

While campaigning, many volunteers and leaders of the AAP, told voters of informal settlements to accept any money that they were offered by other 'corrupt' political parties, and report the same to the Election Commission.[36] The rationale for this, AAP explained, was that this was 'their own money', which had been previously taken by one of the 'corrupt' political parties, either through bribes or other forms of rent extraction, and the public deserved to have the money back. This was repeated to us by many of the residents during interviews.

We heard widely varying accounts of distribution of *actual* money and alcohol, in the weeks prior to the elections, and the impact this had on voting behaviour. An INC party worker from a JJC explained, '[The] electorate here gets swayed by money and alcohol. They are not smart and will believe anything. They make these people win and then complain later. They admit openly that they will only vote for those who provide them alcohol and money.'[37] Several months prior to the 2013 election, a resident from this settlement had told us, *'Jisne pilaaye* whiskey, vote *hai uski'* ('Votes go to he who offers whiskey').[38] On the other hand, a few weeks prior to the election, another resident said, 'Why should we refuse money and other things … we accept whatever is distributed … but we vote for the one we think will be good for us.'[39]

ACCELERATING 'DEVELOPMENT WORKS'

Given that the electoral promises of service delivery, especially those relating to water and sanitation, were so crucial to the election campaigning in informal settlements, our observation of accelerated 'development works' in the weeks prior to the elections was significant.

In a JJC settlement located close to a large industrial area where the issue of lack of toilet facilities had been time and again raised by residents with their MLA, we observed construction of two toilet complexes two months prior to the elections in December 2013. Residents reported that their MLA, a member of the BJP, and MCD officials had laid the foundation stone for these toilet complexes in September 2013. It is interesting to note that in this specific case, the incumbent MLA was voted back to power in December 2013, and he subsequently stood for the post of the MP in the 2014 parliamentary elections as well. In the meantime, the construction of the toilet complexes was completed, but they remained locked and were only opened and made operational in May 2014 after the elections. The same person who had been the incumbent MLA in 2013 and re-elected as MLA in December 2013 was elected as an MP in May 2014. It was only after this that the toilet complexes became operational.

During our discussions with residents in the intermittent period, they spoke of varied reasons for the continued locked status of the toilet complexes. While some told us it was because of some problem with the water supply, others said it was possibly because the toilet complexes could only be 'inaugurated' after the elections, still others believed that it was because the MLA, who was contesting for the post of the MP, wanted to ensure he had secured votes from the JJC before the toilet complexes were made accessible. If the last reason were true, it suggests that the MLA may have tried to use the toilet complexes as 'bait' to get residents from the JJC to vote for him.

In Sangam Vihar, we noticed work underway to build roads and drainage systems less than a month before the elections. While some residents believed that this work had been fast-tracked by the incumbent MLA only in the wake of the election, supporters of the incumbent MLA explained that the work had been delayed and their timing had no link with the upcoming election. Residents in a block of Sangam Vihar said, 'This work is happening only because it is election time.' At a JJ resettlement colony, one group of women told us a few weeks before the general elections in 2014 that no party had come for campaigning to the settlement. They added, 'a few days before the polling, sweepers start coming and start cleaning streets, which is unusual … Candidates disappear after elections.'

Conclusion

One of our interviewees, an office bearer of an RWA in a JJC told us, '*Insaan ko bhookha rakha jaaye to wo jaagta rehta hai par agar usey khana mil jaye to wo so jaata hai.* Parties *humein paani, ration aur in sab mein hi uljha kar rakhna chahti hain*' ('If you keep a person hungry, they will stay awake, but if you give them food, they will go to sleep. Political parties want to keep us occupied with water, rations, and other issues). This quote is particularly telling of how the residents from informal settlements view their relationship with political parties—a relationship which is shaped by the decades of failure of planning in Delhi. It is the failure of planning that makes the key issues—such as basic services and housing—so strikingly similar in both parliamentary and assembly elections.

Due to the exclusion of a large share of Delhi's population living in resettlement colonies, jhuggi jhopri clusters, and unauthorised colonies from the 'planned' city, the political discourse is shaped by issues of basic services and the resultant vulnerabilities of these residents, which includes not only the urban poor but also the urban 'middle classes'. Electoral politics in these settlements remains dominated by services such as water, electricity, and sanitation on the one hand, and processes which 'formalise' the status of informal settlements such as regularisation, and resettlement/rehabilitation on the other. This signifies both the persistence of the problems and, in many cases, unfulfilled election promises made year after year.

The repetitive nature of electoral promises and the ad-hoc measures of service provision trigger scepticism within voters on whether the promises will ever be fulfilled. It is important to highlight that the 'blame-game' between political parties arising out of Delhi's 'limited statehood' also becomes a perpetual feature of electoral politics in the context of informal settlements. Furthermore, the intensity of election campaigning in these settlements, which reflects a very high interface between the voters and the campaigning parties, is a testament to how the very nature of settlements provide fertile ground for the kind of electoral politics we observe in Delhi.

Electoral promises give us insights into how citizenship in unplanned settlements is negotiated through electoral politics. This high degree of interactions, again, could be located in the vulnerabilities that the residents of the informal settlements live with. These vulnerabilities vary across settlements and so do the residents' strategies of negotiating them with the state during the elections.

The research demonstrates that the recurring nature of unfulfilled promises is primarily responsible for the cynicism among the voters. The possibility for different political parties to make the same promise repeatedly without delivering on them is enabled by a lack of transparency in policy-making. Which JJC is demolished and which UAC is regularised still remains ambiguous due to the manoeuvring of political parties. This lack of transparency in policies causes cynicism among voters when their demands are not met, and they continue to remain vulnerable and excluded. The result is that empty election promises serve as a tool through which parties systematically sustain the perpetual exclusion of the residents in informal settlements. Furthermore, the service provision that follows electoral promises is often incremental in nature. Such incremental provision offers immediate relief to the residents but in the long run, leaves room for further improvement and hence scope for intervention and (repeated) promises by the political parties.

Each political party's workers campaign and convey electoral promises to voters in a different manner. How these promises are conveyed determines their effectiveness in terms of their conversion into votes. Based on our field observations, if we had to situate the enthusiasm and the presence of the workers of different parties on a spectrum, then the BJP and the INC would be situated at the opposite ends of the spectrum, while the AAP would be somewhere in the middle. BJP cadres worked more strategically in relation to other party workers. They assessed voters' voting inclinations before polling day, and strategised accordingly. The AAP workers were in the field talking about the issues with people and also included more detailed information about the party's plans in their manifestos. INC workers, on the other hand, were the least enthusiastic and motivated in engaging voters.

A voter identity card is one of the first official documents that the residents of informal settlements obtain in their attempt to eventually become citizens of the city. The fact that residents of these unplanned settlements possess voter identity cards confirms their status as 'formal citizens'. However, the struggle for access to basic services and secure housing shows that formal citizenship does not necessarily translate into substantive citizenship. Rather, residents of informal settlements are the subjects of manipulation in the process of electoral politics with no entitlement either to the land they occupy or to basic services. Political parties often use this insecurity to their advantage, making unfulfilled promises in order to win votes, deliberately keeping residents 'hungry' until the next election comes around.

NOTES

1. This chapter is based on research carried out as part of the *Cities of Delhi* project at the Centre for Policy Research, New Delhi.

2. Although the party was launched in November 2012.

3. New Okhla Industrial Development Authority borders Delhi on the south-eastern side and is a part of the neighbouring state of Uttar Pradesh.

4. Municipal councillors are elected for each ward comprising about 50,000 voters every five years, and for each DMC, councillors elect a mayor each year. The three DMCs were preceded by a single corporation called the Municipal Corporation of Delhi (MCD) until 2011.

5. The GNCTD's legislative body has 70 Members of the Legislative Assembly, each representing an assembly constituency of about 200,000 voters.

6. Apart from State Assembly and municipal elections, voters in Delhi also participate in the Indian Parliamentary Elections, which are held once every five years. Delhi's area is divided into seven parliamentary constituencies, each including ten ACs, averaging about 2,000,000 voters. The most recent Indian Parliamentary Election was held in May 2014.

7. Rural villages located in Delhi's peripheral 'rural' area are characterised by agricultural activity, and their residential buildings are not required to comply with the same planning restrictions as in other settlements. Until the early 1990s, Delhi's rural villages had received notifications incorporating them into the 'urban' area, changing their status to 'urban villages'. Once a rural village becomes an urban village, certain planning provisions become applicable.

8. These settlements are governed under the Slum Areas Act of 1956—a central legislation—but the last time a settlement was designated as a slum in Delhi was in 1994. Slum areas which have not received any formal notification are called jhuggi jhopri clusters (or JJCs), also referred to as 'squatter settlements'.

9. 'Due process', in the context of demolition and eviction of slums in Delhi, includes the following steps: a clear statement of requirement of land on which a JJC is located for a 'public purpose', survey of residents of the JJC for determining eligibility for rehabilitation/relocation, decisions on eligibility and release of concerned lists, distribution of possession letters for relocation plots/flats, notice for eviction, and service provision both at the site of eviction and the site of rehabilitation/relocation. For details, see Banda and Sheikh, 2014.

10. 'Public land' is land which is owned by a government agency. In Delhi, each JJC is located on land owned by a government agency, belonging to either the Government of India, the GNCTD, or one of the local government bodies.

11. See, for instance, Banda and Sheikh, 2014.

12. From the 1960s to the early 1980s, unauthorised colonies were 'regularised' either by the DDA or by standing committees of the erstwhile MCD bringing into existence the 'regularised-unauthorised colonies', which is also another category of settlements.

13. For details, see Heller, Mukhopadhyay, Banda and Sheikh, 2015.

14. The reason for placing the word owner in quotes is that in informal settlements, even those who claim to be 'owners' may not have complete ownership rights over their house. For instance, for Delhi's resettlement colonies, the ultimate owner of the properties remains the Delhi Urban Shelter Improvement Board (DUSIB); in case of unauthorised colonies, which are partly or fully on public land, the ultimate owner of the land, according to official land records, is a government department or agency. (See for details, Sheikh and Banda 2014b.)

15. According to the Election Commission of India, a driver's license, passport, bank passbook, ration card, or the latest telephone/electricity/water/gas connection bill which state the name of the applicant and the residential address are needed to satisfy this requirement. 'Form 6: Application for inclusion of name in electoral roll' and 'Guidelines for filling up the Application Form 6' by the Election Commission of India.

16. In contrast, the Bahujan Samaj Party (though not analysed in this chapter), maintained that they did not prepare a manifesto because they simply did not believe in manifestos and that instead 'they believed in actually doing work'.

17. Aam Aadmi Party, Delhi Election Manifesto 2013.

18. Interview with a representative of the Aam Aadmi Party at AAP's office in Prem Nagar, Patel Nagar Assembly constituency, on 25 November 2013.

19. During a *padyatra*, the political party candidate and party workers/volunteers walk through the main streets of the constituency while sloganeering and making electoral promises.

20. Interview with a representative of AAP during a *padyatra* in Tekhand, Tughlaqabad assembly constituency on 24 November 2013.

21. INC manifesto, Loksabha manifesto 2014, and INC Delhi Assembly Election manifesto 2013.

22. Interview with AAP's candidate who contested the 2013 Delhi State Assembly elections on 5 November 2013.

23. Observations during the AAP Jan Sabha in Deoli assembly constituency (about half of which is inhabited by unauthorised colonies of Sangam Vihar), on 21 November 2013.

24. BJP Loksabha election manifesto 2014b and BJP Delhi Assembly election manifesto 2013.

25. Field visit to Savda Ghevra Resettlement Colony, 2014. For a detailed case study of the Savda Ghevra Resettlement Colony, see Sheikh et al. 2014.

26. Speech of this former MP during a public meeting at the transit camp for the in-situ rehabilitation project for the Kathputli Colony JJC on 8 April 2014.

27. See for details Sheikh and Banda 2014b.

28. A *mandal* is an administrative and spatial unit as decided by a concerned political party. These *mandals* neatly fit into the larger, hierarchical organisational structure of this political party. Each

mandal may have as many as thirteen office bearers: one *adhyaksha* (president), five *up-adhyaksha* (vice presidents), two *mahamantri*, one *kosh adhyaksha* (treasurer), and four *mantris*. Each *mandal* is also likely to have different *morchas* (fronts), including: the *yuva* (youth) *morcha*, *mahila* (women) *morcha*, *alp-sankhyak* (minorities) *morcha*, *SCs/STs* (scheduled castes/ scheduled tribes) *morcha*, and *kisaan* (farmers) *morcha*.

29. Interaction with BJP workers at BJP's office in Sangam Vihar on 2 December 2013.

30. Interview with an AAP Assistant Campaign Manager for the Mundka Assembly Constituency on 29 October 2013.

31. 'Purvanchal' refers to the eastern part of the Indian state of Uttar Pradesh (UP). Historically, it also included the area of UP which is now the Indian state of Uttarakhand.

32. Interview with BJP's campaign in-charge for Patel Nagar assembly constituency on 15 November 2013.

33. Interview with BJP's S. C. L. Gupta who was the MLA of Sangam Vihar assembly constituency from 2008 to 2013 and contested the election in 2013 on 9 November 2013.

34. Interview with a BJP Mandal Adhyaksh (President) for the Deoli assembly constituency in March 2014.

35. Interaction with AAP 'volunteers' during a rally in Deoli assembly constituency on 2 December 2013.

36. AAP even distributed pamphlets which urged voters to report any illegal distribution of money or alcohol to the Election Commission.

37. Interaction with an INC party worker at Indira Kalyan Vihar JJC on 20 November 2013.

38. Interaction with residents of Indira Kalyan Vihar JJC on 7 April 2013.

39. Interaction with residents of Indira Kalyan Vihar JJC on 24 October 2013.

REFERENCES

Aam Aadmi Party (AAP), *Delhi Election Manifesto 2013*, (English and Hindi versions), 2013.

Auerbach, Adam M., 'Clients and Communities: The Political Economy of Party Network Organization and Publications Development in India's Urban Slums', *World Politics*, 68, 1 (2016), pp. 111–48.

Banda, Subhadra, and Shahana Sheikh, 'The Case of Sonia Gandhi Camp: The Process of Eviction and Demolition in Delhi's Jhuggi Jhopri Clusters', A Report of the Cities of Delhi project, Centre for Policy Research, New Delhi, 2014.

Baviskar, Amita, and Nandini Sundar, 'Democracy Versus Economic Transformation?', *Economic and Political Weekly*, 43, 46 (2008), pp. 87–9.

Bharatiya Janata Party (BJP), Election Manifesto 2014: *Ek Bharat Shreshtha Bharat – Sabka Saath Sabka Vikaas*, 2014a.

————, Loksabha Election 2014: Election Manifesto – *Abki Baar Modi Sarkar*, Delhi Pradesh, 2014b.

_____, *Manifesto for the Delhi Vidhan Sabha Elections 2013*, (English and Hindi versions), 2013.

Das, Veena, and Michael Walton, 'Political Leadership and the Urban Poor: Local Histories', *Current Anthropology*, 56, 11 (2015), pp. S44–S54.

Government of National Capital Territory of Delhi, *Chapter 14 on Urban Development*, in: Economic Survey of Delhi 2008–09, (2009), pp. 164–76.

Heller, Patrick, Partha Mukhopadhyay, Subhadra Banda and Shahana Sheikh, 'Exclusion, Informality, and Predation in the Cities of Delhi: Overview Report of the Cities of Delhi Project', Working Paper, *Centre for Policy Research*, New Delhi, 2015.

Indian National Congress (INC), *Manifesto: Delhi Elections 2013*, (English and Hindi versions), 2013.

_____, *Lok Sabha Elections 2014: Manifesto – Your Voice Our Pledge*, 2014.

Jha, Saumitra, Vijayendra Rao and Michael Woolcock, 'Governance in the Gullies: Democratic Responsiveness and Leadership in Delhi's Slums', *World Development*, 35, 2 (2007), pp. 230–46.

Lemanski, Charlotte, and Stéphanie Tawa Lama-Rewal, 'The 'Missing Middle': Class and Urban Governance in Delhi's Unauthorised Colonies', *Transactions of the Institute of British Geographers*, 38, 1 (2013), pp. 91–105.

Roy, Ananya, and Nezar AlSayyad, *Urban Informality: Transnational Perspectives from the Middle East, Latin America, and South Asia*, Lanham, MD: Lexington Books, 2004.

Sheikh, Shahana, and Ben Mandelkern, 'The Delhi Development Authority: Accumulation Without Development', A Report of the Cities of Delhi project, *Centre for Policy Research*, New Delhi, 2014.

Sheikh, Shahana, and Subhadra Banda, 'The Thin Line between Legitimate and Illegal: Regularising Unauthorised Colonies in Delhi', A Report of the Cities of Delhi project, *Centre for Policy Research*, New Delhi, 2014a.

_____, 'The Delhi Urban Shelter Improvement Board (DUSIB): The Challenges Facing a Strong, Progressive Agency', A Report of the Cities of Delhi project, *Centre for Policy Research*, New Delhi, 2014b.

Sheikh, Shahana, Subhadra Banda, and Ben Mandelkern, 'Planning the Slum: JJC Resettlement in Delhi and the Case of Savda Ghevra', A Report of the Cities of Delhi project, *Centre for Policy Research*, New Delhi, 2014.

8

City Boundaries and Waste Frontiers: Exploring Nayandahalli as an Ecosystem where Waste is Transformed into Resource[1]

Pinky Chandran and Kabir Arora

Introduction

Waste,
The all-pervasive reminiscent
Of a love affair gone awry
Discarded without a thought ...
Lies on the road, on the footpath, on the beach
Or tossed carelessly in the bin ...
Raw, fizzy, bubbling, visceral
Waste,
Is caught in the binary of dirty and clean and
The fragility of trash and aesthetics ...
Implicating, threatening, surrendering
But to those who make a living,
Waste, is not void of value ...[2]

Today, our cities are marked by novel forms of self-indulgence and striking social inequities that encourage unencumbered wastefulness. We happily discharge our duty of mass consumption to boost economic growth. The negative externality of this sanctimonious duty is generation of waste. 'Waste', the word used in common parlance, is something that we discard or throw away as it carries no value. On the other hand, Bengaluru's waste workers often use the term '*maal*', essentially meaning 'material', instead of waste to describe the contents that they work with. The term 'material' is usually described as an object or substance that has inherent value, with a potential to continue, change, and transform. In this way, the concrete relationships that we build with the waste produced in our urban centres bears a striking resemblance to those imagined in Calvino's fictional cities.

> The city of Leonia refashions itself every day: every morning the people wake between fresh sheets, wash with just-unwrapped cakes of soap, wear brand-new clothing, take from the latest model refrigerator still unopened tins, listening to the last-minute jingles from the most up-to-date radio. On the sidewalks, encased in spotless plastic bags, the remains of yesterday's Leonia await the garbage truck. Not only squeezed tubes of toothpaste, blown-out light bulbs, newspapers, containers, wrappings, but also boilers, encyclopaedias, pianos, porcelain dinner services. It is not so much by the things that each day are manufactured, sold, bought, that you can measure Leonia's opulence, but rather by the things that each day are thrown out to make room for the new (Calvino 1974/1997).

Garbage has been the focus of increased social, political, economic, and scientific attention given its increased quantities and the new forms in which it manifests itself. Moreover, as social scientists have remarked, waste is a social construct, with varying meanings and practices attached to it across history and society (Douglas 1966/2002). This makes an analysis of how various societal actors engage and deal with waste as an important research subject, critical to the crafting of a sound waste management policy.

Bangalore (Bengaluru), like most cities in developing countries, has an infra-economy.[3] 'Infra-economy' denotes on the one hand, an economy that is denied recognition, and on the other, one that is critical to the production of urban space. In our context, it is a place where waste (material) is recycled, repurposed, and reprocessed, and operates in the shadows. In order to examine this economy more closely, we focused on Nayandahalli, a locality in Bangalore also informally known as the plastic recycling hub as our research site for the period of one year.

During this time, we approached this site as an ecosystem where waste is transformed into a resource. We tried to make sense of the many questions that remain unanswered regarding urban informality and the informal waste economy in particular. These included: who are the important actors in the informal waste economy? What role do they play? What is the value chain in the informal waste economy? Why and how are they vital to urban ecology? And what are the challenges faced by them?

Methodology

Work on this research project started in May 2015. An informal meeting with the recyclers of Nayandahalli, scrap dealers, and dry waste collection operators contributed to the development of the research process. Salma and Siddique, residents of Nayandahalli, volunteered to initiate the research by introducing the research team. It was also decided that the local community radio station—Radio Active CR 90.4MHz—would be extensively used in documenting stories, given that the radio jockeys were also residents of the area. The methodology involved both primary and secondary data collection and analysis. The primary data included qualitative data and was complemented by quantitative data. The authors walked around the recycling hub once in three weeks for 15 months to build appreciation of the informal spaces and to observe and seek historical narratives of the place, in addition to seeking out a more lived experience of Nayandahalli. Participant observation was also used with field notes recorded in audio and written form in a log book. Photo-documentation was done extensively. A formal survey in the form of questionnaires was administered to 100 godown (storehouse and sorting centres) owners, 18 factory owners and 10 home-based workers. Informal and semi-structured focus group discussions were conducted in batches with godown owners, waste sorters, truck/tempo drivers, and home-based workers. Separate radio interviews with godown owners, sorters, and factory owners were also conducted. Furthermore, visits were undertaken at different informal recycling spaces in Bangalore, Delhi, Mumbai, Mysore, Tumkur, and Udupi.

A two-day national roundtable was held with recyclers to consolidate the understanding on the hierarchies within the informal waste economy on the need for a recycling policy, followed by a group discussion with local scrap dealers, dry waste collection operators, and recyclers from Jolly Mohalla and Nayandahalli. Both the primary researchers are part of Hasiru Dala—a collective of waste-pickers and informal waste collectors. Thus the orientation towards the research is empathetic and participatory. In many ways, this research project is community-led, with collective generation of knowledge on the basis of day-to-day lived experiences.

This essay is a reflection on the flow of matter where waste becomes a valuable resource, and stories of people who are a part of the process of transformation are central to it. There are poems, first-hand narratives, and pictures used to make what is generally invisible, visible. The poems are written by Pinky Chandran and appear after the title of each sub-heading to set the introductory tone for each section. The paper begins with the question of the identity of the informal waste workers of Bangalore. It describes the material flow chain, maps the important actors, and displays the centrality of place in the urban infra-economy which is threatened by the process of gentrification, with large-scale infrastructure projects like that of the metro rail and the widening of roads resulting in large-scale real estate development. The paper concludes with a sense of hope as recent policy directions have recognised the role played by the actors in the infra-economy.

The Identity of the Informal Waste Workers of Bangalore

In 2010, Bangalore, known as the Silicon Valley of India, was warming to the concept of decentralised management of waste, as the citizens group, Solid Waste Management Roundtable (SWMRT), had appealed to the Lok Adalat (People's Court)—a non-adversarial alternative dispute resolution system set up under the Legal Services Authorities Act, 1987 from mid-2010—which led to a shift in direction for the Bruhat Bengaluru Mahanagara Palike (Greater Bangalore Municipal Corporation or BBMP), the institution responsible for implementing decentralised waste management across the city, including the construction of dry waste collection centres (DWCCs). This was further endorsed by the Karnataka High Court in 2012. DWCCs, which were first set up in Bangalore (Chandran and Narayanan 2016), are an important aspect of decentralised waste management. The concept was modelled around neighbourhood recycling centres. The DWCCs are charged with facilitating the collection/purchase of all recyclable waste from residents, sanitary workers, and waste-pickers or scrap dealers.[4] Installation of DWCCs also included the integration of waste-pickers and informal waste collectors in the operations of these centres and encouraged extended producers' responsibility[5] for packaging materials that are not being recycled presently. Thus, these centres were intended to serve as models for sustainability.

Given the acknowledgement for decentralised facilities, the Alliance of Indian Waste-pickers, a national coalition of waste-pickers organisations, and the Mythri Sarva Seva Samithi (MSSS), a member of SWMRT, appealed to the Lok Adalat to recognise the efforts of waste-pickers, sorters, and itinerant buyers (Chandran, Shekar, Abubaker, and Yadav 2014). Following directives from the Court, the Commissioner of BBMP issued a circular to enumerated waste-pickers, scrap dealers, and itinerant buyers. This decision helped the BBMP become the first local body to initiate the process of registration as per recommendations of the Audit Report on Management of Waste in India (Comptroller and Auditor General of India [CAG] 2008).

Thus began the recognition of the waste-pickers in Bangalore.

Figure 1: Waste-picker on the way to trade her day's collection
Source: Pinky Chandran/*Seminar Magazine*

The city's dirty secret
Scattered on the streets,
A faceless figure, in unkempt clothes
Wanders around searching, rummaging, picking;
Empty bottles, discarded tea cups, crumpled paper,
Dirty plastics bags and empty shampoo bottles;

From the rubbish pile of rotting food, egg shells and sanitary napkin
A passer-by frowns in disdain and covers his nose
Unconcerned, she goes about picking
With the growls of the dogs for company, amidst the blaring horns
Unconcerned she meticulously goes about the business of picking
Oh you thief, says the lady of the house, I don't want you nearby
Halt, who goes there, says the cop
I know not who I am, for the city does not identify me, she says
Unconcerned, she continues picking, silently keeping the city clean
She is the waste-picker![6]

The informal waste economy is heterogeneous and multi-faceted (Gill 2010; Chikarmane and Narayan 2000). It consists of an economically dynamic population that forms a vital link in the solid waste management system of any city in a developing country. This economy incorporates a range of activities from waste-picking, to the marginal operations of petty scrap dealers, to those linked with large-scale enterprises. Most operate without significant legal recognition or protection. The World Bank estimates that 1 to 2 per cent of the urban population in developing countries earns a living through work in this sector (Medina 2008). In 2012, the International Solid Waste Management Association established a taskforce to study the linkages between globalisation and solid waste management. The report released estimated that the number of informal sector recyclers (ISRs) is around 20 million worldwide, with almost 50 per cent of the labour force involved in waste management (ISWA 2012).

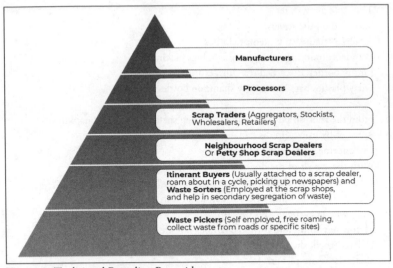

Figure 2: Traditional Recycling Pyramid
Source: Pinky Chandran/Hasiru Dala

Entry into this sector for newcomers is usually a last resort survival strategy and, for some, a family affair, passed down from generations (Chikarmane and Narayan 2000). Further up the ladder, entrepreneurial drive is the hallmark of scrap dealers/traders. These economies are socially constructed based on market principles. Often unregistered, these entrepreneurs have limited access to credit, infrastructure and other facilities, although their economic output is much higher (Chikarmane, et al. unpublished). Very little data exists on the actual contribution of the sector as most of its activities go unrecorded.

A 2013 study, titled 'Informal Waste Workers' Contribution', documented the BBMP's role in formally recognising the importance of waste-pickers in the city, along with providing a demographic profile of waste-pickers and highlighting the contribution of informal recycling to the city's economy. The study revealed that 15,000 waste-pickers were retrieving about 1,050 tons of recyclable waste, saving the municipality about 84 crores annually (Chandran, et al. 2014).

Bangalore's Material Flow Value Chain

We first met Salma and Siddique at an informal gathering of waste-pickers assembled to discuss the formation of a membership-based organisation of waste-pickers in Bangalore in 2011, which was called Hasiru Dala, meaning 'green force'. Confused and shy at the gathering, they kept to themselves. Salma used to work as a waste sorter at a godown segregating plastics in Nayandahalli, and Siddique used to drive a truck that transported 'material' (waste).

At the second gathering of waste-pickers, the vision for the organisation was taking shape. The mood was jubilant. Salma and Siddique were eager to participate in the mobilisation process. They also wanted to apply to operate dry waste collection centres allotted to waste-pickers and other informal waste collectors. They became a part of Hasiru Dala. Later, they started hosting a daily radio programme titled *Kasa Shramika Parisara Rakshka* (Waste-pickers are the Saviours of the Environment), on Radio Active CR 90.4 MHz, Bangalore's community radio station.

In the two-year period, from 2012–14, Salma and Siddique profiled a number of waste-pickers, waste sorters, scrap dealers, godown owners, waste-picker colonies, and migrant workers. Soon we in Hasiru Dala realised that there is a world beyond waste-pickers about which we need to learn. Salma and Siddique became our mentors, helping us to explore the wider informal waste economy in Bangalore. With them we visited Nayandahalli, and made it our field site for many months to come.

> What happens to the things we trash out?
> What about them?
> Have we ever stopped to notice?
> What trails does trash undertake?
> What about them?
> Have we ever stopped to notice?
> What stories do they hide or collect?
> Of their journey,
> To the aggregation and recycling centres…!

Bangalore's dry waste chain is a complex emergent network that both spans and blurs the line between the formal and informal economy. It is interconnected at different levels, converging at recycling markets and recycling hubs like that of Nayandahalli. The two figures presented below represent the complexity and diversity of the informal economy and its actors.

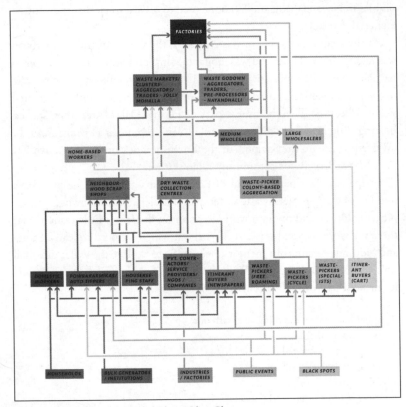

Figure 3: Bangalore's Material Flow Value Chain
Source: Pinky Chandran/*Seminar Magazine*/Hasiru Dala

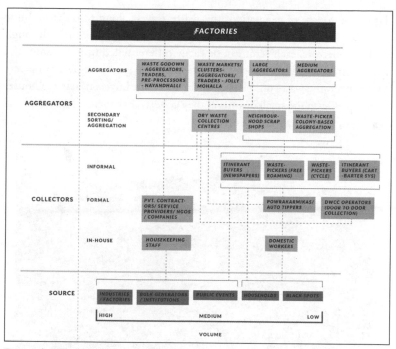

Figure 4: Value Chain Reinterpreted
Source: Pinky Chandran/*Seminar Magazine*/Hasiru Dala

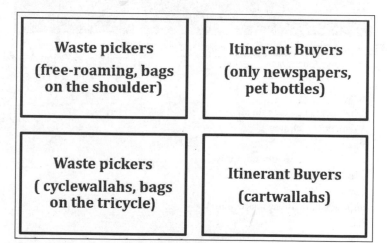

Figure 5: First Level Actors in the Recycling Value Chain
Source: Pinky Chandran/*Seminar Magazine*/Hasiru Dala

From the source of generation, the waste travels along through multiple agencies and formal and informal actors termed 'collectors', although within collectors, each actor can be easily differentiated from the source of collection, method, and type of collection. While the waste-pickers operate purely from the waste on the streets, the itinerant buyers usually go house-to-house. Given the small quantities they collect, they then sell it to the local neighbourhood scrap shop.

Figure 6: Scrap loaded truck on the way to Nayandahalli
Source: Pinky Chandran

Scrap,
A fragment, a piece, a shred,
A remnant, a leftover
Scrap,
Something that we discard, throw,
Eliminate, remove or dump,
Scrap,
Impersonal, invisible, unaccounted,
Scrap is,
Intermingled, Bundled, Flattened,
Combined, Boxed and placed in trucks
to the godowns of Nayandahalli ...

Destination Nayandahalli

Most cities in developing countries contain spaces containing large quantities of urban waste—Dharavi in Mumbai, Orangi Township in Karachi, City of God in Rio de Janeiro, Old Fadama in Ghana, Mokattam Village (also known as the 'Garbage City') in Cairo. Bangalore is no exception. More often than not, most do not notice these places. These areas act as a perfect setting to cast away waste workers. In Bangalore, Nayandahalli occupies this space.

> Nayandahalli, twenty-five years back, was jungle. There was no electricity, water, or roads. On a vacant plot, the landlord gave us permission, and we put up a hut, as my husband found a job as a watchman.
>
> (Zarina, Sorter and Co-owner of godown)[7]

However, the area found itself within the city limits of Bangalore after the agglomeration in the 1970s. Located along the Mysore Road, on the State Highway no. 17, it has the Vrishabhavathi River, a tributary of the Arakavati on one side—a river that seems more like a historical relic than active water body given its current form as the location for the city's sewage streams. It shares borders with Banshankari, Rajarajeshwarinagar, and the Bangalore University campus. Nayandahalli boasts a railway station connecting Bangalore and Maddur and a passenger train connecting Bangalore to Mysore. Today, Nayandahalli is districted as Bangalore Municipal Ward no. 131 and is spread over 2.07 sq. kms. The ward consists of the following localities: Nayandahalli town, Chandra Layout Extension, Chandra Layout II stage, Metro Layout, and Dr Ambedkar Nagar.[8] The area is dominated by single dwelling units, with lower-middle class and middle class households.

> Far away in the city,
> Past the Vrishabhavathi river,
> A tributary of the Arakavathy,
> Now
> An open drain of green waters,
> Emitting pungent aromas …
> Way past the constructions of the metro and the tall buildings
> Nestled inside, are a gaggle of tins/asbestos sheet sheds …[9]

In addition to carrying Bangalore's sewage, the Vrishabhavathi River is also fed discharge from the surrounding industrial area, and the illegally dumped waste. It is also known as the 'Kengeri Mori'.[10] The foul smell emanating from the river and the white froth bubbling inside has contributed to the image of Nayandahalli as an aesthetically unappealing place. The negative image of Nayandahalli, which is home to a large number of informal waste workers, is intrinsically tied to the negative image of waste and waste workers in general. As has been written by Mary Douglas: 'Dirt is a matter out of place, suggesting that the label "dirt" does not describe the nature of something, but instead implies an infringement on the boundaries of a social order' (1966/2002). Public discourse often frames such areas as eyesores, bereft of any hope, and disempowered. Such a perspective does much to camouflage the city's unencumbered consumption and glaring social inequities.

> Is there anything more naked?
> Than the glinting tin shed
> Hiding the city's rubbish,
> In a cloak of anonymity
> Ever wondered,
> What transpires inside?[11]

Figures 7–8: The tin sheds at Nayandahalli
Source: Pinky Chandran

Bangalore's waste, in particular its plastic waste, passes through the hands of different actors, as illustrated in Figure 2, to reach Nayandahalli. As one makes their way to interior roads, one can spot miniature mounds of plastic bottles, milk covers, helmets, buckets, broken chairs, slippers, old CDs, wires, disposable cutlery, take-away boxes, discarded shoes, toothbrushes, helmets and more spread out on blue tarpaulin or directly on the street. Alongside these items are plastic crates and plastic non-woven bags for storage. Upon closer inspection, one can discern in the clutter the industriousness of agile hands and observant eyes that organise, sort, and aggregate materials into multiple categories of plastic, metal, paper, and cloth. And within plastics categories includes polyethylene, polypropylene, PET, or polyvinyl chloride (PVC)—categories inconceivable to laypeople who perceive the discarded items mainly in 'use and throw' terms.

> I did not know what a plastic was. But I learned! It took me a year! Now, I can proudly say that I can sort in about 60–70 varieties. But unfortunately, I do not have space, and so I sort at home. And when I do so, I cannot accumulate large quantities of each type of material, and so I do not get the right rate. On the flip side, working at home has more disadvantages, with children around, we have to be doubly careful as they think we are playing. We cannot afford to invest in a godown as the down payment is huge. For a person earning Rs. 200–300 a day, we cannot [do] this. [It] is impossible.
>
> (Peersaheb, Itinerant Buyer)[12]

Figure 9: Waste sorters at Nayandahalli
Source: Pinky Chandran

The Makings of a Plastic Recycling Hub

> Rich people's garbage was every year more complex, rife with hybrid materials, impurities, imposters. Planks that looked like wood were shot through with plastic. How was he to classify a loofah? The owners of the recycling plants demanded waste that was all one thing, pure.
>
> (Boo 2012/2013)

Depending on the type of godown, materials are sorted into over 35 to 70 categories. Women and men sit with plastic trays in front of them and sort mixed plastics based on the resin or type: HDPE (High-density polyethylene), PP (polypropylene), polyvinyl chloride (PVC), polyurethane (PUR), polyethylene terephthalate (PET), and polystyrene (PS), polyethylene (PE), etc. The people who sort, go a step further to sort them based on colour and grade (virgin, or recycled once or multiple times). They are also skilled enough to perceive the hardness and softness of a particular material. Most sorters are experienced in identifying materials based on appearance, touch, sound, smell when burnt, and also by biting into the plastic. Further up the chain, larger godowns accept only specialised material from what has been sorted, which is further sorted based on colour. The sorters separate the bottle lids from the bottles before they are thrown in the pile based on colours which are then taken away to be bailed or flattened. Some of the godowns engage in further segregation, manually cleaning, cutting, and grinding materials. The ones that do not make the cut are transported to the large godown known as the Delhi Godown.[13]

Many products that enter the market are a complex mix of plastic, metal, glass, paper, foam, or rubber. Many sorters go the extra mile to sort these and isolate the plastic:

> The market is inundated with new and newer materials. It is tricky for a new comer to decipher. However, having worked in this space for over five decades, one is trained to differentiate and we are trying to catch up.
>
> (Peersaheb)

Given the diversity in the dry waste stream, and based on high value and low value material, rates for the materials vary from scrap shop to scrap shop, at the ward level, and higher up the aggregator levels. While medium and large-scale aggregators located within the city have links with processors for specific material, the majority of the material is sent to the informal waste clusters for aggregation, trading, or processing.

Shailender Kumar, a plastic waste reprocessor, recounts how he got into the plastics recycling business:

> I started the godown [for aggregating and sorting plastic]/factory [for reprocessing plastic waste and making yarn out of it] about four years ago. My starting investment was about INR 5 lacs and I gave one lac in advance. The size of my godown/factory is about 30/40 square feet. I collect Grade A quality plastics from different factories (generated as waste), bring it my godown, and segregate it, and then put it in the machine to make yarn and sell it back to the factories that make plastic chairs, water drums, water pipes, carry bags, hand covers, suitcases, nursery covers, Syntax drums, and other items. I go about six to seven times for collection in a month. And collect about eight to nine tons of plastic (waste) during that time.
>
> There are two types of yarn that we make: first quality and second quality. It is filtered to make plastic items. Per month, we segregate between six to seven tons of plastic. Per day it will amount to 300–350 kilograms of plastic for reprocessing. I run the machine weekly two or three times, depending on the load. After I send the yarn to the factory, they test it for quality, before paying me. On an average month, I send ten loads of yarn to different factories located in Tamil Nadu and Andhra Pradesh and I decide my selling price for the yarn. However, the market is not stable and rates fluctuate severely. I have eight people under me. For men, I pay Rs. 300 per day and for the women I pay about Rs. 220 per day. I also provide lunch, coffee/tea, and bonus once a year. I also give them advance as and when they ask.[14]

Jolly Mohalla[15] and Nayandahalli have been two major markets for recycling waste materials in the city with a history of over fifty and thirty years respectively. Following finer secondary sorting and grading, the materials, depending on the type, go into primary processing. The process includes bailing, washing, beating, grinding, etc. Secondary processing includes other steps such as melting, granulation, and pulping.

Digging deeper into the history of Nayandahalli, one begins to uncover an area that slowly began harbouring the city's dirty secrets, silently transforming Bangalore's detritus into raw materials, which were then sent to factories for processing. These recycling and reprocessing enterprises soon spilled over from Nayandahalli into surrounding areas such as JJR

Nagar, Gowripalya, Deepanjalinagar, and Gangondanahalli. The area began developing during the late 1970s and early 1980s, when plastic waste made it to the streets from both industrial and municipal sources. Today, there are over 250 godowns scattered across Nayandahalli and neighbouring wards. The recycling godowns and some factories situated there have no formal structure. Instead, they are spread out quite sporadically, with godowns spread across Metro Layout, Telecom Layout, and Revanna Badavane. There exists a vague semblance of area-based specialisation in Nayandahalli. Across the town's main railway track, one comes across areas that specialise in washing, drying, and de-inking. Areas that reprocess plastic are scattered primarily around Muthuchari Industrial Estate and Azeez Seth Industrial Estate, Metro Layout, and Pipe Line Road. Other areas like Kamashipalya, Kumbalgod, Sunkadakatte, Magadi Road, Peenya Industrial Estate, Bommasandra Industrial Estate, KSSIDC industrial area, and Deepanjalinagar host larger plastic manufacturing factories. When interpreting this economic geography, one can discern that formal and informal enterprises in Nayandahalli are intimately connected, with formal entities in close and persistent contact with informal ones while facilitating the smooth flow of materials.[16]

Today, given its strategic location, Nayandahalli has housed several major infrastructural projects such as the NICE Road, the Mysore Road flyover, and the metro rail line. These developments have helped boost real estate speculation in the area and have suddenly transformed what was once thick forest into one of the most sought after property markets in Bangalore. Slowly and steadily, gentrification is happening and many godowns and recycling units have been asked to move out. The informal waste workers of Nayandahalli are urban nomads who are now looking for other spaces to set up their units.[17]

Conclusion

In this chapter we have tried to provide an overview of the informal waste economy in Bangalore and the players involved. Actors in the waste economy, though often ignored by the rest of the city and policymakers, are central players in the infra-economy, providing essential environment services. Informal waste workers play a vital role in the economy of the city as a whole. The poems, photographs, and stories amplify the need for recognition by the rest of the city and policymakers of these actors as vital citizens who keep the city's economy ticking. Informal waste workers play a crucial role in the economy and the city as a whole, transforming what others deem to be 'waste' into marketable goods, which can be resold and reused.

The Solid Waste Management Rules, 2016, notified by the Union Ministry of Environment, Forest, Climate Change (MoEFCC) for the first time since the first set of rules in 2000, defined the terms 'waste-picker and informal waste collector'. It further mandated incentivising the informal recycling industry. However, the details of this incentivisation were left ambiguous by the MoEFCC, which has left scope for interpretation.

While the recent law envisions inclusion, in actuality, the opposite is happening as those units which provide basic environmental services are displaced through large-scale urban infrastructure development projects and market-led gentrification. Many units have moved out and many are moving out from Nayandahalli in search of newer places where they can operate, thus, becoming urban nomads. Whenever these workers are asked what they desire for their work, their answer is always security of workplace and an end to displacement. Their existence and security is crucial for the city to be able to manage its discarded materials.

NOTES

1. This chapter forms an important part of the study titled *Valuing Urban Waste: The need for a comprehensive material recovery and recycling policy* by Hasiru Dala. The quotes from the interview were aired on Radio Active 90.4 MHz, a community radio station in Bangalore and some of the transcription appears on their blog <www.radioactivecr.wordpress.com> and on the blog run by Hasiru Dala <www.wastenarratives.com>. We are grateful to our colleague Malleshwari from Hasiru Dala who served as the research assistant and helped with primary interviews of the recyclers. In addition, we are thankful to Salma and Siddique, residents of Nayandahalli, for accompanying us through all the surveys, immersion trips and tours, and for scheduling meetings and interviews with various stakeholders. Our special acknowledgement to Usha from Radio Active CR 90.4 MHz, for recording and editing the interviews for broadcast. We are also grateful to our colleague Marwan Abubaker and to Nalini Shekar who assisted us greatly with this research. Our deepest gratitude to Shreyas Sreenath for all his support and suggestions. The funding for this research came from the Indian Institute of Human Settlements (IIHS) Bangalore, as part of their Case Development Series towards 'Re-framing Urban Inclusion', Wipro Limited and Global Green Grants Fund. We are also grateful to the following organisations for their advice: Kagad Kach Patra Kashtakari Panchayat, Global Alliance for Incineration Alternatives, Solid Waste Management Round Table, Bangalore,

and Jain University. We would also like to give a special acknowledgement to Karnataka State Pollution Control Board for hosting the deliberations with the recyclers.

2. The poems and photographs are by Pinky Chandran and first appeared on the primary author's personal social media pages and the dedicated social media page @wasteframes (includes a blog, Twitter and Instagram handles) that she runs and forms a part of her collection of 2,500 photographs collected during the study.

3. As defined by Vinay Gidwani (2015: 576), the term 'infra-economy' has a double valence: 'it denotes, on the one hand, an economy that is denied recognition by state and civil society (and is 'seen' only at moments of crisis, as an object of condemnation or reform), and on the other, an economy that is critical to the production of urban space such that it is conducive for capitalist accumulation. Correspondingly, the labour of waste transformation—recycling, repurposing and reprocessing—that is undertaken …'.

4. Dry waste in Bangalore includes recyclables, including low/no value waste.

5. According to Solid Waste Management Rules 2016, 'extended producer responsibility' (EPR) means responsibility of any producer of packaging products such as plastic, tin, glass, and corrugated boxes, etc., for environmentally sound management, till end-of-life of the packaging products.'

6. The waste-picker poem by Pinky Chandran has appeared in many web portals and has been read out in many public forums <https://radioactivecr. wordpress.com/2016/08/16/daastan-e-nayandahalli-a-photo-exhibition-by-pinky-chandran-and-marwan-abubaker/> and <http://www.india-

seminar.com/2017/694/694_pinky_chandran.htm>.
Note: There exist different versions of the poem by the author.

7. This interview was conducted in Dakhini and was later translated in English.

8. A photo essay and parts of the chapter appeared in the *Seminar* Magazine titled 'Bangalore's Great Transformation' June 2017 under the sub title: 'Nayandahalli: transforming waste into resource' by Pinky Chandran <http://www.india-seminar.com/2017/694/694_pinky_chandran.htm>.

9. This poem was part of the photo exhibition exhibited in Bangalore and appeared on <https://radioactivecr. wordpress.com/2016/08/16/daastan-e-nayandahalli-a-photo-exhibition-by-pinky-chandran-and-marwan-abubaker/>.

10. 'Mori' means drain and Kengeri is the name of the area adjacent to Nanyandahalli.

11. This poem was part of the photo exhibition exhibited in Bangalore and appeared on <https://radioactivecr. wordpress.com/2016/08/16/daastan-e-nayandahalli-a-photo-exhibition-by-pinky-chandran-and-marwan-abubaker/>.

12. Interview was conducted in Hindi and later translated in English.

13. 'Delhi godown' is a local term used for materials aggregated to be sent to Delhi for further segregation and processing.

14. The interview was conducted in Hindi and translated in English.

15. Situated in the heart of Bangalore, Jolly Mohalla is a hub of recycling-aggregation and trading. The place was formed after the shops around the area began throwing out gunny bags or *thailas* from the packaging. Jolly Mohalla grew from the need to accumulate the discarded materials, as the entrepreneurial informal

waste sector saw an opportunity in recycling. In the fifty years of its existence, different kinds of materials have passed through Jolly Mohalla—from paper, plastic metal, glass, and jute, with shops specialising in the aggregation of each.

16. A modified version of this text, appears in the article written by the author for *Seminar* magazine <http://www.india-seminar.com/2017/694/694_pinky_chandran.htm>.

17. Ibid.

REFERENCES

Boo, Katherine, *Behind the Beautiful Forevers*, New Delhi: Random House India, 2012/2013.

Calvino, Italo, *Invisible Cities*, (W. Weaver, Trans.), London: Vintage, 1974/1997.

Chandran, Pinky, and Sandya Narayanan, 'A Working Observation on the Dry Waste Collection Centers in Bangalore', *Procedia Environmental Sciences*, 35, pp. 65–76, 2016.

Chandran, Pinky, Nalini Shekar, Marwan Abubaker, and Akshay Yadav, *Informal Waste Workers' Contributon in Bangalore*, Hyderabad: International Society of Waste Management, Air and Water (ISWMAW), 2014.

Chaturvedi, Bharati, and Vinay Gidwani, 'Poverty as Geography: Motility, Stoppage and Circuits of Waste in Delhi', in J. S. Anjaria, and C. McFarlane, (eds.), *Urban Navigations, Politics, Space and the City in South Asia*, New Delhi: Routledge, 2011, pp. 50–78.

Chikarmane, Poornima, and L. Narayan, 'Formalising Livelihood: Case of Waste Pickers in Pune', *Economic & Political Weekly*, 34, (2000), pp. 3639–42.

————, (Unpublished), 'Report on Scrap Collectors, Scrap Traders and Recycling Enterprises in Pune', International Labour Organization-SNDT.

Comptroller and Auditor General of India (CAG), *All India Audit Report on Management of Waste in India*, Performance Audit - Report No. 14 of 2008, New Delhi: Comptroller and Auditor General of India, 2008.

Douglas, Mary, *Purity and Danger*, London: Routlege, 1966/2002.

Gidwani, Vinay, 'The Work of Waste: Inside India's Infra- Economy', *Transactions Of The Institute of British Geographers*, 40, 4 (2015), pp. 575–95.

————, and Rajashree Reddy, 'The Afterlives of "Waste": Notes from India for a Minor History of Capital Surplus', *Antipode*, 43, 5 (2011), pp. 1625–58.

Gill, Kaveri, *Of Poverty and Plastic: Scavening and Scrap Trading Entrepenuers in India's Urban Informal Economy*, Delhi: Oxford University Press, 2010.

International Solid Waste Association, I. S., *Globalization and Waste Management*, International Solid Waste Association, 2012.

Medina, Martin, 'The Informal Recycling Sector in Developing Countries', *Public Private Infrastructure Facility*, 44, 1 (2006).

Ministry of Environment, Forests and Climate Change (MoEF& CC), Government of India, *Solid Waste Management Rules 2016*, New Delhi: Controller of Publications, 2016.

'*Scientists Find Great Pacific Ocean Garbage Patch*', National Science Foundation, <https://www.nsf.gov/news/news_summ.jsp?cntn_id=115481>, last accessed Oct. 2016

9

'Studying in the *Mahol*': Middle-class Spaces and Aspiring Middle-class Male Subjects in Urban Pakistan

Muntasir Sattar

Introduction

A mixture of infrastructural investments and public–private partnerships has dramatically transformed Lahore. Signal-free corridors, a rapid bus transit system (the MetroBus), and a host of municipal services outsourced to Turkish companies index elements of an urban transformation. To Ayub Sahab, a tall, imposing hostel manager in central Lahore, these changes were part of the Chief Minister's attempt 'to make Lahore like Paris'. While on a motorbike ride not far from the Choudhury Mansion hostel, Ayub pointed to a freshly paved road that was once bustling with activity. The Paris model signals a far deeper transformation that goes beyond infrastructure or state-directed development.

A marker of that transformation has been the recent rise of single-sex hostels found in Lahore's busy transit hubs, many of which are private and unaffiliated with colleges or universities. They cater to migrants in a city reputed for its educational and professional opportunities, attracting young people from all over Pakistan. While the city's historic institutions of education have attracted students for generations (Glover 2007), what is important about hostels built after the Higher Education Commission reforms in 2002 is the *mahol* or environment engendered by the size, scale, and concentration of this urban housing. The hostel reflects how Pakistan's social change articulates within a dynamic urban landscape. The space of the hostel thus serves as a crucial linkage between some of these larger socio-economic processes and an emerging class of men.

Rapid rural–urban migration (Hasan 2006), economic growth (Zaidi 2015), and an increasingly educated and young population (Sattar 2015) serve as the context of an urbanised Pakistan. The gradual rise of the services sector (Zaidi 2015), the changing nature of work (Z. Y. Zaidi 2011), and shifting class dynamics (Maqsood 2014) make Lahore, and by extension Choudhury Mansion, important sites of inquiry. The vantage point of central Lahore that offers perspective into the everyday life of male graduates from all over the country who come to fulfil their career goals illustrates how these larger conditions are intertwined.

Ayub Sahab's hostel, Choudhury Mansion, is one among a dozen catering to about 1,200 men in a space nestled between two major roads in Mazang. The hostel is a hub in a network of spaces that includes Lawrence Garden, Quaid-e-Azam Library, and periodically, Punjab University. Young men circulate in this network—and the environment that it engenders—to prepare for the annually administered merit-based exam for the elite Civil Service, referred to as the 'CSS exam'. Men occupy these spaces for months or years at a time, in which many study at private 'academies' where they work in small groups and listen to lectures from teachers and current civil service officers to learn how to write essays, briefs, and revise their knowledge of a wide range of topics from biology to Islamic law. While several languages can be heard, Urdu is the lingua franca.

Though few men pass the exam, the experience of those aspiring civil servants who circulate between these spaces is illustrative of some of the processes of transformation of Lahore's urban landscape. This chapter makes the argument that the space of the hostel is a classed urban milieu in which men with similar backgrounds collaborate in shaping their subjectivity. In providing insight into a less-explored but important masculine and transient urban space, this chapter explores the relationship between urban space and class subjectivity.

Ethnography of an Urban Middle Class

Amidst Pakistan and Lahore's transformation, an important element that is far less explored in the Pakistani context than in India is the formation of what Zaidi (2014) refers to as a 'middle class' and what has been explored in

South Asia as a 'new' middle class (Fernandes 2006; Mazarella n.d.). Recent ethnographic work in urban settings in India and Nepal has helped broaden Weberian and Bourdieusian approaches to class in the subcontinent (Leichty 2003). They help focus analytical attention away from consumption towards subjectivity and into the middle class as a dynamic cultural position.

Though elements of Pakistan's urban transformation have been studied separately (Durr-e-Nayab 2011; Ali 2002) through quantitative research, this study weaves together disparate analytical strands that are encapsulated in one neighbourhood of Lahore. Bringing these changes into one analytical frame, this study links larger macroeconomic and political changes through ethnographic description of a rapidly transforming neighbourhood and how it is navigated by young men. In exploring the *mahol* of recently developed housing for migrant men, this chapter builds on the contributions of Hasan (2006) to help understand the social and cultural implications of an urban transformation.

A focus on the educational and career strategies of unemployed men as they unfold day to day at Choudhury Mansion allows insight into the enormous changes that cities—particularly in the subcontinent—are undergoing. As a resident of the hostel, the author was able to document the formation and maintenance of the *mohalla* as well as the everyday strategies and activities of aspiring bureaucrats in a hostel over the course of one year. Looking at the relationships that form between residents and the educational activities provides a view on how an actively maintained space is conducive to a transformation of one's subjectivity.

On the other hand, exploring Lahore's transformation through the everyday life of a large hostel is to provide perspective on Lahore's changing landscape. To do that, this chapter focuses on oral history accounts of the development of the *mohalla* or neighbourhood and on the way the young men who live in that area make use of the space. While I refer to the *mohalla* as a geographical reference in a physically-bounded space, I refer to the '*mahol*' that it engenders as a 'lifeworld socially produced through associations' (Appadurai 1996). Using ethnographic methods, this chapter explores the impact of market forces, urban planning, and the flow of young people—mainly from rural Pakistan—on the transformation of one locality in Lahore.

A perspective into the interdependent processes of social and spatial transformation illustrates unique patterns of stratification anticipated by research on urban poverty in peripheral areas in Latin America (Safa 1986), South Asia (Tarlo 2003; Roy 2002; Van der Linden 1983), or North America (Stack 1997). In exploring how space is configured by larger forces and navigated, the aforementioned studies highlight poverty in their explorations of urban stratification. Applying this approach to a middle-class locality in Lahore, this chapter contributes to more focused work on the emergence of a 'new' middle strata characterised by consumption and taste (Liechty 2003), precarious employment (Fernandes 2006), and a new politics (Mazarella n.d.).

How unemployed educated young men from rural backgrounds position themselves and utilise the *mahol* to work to better their social and cultural capital is exemplified in the vignette below. What the city means to young educated men, and how it plays a role in their lives, provides rich insight into what this *mahol* is and how it is experienced.

Vignette

The 'CSS *mahol*' on offer in Lahore was both what attracted young men from around Pakistan and what was created by them. In spring, each annual cycle of arriving aspiring elite government officers replenished and sustained the *mahol* as others left. 'CSS aspirants', as they would refer to themselves, would study with current elite government officers, read, or study old exams in their hostels or at libraries. They would concentrate in hubs largely around Quaid-e-Azam Library in Lawrence Garden (officially renamed Bagh-i-Jinnah) in the centre of Lahore, often arriving in pairs. One could hear them practicing English in the lush gardens and could identify them from their smart pant-shirt dress and the books they carried. These would include books published for specific exams like Everyday Science, Pakistan Studies, and Islamic History. Some of the books in circulation included a photocopied contemporary book like *Why Nations Fail* by Acemoglu and Robinson or a book published over a hundred years ago such as *Precis Writing* by R. Dhillon.

One such pair was Adam and Zain, who had recently arrived from Sukkur in Sindh when I met them. They lived in Patiala House where hundreds of other CSS aspirants lived, at walking distance from the library and Bagh-i-Jinnah. Dozens of fliers were stuck to the walls in this area advertising CSS academies, teachers, and 'notes' that could be used for exam preparation.

On a cool evening in the early spring of 2014, we chatted sitting on the concrete floor of the sparsely furnished room, one of about a dozen such rooms in a modest three-floored, brick building. We sat with our backs against a wall in the faded-blue first floor hostel room that they shared. I was familiar with this room arrangement; CSS notes lying about, a laptop, and thin bedding, and sheets and pillows shoved into a corner.

Adam and Zain were an unlikely pair. Adam is short, clean shaven, and struggles with English while Zain is of medium-build with a smart beard and speaks with near fluency. Adam, who had never held a job, had come a little earlier and found the room. His father is a doctor and several of his family members work in the government in Sindh. On the other hand, Zain, whose father was a shopkeeper, previously worked for an NGO in Sindh.

While in Lahore, Zain took 'tuitions' (lessons) with a Persian teacher but mostly studied on his own at the Dar-us-Salam Library. This library was Bagh-i-Jinnah's smaller library where practically anyone could sit without becoming a member provided they came early enough to claim a desk. Meanwhile a dozen yards away, Adam would be sitting on the floor, at the feet of his teacher, Sir Fawad, at the *baaradari* (12-arched brick structure) before finding his way to the library in the early afternoon.

It is a more general *mahol* that these two young men and many other of my fellow hostelites had come for from far flung areas of Pakistan. As Zain put it, they can easily find a place to study in the library and coordinate with fellow aspirants, especially seniors who have experience. 'Just today, one of my seniors who failed his CSS English essay told me about the importance of keeping calm and nerves in check.' Access to such a network and space would be unlikely in his hometown.

Theorising Class in the South Asian City

The rapid growth of hostels catering to young educational aspirants in the city reflects the perception of Lahore as a city that is particularly developed and resource-rich. As hostelites and friends in the *mohalla* told me, the city is not cheap but has resources that few other cities do. Lahore's wider 'CSS *mahol*' brings together many young men in hostels and study groups with little in common besides education and aspirations. Entire buildings, and in fact neighbourhoods, are dominated by the CSS aspirants. To study the way these spaces are maintained and lived in is to explore the spatialisation of class (Zhang 2008; Srivastava 2012) in an urbanising society. More specifically, it is to explore the relationship between space and the shaping of habitus, particularly how young men endeavour to attain the social and cultural capital to become 'officers' through daily study and socialising with certain individuals in these spaces. This means differentiating between the *mahol* and *mohalla* and then exploring the cultural production of a *mahol* or milieu that enables this socialisation.

In her study of private housing developments in Kunming (China), Zhang (2008) highlights subjectivity as she shows how residents' habits and dispositions change according to their own expectations in a new real estate development. She argues that 'exclusionary residential space provides a tangible place where class-specific subjects and their cultural milieu are created, staged, and contested' (Zhang 2008: 25). Zhang's work demonstrates how exclusionary practices on the one hand, and competing claims made of status through lifestyles and consumption on the other, illustrate the formation of classed subjectivities of residents in new private housing developments. In the context of the transformation of the Indian political economy, Srivastava (2012) explores subjectivity of residents in private residential gated communities and lifestyles. Thus, such residential communities are the locales of identity, which create a model of 'post-national citizenship that constitutes a gloss on the relationship between the state and its citizens' (Srivastava 2012: 62). Both authors point to the relationship between space and subjectivity in highlighting the importance of class in understanding urban space.

While both Zhang and Srivastava focus on planned housing developments in their research, the exploration of Lahore's urban transformation is of a less-organised neighbourhood or a locality, one that Appadurai (1996) would refer to as a physical reference. The area is considered to be a commercial *mohalla* with a market on one end and hostels on the other; it is a de-territorialised place that houses a transient population. This heterogeneous space contrasts with other types of urban space studied in the subcontinent, which are formed on the basis of caste or religion (Jaffrelot and Van der Veer 2008; Kumar 1988). Next, I present accounts from hostel managers and owners about the formation and maintenance of the *mohalla*. This section highlights the significance of class for understanding the formation of the urban *mohalla* and provides a description of the changing urban landscape in the city of Lahore.

Exclusivity and the Development of the Milieu

Lahore's hostels vary greatly—some are purpose-built and others are simply homes in which families informally rent rooms to guests. Many of the hostels in Mazang are purpose-built and accommodate at least half a dozen rooms and most are multi-storey occupancy buildings.

A businessman and long-time resident recounts how this part of the city became increasingly dense. Mr Yusuf, whose family moved into the house behind what is now Choudhury Mansion around Partition, recounted how five large bungalows occupying this area were sold, demolished, the land split up, and converted into commercial properties including auto showrooms and more recently, hostels. Mr Choudhury, the owner of Choudhury Mansion and several other hostels, explains that the Mansion, built by his late father in 2004, was the first hostel in this Jail Road *mohalla*. Since then, other developers followed, with nearly a dozen others coming up over the years. The result, as Ayub Sahab put it, is that well over a thousand *pardesis* (outsiders) now populate the area, with only a handful of locals like Mr Yusuf. The hostelites, managers, chowkidars, and the cleaning staff are all from outside Lahore.

One of Mr Choudhury's employees, Mr Gul, explained the rapid growth of hostels: 'It's the best business right now'. Mr Gul explained this happened at the same time as Punjab College and other institutions opened up in Lahore in the mid-2000s, attracting students from all over the province. 'At one time there were only two; now there's a hostel on every corner.'

Dr Grace Clark, head of the Sociology Department at Forman Christian College, supported Mr Gul's assertion. She explained that Pakistan has experienced an education boom since the University Grants Commission was reformed and became the Higher Education Commission (HEC) in 2002 (personal communication 2013). Indeed, data on the HEC's website indicate enrolments have quadrupled; nearly a million students are enrolled in higher education in Pakistan (HEC 2012a). Lahore has the highest number of educational institutions per capita (HEC 2012b).

While both Mr Yusuf and Mr Choudhury see the open market at work, a former councillor notes the role of planning and state involvement in these changes. Mr Malik, who works in a property management office in the adjacent *katchi abadi*, attributes some of the change to the Lahore Development Authority management. He explains that the zone of hostels and adjacent *katchi abadi* emerged partly thanks to the construction of the Metro BRT system, the development of Ferozepur Road, and—going further back into the 1990s—the relocation of Tollington Market from Mall Road. Additionally, the LDA's neglect of the *ganda nala* (sewage canal) and recent interest in clearing it to build a highway plays a part in making this *mohalla* what it is today. According to him, the area has become commercial, busy, and foul-smelling.

I have described the development of housing for young university graduates to show how the area is shaped by migration, city planning, education institutions, and larger changes that have been happening in the area and the city as a whole. The development of this formal housing arguably grew with and around the *katchi abadi*. As Haji Sahab describes, 'Ten years ago there was a *khokha* [small stand selling food items and cigarettes] and now there are a dozen businesses catering to the residents of the diverse *mohalla*.' The area has thus seen a gradual commercialisation stimulated by migration, property investment, and indirect urban planning. The commercial *mohalla* defies easy categorisation, bringing together an assortment of labourers, businessmen, and hostelites. In this larger *mohalla*, how do hostels distinguish themselves?

Production and Maintenance of VIP Milieu

Choudhury Sahab, the owner of Choudhury Mansion, pointed out that his hostel was not for everyone: 'It is one of the most expensive hostels in Lahore.' Some comparison is in order. Hostels are differentiated by their amenities as well as cost. Haji Sahab, the owner of Sana Mansion, explains that his hostel offers 'VIP rooms', which include television, cable, fridge, and carpeting, and are mainly rented by doctors. He has a second tier of rooms that are cheaper but do not have these amenities.

In Choudhury Mansion, being able to pay the rent did not guarantee a room. Hostelites must sign a contract, provide two passport-size photos, a copy of their CNIC (national government-issued identity card), a letter indicating salary, or a copy of their student ID. Applicants must go through an interview with Ayub Sahab too. It is a fairly rigorous process. How does Ayub Sahab select people? 'We only select people we like. We first prefer people who have lived here, people whom we know. If there is not someone like that, then we show the room, and keep a waiting list.' Ayub Sahab shows me a small note with some names. He explained further. 'If we don't find someone we know, then we go to the list. We show the rooms, look at the list and see who we like.' I asked how he determined who he liked. 'I ask them what they do, if they're government workers, or I ask what college, and see if it's a good college. Then I decide whether to give them accommodation.'

One of the reasons for this selectivity and concern with security was the police who would take lists of residents and copies of ID cards regularly. Ayub Sahab would patrol the hallways from time to time, as if to inspect them; he would ask people who they were and where they were going. The reality was that the hostels in the hostel zone were quite open; it was not too difficult for anyone to go in and out, although there were cameras placed at the entrances.

Ayub Sahab also used the effect of posters and signs put up around the hostel in the maintenance of day-to-day security.

Figure 1: Notice
Source: Muntasir Sattar

Ayub Sahab says that he made the sign:

> To scare people, and to keep the *chawwal* [idiots] out. I want people to think that the SHO [station house officer] wrote it. I had printed it myself though! I wanted people to believe that there's an active watch.

His objective is to create an environment in which residents study. Like Haris Heights' manager said, he asks people to leave if they are not studying. 'We don't allow *hulla gulla* [partying] … If you came for studies, study.' Ayub Sahab echoed this point saying, 'we call their parents if they're not behaving and tell them how they're spending all this money and not studying.' Reinforcing this carefully managed environment, the neighbouring hostel manager explained he offers backup universal power supplies (UPS) in each room. 'Otherwise, how will the residents study?'

Ayub Sahab highlighted management and control to stress the difference between other hostels, particularly those at public universities. News reports indicated that Punjab University hostels were raided in the fall of 2013 and criminals were found to be residing there. One resident at a public university hostel told me he was staying there illegally for free, his cousin having paid the entire year's fee in one go—Rs 30,000—for a room that accommodates two people. There was no checking he explained; he and many others went undetected.

In a way Ayub Sahab seemed to be pointing to a marker of distinction, separating other hostels from the one he managed not only in cost but by the way the space was managed. One element of making this organised VIP *mahol* was about crucial exclusion. When I asked Choudhury Sahab himself what made his hostels successful, he explained, 'We do not allow women. They are strictly forbidden in the Choudhury Hostels.' Choudhury Sahab's response, like Ayub Sahab's, 'naturalise[s] economic privilege by couching it in a language of honour and morality that excludes its class others' (Liechty 2003: 20). In their careful selection and attention to security, there is a signal of legitimising Choudhury Mansion, while exclusion is made to appear natural as a means of producing a particular kind of space.

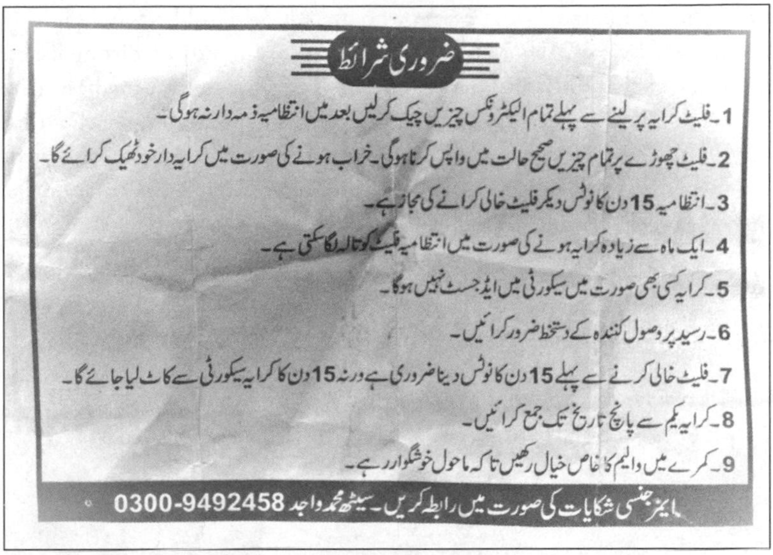
ضروری شرائط

1۔ فلیٹ کرایہ پر لینے سے پہلے تمام الیکٹرونکس چیزیں چیک کرلیں بعد میں انتظامیہ ذمہ دار نہ ہوگی۔

2۔ فلیٹ چھوڑے پر تمام چیزیں صحیح حالت میں واپس کرنا ہوگی۔ خراب ہونے کی صورت میں کرایہ دار خود ٹھیک کرائے گا۔

3۔ انتظامیہ 15 دن کا نوٹس دیکر فلیٹ خالی کرانے کی مجاز ہے۔

4۔ ایک ماہ سے زیادہ کرایہ ہونے کی صورت میں انتظامیہ فلیٹ کو تالہ لگا سکتی ہے۔

5۔ کرایہ کسی بھی صورت میں سیکورٹی میں ایڈجسٹ نہیں ہوگا۔

6۔ رسید پر وصول کنندہ کے دستخط ضرور کرائیں۔

7۔ فلیٹ خالی کرنے سے پہلے 15 دن کا نوٹس دینا ضروری ہے ورنہ 15 دن کا کرایہ سیکورٹی سے کاٹ لیا جائے گا۔

8۔ کرایہ یکم سے پانچ تاریخ تک جمع کرائیں۔

9۔ کمرے میں والیم کا خاص خیال رکھیں تا کہ ماحول خوشگوار رہے۔

ایمرجنسی شکایات کی صورت میں رابطہ کریں۔ سیٹھ محمد واجد 0300-9492458

Figure 2: Back of the monthly rent bill with the list of rules
Source: Munstasir Sattar

Perhaps the most important marker of the classed milieu are the residents. Another hostel owner explained that his tenants studied and succeeded in attaining government and other professional positions. I understand this selectivity as a form of erecting boundaries. These sorts of markers were attributed to residents' 'cleanliness' and a lack of 'troublemakers' hinting at how the space came to be associated with certain qualities, communicating through these distinct symbols what prospective tenants could understand as 'suitable'. Amir, a recent engineering graduate from southern Punjab who had come to launch a singing career, told me that the reason he came to Choudhury Mansion is because there is no *shor sharaba* (rowdiness).

To illustrate this point in another way, on the eve of the first day of Ramazan (the Islamic month of fasting) 2014, Dr Kamran, a homeopathic doctor from Karachi, recounts how a neighbour near his shop in Lahore showed him some hostels that were 'dirty'. On the other hand, he liked Choudhury Mansion as it had a fridge and TV and he did not have to go buy them. Dr Kamran said, 'education makes a difference—in the sense of cleanliness'. I prodded him to explain what education has to do with it, to which Dr Kamran said: 'Those who are educated—like people in this hostel—are cleaner.' Choudhury Mansion then came to be distinguished from less costly hostels not just on the basis of cost, but on the basis of a marker of class. The space mattered as much as the type of people who lived there. This dovetails with local ideas of distinction, in which being 'educated' is a metaphor for class distinction; as Murphy puts it: 'Representations of literacy and education are often conflated with class' (Murphy 2013: 345).

Figure 3: Laptops are an important study tool at Choudhury Mansion, electricity or no electricity
Source: Muntasir Sattar

Frogs in a City Well

What are the implications of policed boundaries, solitude, and geographic proximity for Choudhury Mansion's residents? Below, I show how groups of CSS aspirants in Choudhury Mansion and similar areas like Patiala House (where I lived) form class-cultural milieus in which subjectivities are crafted. I show how in the milieu (i.e. hostels and zones of hostels), collaboration— not strictly competition—such as guidance and moral support as well as education, can shape a kind of rite of passage that involves learning as well as constant practicing or performing their skills and knowledge.

Like the aspiring government officers in the hostel, Dr Parvez spoke of his inability to study at home in his village. Achieving his goal would have to be done here in the hostel, and that really is all that he did—sometimes sitting on a chair in the hall, at other times on the floor of his room. He described himself as a '*kuein ka maindak*' (frog in a well*), admitting he did not even know where Main Market in Gulberg was.** Indeed, all he did was study for his upcoming medical exams.

Having visited two other villages of unemployed men, I could see why the hostel was so important. In two village visits in Punjab, I observed that electricity and Internet access is sporadic, while duties and obligations at home kept young men busy. On the other hand, being in Lahore (and at the hostel) gave hostelites the opportunity to access resources easily and study with others as well. CSS aspirants and medical students alike could pick up the books and materials required from bookshops, academies, and from each other with little or no difficulty. No degree or diploma-granting institution required attendance in Lahore; in other words, they did not need to be here, but it seemed to be the correct *mahol* to help them get their preparation done. The hostel and hostel zone's carefully managed peace and quiet, the abundance of fellow test takers, and youth-oriented local economy of services played an important role.

Thus, one of the most attractive elements of the hostel was its environment for studying. One of the consequences of Ayub Sahab's selectivity (and the hostelites' own self-selection) is to create a space that is conducive to studying, allowing a 'convergence', to borrow one hostelite's term. It was attractive to professionals like Kamran and Amir and especially to students like the CSS aspirants. 'I'm middle class, and I came here to study,' said Hamza who stayed in the hostel adjacent to Choudhury Mansion. The city itself is a draw—he learns English from a teacher and came here because he could not find a job in engineering in Pano Aqil (Sindh). He came to Lahore to 'kill time, for a short period, and also for gain'. 'Anyway,' Hamza explained, 'it is better than being at home.'

---

* An Urdu saying used to describe a person who is unaware of their surroundings or is sheltered from the world.
** A well-known shopping and commercial area in Lahore, which was a 5-minute drive way.

Vignette

In an impromptu collaborative session over a cup of tea at the café at the foot of Choudhury Mansion, Umar and Nadeem talk a bit about the expected changes in the CSS exam and about the essay portion. Widely respected and a graduate of the Government College, Umar has been at Choudhury Mansion for years. Dr Nadeem has only been here for six months and is taking the learner's role. As in countless other sessions I participated in, Nadeem and Umar talk about the exam to learn and prepare by sharing experiences, tips, and knowledge gained from other places. Umar, an economics graduate from central Punjab, is well-known and would collect notes from everyone and had a stack of preparation books in his room that friends would come to use. The question they discuss involves violence, and an example Umar gave was terrorism. Nadeem says, 'what's your opinion of terrorism?'

After giving a full account, Umar adds, 'give what the questioners want.' I ask for a clarification: 'so one can tell the truth?'

No, they exclaim. Umar looks at Nadeem again and gets back to the session. Umar asks Nadeem which essay question he did. Nadeem responds that he responded to 'Great nations win without fighting'. Then later at dinner, the scene reproduces itself, this time when Nadeem meets another CSS aspirant originally from Balochistan, Nadeem takes the senior role. The discussion begins with a question: which essay did you choose and how did you answer?

***

The *mahol* and the city more generally are critical to the career strategies of CSS aspirants. As Rasheed, a CSS aspirant and the son of a doctor from Sindh, said, he likes the idea of having people here who are generally in the same position as him. As the space was associated with preparation for one's career, it was seen as fostering a conducive atmosphere. Rasheed, who has lived at Choudhury Mansion for some years, explains how important the hostel is to studying and working toward his goals. A long-time resident and frequent partner of Umar, hostelites help each other, he felt.

> In Choudhury Mansion I can talk to people about what books they use, where they go for tuitions, and I can study at the same time. People here are from the same situation; they have also come for the same purpose. They are facing

the same issues I am. If I'm depressed, I go to Umar *Seth* … he takes me out, he understands what I'm going through.

His friend and sometimes study partner, Dr Nadeem, echoes that view, highlighting the broader city in the shaping of his abilities. Dr Nadeem explains as he packs up his things before going back to Larkana: 'I have learned a lot.' He mentions the ability to think critically, how to read, and how to give constructive feedback. He talks about the cognitive skills he has improved and the study skills too. Nadeem mentions that he studies daily. Then he talks about how he has learned from the city:

> I've learned from different people—different things from different people. From one person, not to waste my time. From you [referring to me], how to plan the day. I didn't just learn from the city, I learned from Shan. I want to come back, to learn and study, and not just [make] money. The city of Lahore has groomed me.

Having spent most of his time with other aspiring officers in the network of spaces that the city provides, Dr Nadeem speaks to the importance of the study group he attended that would not have been possible in his town in Sindh. His experience with officers and fellow aspirants, along with the opportunity to speak English regularly, helps Nadeem prepare for an exam but also gain the social and cultural capital for the cultural position that elite bureaucrats occupy in Pakistan.

One of the clearest examples of how one moulds oneself into that cultural position is the way young men learn the 'correct' perspective on important issues of the day. In discussions with one another, such as between Nadeem and Umar above, aspiring officers are learning 'correct' viewpoints to adopt. With little idea of what to expect on the exams, aspiring officers share their past answers. They learn what viewpoint to hold, at least officially, with regard to issues such as governance, politics, and terrorism.

Two examples relate to conflict. In a discussion that seemed to take place several times, one topic of discussion was a question that appeared on the 2014 exam. After Nadeem and Umar's discussion, I noticed Umar's point about the 'right' answer during responses. The 'right' answer was also shared on Facebook posts by hostelites during their time in Lahore.

Viewpoints like these are shared and circulated online and in study groups in the park and at the hostel in preparation for their exam. In addition, young men socialise with officers and government servants and with one another, giving them ample opportunity to practice employing these viewpoints. They accumulate cultural capital in this manner, prepared to deploy it during an exam or during informal gatherings or interviews. In physical and intellectual proximity along with a kind of mimesis, educated, unemployed men gradually make themselves worthy of selection to the elite bureaucracy.

Conclusion

The *mohalla*'s gradual transformation from a residential area to a thriving and dense zone of hostels is shaped by larger forces, like the influx of migrants, urban planning, and Lahore's renowned education institutions. However, the way the space of the hostel itself is produced creates what one hostelite calls 'convergence'—a specific environment or *mahol* that appeals to highly educated men from across Pakistan. This classed milieu is a collaborative and competitive one, enabling men to study and to transform themselves in ways they deem more effective than preparing on their own in their homes. The space of the hostel serves an important purpose for them; it is not just a neutral background in their quest.

The large, dense hostel in a central location in Lahore is important because of the role it plays in bringing students with similar aspirations together as they prepare for the merit-based process of selection. The way that the milieu shapes the subjectivity is through the community of practice (Lave and Wenger 1991) in which seasoned aspirants share their experiences and guide newer arrivals in preparation for the annual CSS exam. That of course could not happen without the collaborative space that was created and maintained by Ayub Sahab.

In this way, the hostels in Lahore represent a distinct space, which is essential for the cultivation of the educated, urban, cosmopolitan subject. This is not easily done on their own in their home towns, villages, and cities which do not have similar bookshops, CSS academies, and fellow learners. And that is partly thanks to Ayub Sahab but also to every learner and hostelite that is involved in this community of practice (Lave and Wenger 1991). This is not the space necessarily of conformity, as Zhang (2008) describes, but the site of conscious cultivation enabled by the collaboration of what are ostensibly competitors for the same positions.

The hostel and the *mohalla* represent what Zhang refers to as the spatialisation of class. Using symbols, facilities, security, and social networks, the so-called 'VIP' Choudhury Mansion hostel caters to the 'educated' person. Meanwhile, the hostelites in their everyday routine are expected to live up to the expectations of the hostel by studying. On its own, the hostel is not very different from any other hostel in the city including the constant stench of sewage, electricity problems, and cramped rooms where cockroaches roam about. However, because of the peace and quiet and the presence of men from similar backgrounds sharing similar ambitions, this hostel was a space of distinction in the eyes of the hostelites.

While the space of the hostel and its surroundings is important, the city of Lahore also plays an important role in creating this *mahol*. It is perceived as being safe, and it offers 'exposure', as some call it, to a kind of cosmopolitanism that comes with being in a big city. It is a chance to leave the village for an experience of being on one's own, and to be recognised as a 'student'—a much preferable designation over being 'unemployed'.

In a time when security concerns are at the forefront of public discourse in urban Pakistan, this research demonstrates the class-cultural milieu that is produced through the careful management of security and selection within the hostels. While the municipal authority plays an important role in shaping the area, the space of the hostel is produced by keeping up a particular image of respectability. The space is made for 'well-mannered educated people', a naturalisation of class difference that subtly communicates its cultural position. In turn, hostelites value the hostel for the solitude and for the 'type' of people who live there. Furthermore, class subjectivities are cultivated during the daily performances and practice of learners. In this 'community of practice', a milieu is formed in which grooming, teaching, learning, and mentoring shape the emergence of classed subjects. In short, the hostel allows a convergence of people doing similar things, as Rasheed puts it, who can help one another. It is a place to think and speak like an elite bureaucrat.

This chapter describes the complex interplay of class, gender, and age in shaping the space of a particular middleclass *mohalla* in Lahore. With their arrival in central Lahore, these young migrant men drive the growth of the hostel zone and actively reshape the city. In this way, class and space are mutually constituted. The heterogeneous space of this *mohalla* defies the previously easy categorisation of the slum, *basti*, or gated community that dominates urban studies' literature. The emergence of this type of neighbourhood is the product of a rapidly urbanising society that is being reshaped by a massive growth in the education sector and processes of globalisation.

Despite its neglect in studies of urban Pakistan, the *mohalla*, as a complex social formation, plays a vital role in how young men strive to become successful middle class subjects within an uncertain urbanising future. The study of Lahore's hostels demonstrates the way a particular kind of space is carved out in the city, shaped by migration, economic and political conditions, and by urban planning. It illustrates the work that goes into defining the boundaries and characteristics of the locality by multiple actors at the level of their everyday lives. It is through these processes of spatial and social formation at the level of the locality that the fabric of the city itself is made.

REFERENCES

Ali, Reza, 'Underestimating Urbanization', *Continuity and Change: Sociopolitical and Institutional Dynamics in Pakistan*, S. Akbar Zaidi, (ed.), City Press, 2002, pp. 127–32.

Appadurai, Arjun, *Modernity at Large: Cultural Dimensions of Globalization*, Minneapolis: University of Minnesota Press, 1996.

Durr-e-Nayab, 'Estimating the Middle Class in Pakistan', *The Pakistan Development Review*, 50, 1 (2011), pp. 1–28.

Fernandes, Leela, *India's New Middle Class Democratic Politics in an Era of Economic Reform*, Minneapolis: University of Minnesota Press, 2006.

Glover, William J., *Making Lahore Modern: Constructing and Imagining a Colonial City*, Minneapolis: University of Minnesota Press, 2007.

Hasan, Arif, *The Scale and Causes of Urban Change*, Karachi: Ushba Publishers, 2006.

'HEC Graduate Data 2005–2009', Government of Pakistan Higher Education Commission <http://www.hec.gov.pk/InsideHEC/Divisions/QALI/Others/Pages/GraduateData.aspx>, last accessed 2 Dec. 2012.

'HEC Recognized Universities and Degree Awarding Institutions', Government of Pakistan Higher Education Commission <http://www.hec.gov.pk/OurInstitutes/Pages/UniversitiesAffiliatedColleges.aspx>, last accessed 29 Nov. 2012.

Jafferlot, Christophe, and Peter Van der Veer, *Patterns of Middle Class Consumption in India and China*, New Delhi: Sage Ltd, 2008.

Kumar, Nita, *The Artisans of Banaras*, Princeton: Princeton University Press, 1988.

Lave, Jean, and Etienne Wenger, *Situated Learning: Legitimate Peripheral Participation*, Cambridge: Cambridge University Press, 1991.

Liechty, Mark, *Suitably Modern: Making Middle Class Culture in a New Consumer Society*, Princeton: Princeton University Press, 2003.

Linden, J. J. Van der, J. W. Schoorl, and K. S. Yap, *Between Basti Dwellers and Bureaucrats: Lessons in Squatter Settlement Upgrading in Karachi*, Oxford: Pergamon Press, 1983.

Maqsood, Ammara, 'Buying Modern: Muslim Subjectivity, the West, and Patterns of Islamic Consumption in Lahore, Pakistan', *Cultural Studies*, 28, 1 (2014), pp. 84–107.

Mazarella, William, 'Middle Class', *Keywords in South Asian Studies* <https://www.soas.ac.uk/south-asia-institute/keywords/file24808.pdf> last accessed 3 Aug. 2015.

Murphy, Richard, 'The Hairbrush and the Dagger: Mediating Modernity in Lahore', *Urban Pakistan*, Khalid Bajwa, (ed.), Karachi: Oxford University Press, 2010.

Roy, Ananya, *City Requiem, Calcutta: Gender and the Politics of Poverty*, Minneapolis: University of Minnesota Press, 2002.

Safa, Helen, 'Urbanization, the Informal Economy, and State Policy in Latin America', *Urban Anthropology*, 15 (1986), pp. 135–63.

Sattar, Muntasir, 'Education and Power', *Dawn News*, 12 January, 2015.

Srivastava, Sanjay, 'National Identity, Bedrooms, and Kitchens: Gated Communities and New Narratives of Space in India', in *The Global Middle Classes: Theorizing through Ethnography*, Rachel Heiman, Mark Liechty, Carla Freeman (eds.), School for Advanced Research Press, 2012, pp. 57–84.

Stack, Carol, *All Our Kin: Strategies for Survival in a Black Community*, New York: Basic Books, 1997.

Tarlo, Emma, *Unsettling Memories: Narratives of the Emergency in Delhi*, University of California Press, Berkeley, 2001.

Zaidi, S. Akbar, *Issues in Pakistan's Economy*, Karachi: Oxford University Press, 2015.

————, 'Rethinking Pakistan's Political Economy: Class, State, Power, and Transition', *Economic and Political Weekly*, 1 February, 2014.

Zaidi, Zehra Yasmin, *Chaddors and Pink Collars in Pakistan: Gender, Work, and the Global Economy*, Dissertation, Brandeis University, 2011.

Zhang, Li, 'Private Homes, Distinct Lifestyles: Performing a New Middle Class', *Privatizing China: Socialism from Afar*, Li Zhang and Aihwa Ong, (eds.), Ithaca: Cornell University Press, 2008.

Afterword

South Asian Cities in the New Millennium

Writing on an assortment of cities in South Asia, the contributors in this book bring into conversation the myriad complexities of configuring urban life constituted by politico-economic, social, and ecological sets of exchanges. While conventional approaches to South Asian cities often subscribe to a dystopic view of a capitalist-induced declining future, an expanding body of scholarship advances a view that contextualises South Asian cities within a diverse range of distinctive urban contexts. In doing so, it has opened new ways of considering cities in general (Rao 2006; Roy 2009; Ghertner 2011; Rademacher and Sivaramakrishnan 2013; Anwar 2016; Benjamin 2008, to name a few). As the Global South has become the new epicentre of urbanism, South Asian cities account for a significant shift in demographic changes and economic transformations, a reality that has not yet been fully acknowledged especially with respect to Pakistan. As analysts turn today to the urban question in Pakistan, estimates of scale and urban change proliferate. Despite the current controversy over methods of rural–urban classification in the 2017 Census, the results do show that an increasingly greater proportion of Pakistanis live in cities today, where all net new employment will be generated. For Pakistan's young and mobile population, cities are undeniable magnets for resources and their aspirations for securing a 'good life'.

The essays in this book deal with issues that are specific to the Global South, such as informality, rural–urban migration, and peripheral urbanisation. But what marks this collection of interventions are the divergent views within a new cohort of upcoming scholars who collectively assert the imperative of framing urban issues from a South Asian vantage point. For instance, by examining resettlement projects in the city of

Amritsar (India) from below, Helena Cermeño highlights the importance of conceiving new methodological and theoretical approaches that disrupt universal understandings of urban development in India. She creatively uses ordinary citizens' cognitive maps to explore everyday access to a city where a new development calculus is unfolding in the broader context of India's developmental objectives. At the core of this collection is an interest in drawing South Asian—specifically Pakistani and Indian—cities into closer conversation with urban theory that departs from the Eurocentric epistemic trap to which studies on urbanism and urbanisation are generally confined. In this spirit, the essays in this book bring a fresh perspective to the project of engaging with South Asian cities on their own terms.

The essays provide eclectic approaches to what constitutes the South Asian city, inspired by the experiences of everyday urban life, new configurations of postcolonial governance, and the redevelopment of urban futures. This has important consequences for comparing (Kirmani, 'Introduction') ongoing dynamics of policy circulations, worlding aspirations, city modelling, security imperatives, and related impacts in an era of planetary urbanisation. Moreover, the essays bring into conversation for the first time exclusively the diverse yet historically analogous experiences of Indian and Pakistani cities, which is, I think, a thought-provoking contribution for our comparative imagination and for forging new conversations. Given the relentless dynamics of socio-spatial restructuring since Partition, boundaries, scale, and the morphology of urbanisation and related ecologies have been continually reworked in India and Pakistan.

What might we learn, then, about South Asian cities, and Pakistani and Indian cities in particular, from these essays? The two things that emerge strongly in these essays are the dynamics of peripheral urbanisation that pivot on a fluctuating agrarian space, and the imminent commons in which the primeval elements like air and water have become artificial and politicised. These themes connect with a third and equally important topic concerning aspirations and anticipations about new futures—whether such futures involve the politics of security and ecological disaster, or are expressed through everyday hopes and the agency of individuals placed within wider cultural milieus and socio-spatial structures of power (Anderson 2010).

Agrarian Spaces

Cutting across several essays is an awareness that urbanisation and everyday life in South Asian cities increasingly hinge on socio-spatial transformations of the agrarian hinterlands. As a predominantly agrarian and one of the least urbanised regions of the world with approximately 35–40 per cent of its population defined as urban, South Asia is projected to become one of the most urbanised regions within the next few decades. This unprecedented urban transformation is taking place not in the cities but on their peripheries that are largely agricultural. Suburbanisation, de-agrarianisation, peripheral urbanisation—all these processes are interconnected, and they index new modes of urbanisation, new modes of the production of urban space located at the limits of our planetary existence. This of course is not unique to South Asia, but peripheral urbanisation often accompanies de-agrarianisation and constitutes a distinctive feature of urban change in South Asia. Both Rajani and Islam as well as Rashid and Moulvi capture this process succinctly when they discuss, in the cases of Karachi and Lahore, the prolific housing schemes, real estate developments, and intense property speculation that is transforming these cities' peripheries, attendant village economies, and indigenous histories and practices. In this emergent process, it has become increasingly difficult to separate the state from capital. As Rashid and Moulvi note in their discussion about the role of the powerful parastatal, the Lahore Development Authority, in acquiring agricultural land: 'The case of LDA City lays bare how increasingly the state, rather than clearing the way for capitalists, is becoming indistinguishable from them.'

Notably, these essays bring to the forefront the complex relationship between the rural and the urban, and underscore the socio-spatial fluidity that characterises our global urban condition under modern capitalism, where intensifying and interdependent socio-spatiality blurs the boundaries between rural and urban, and destabilises longstanding ecologies of the agrarian. But they do so by keeping in context the colonial–postcolonial interplay of governance specific to South Asia. The circulation of the grand narrative of the nation's economy and social growth can also be traced in these essays, as both dynamics are not only co-constitutive, but also engage peripheral urbanisation in myriad ways. A case in point is Sheikh, Sharma, and Banda's essay on the process of electoral politics in New Delhi's informal settlements or its rural villages and resettled colonies where citizenship is negotiated through the recurring, unfulfilled promise of service delivery. These issues of socio-spatial transformations and the related politics of informality get to the heart of the rural–urban relationship, and show the extent to which, for ordinary citizens, new opportunities of mobility are deeply entangled with vulnerabilities and exclusions that resonate in the contemporary postcolonial political order of violence and corruption in South Asia.

Imminent Commons

While urban spaces materialise through dynamics of movement, connectivity, circulation of commodities, and reconfigurations of identity and attachments, these are also spaces of the privatisation of common resources and the urbanisation of nature, where deforestation, concretisation, encroachment, and land reclamation for development produce ecological ruptures. For South Asian cities in the new millennium, the 'environment' constitutes a new element of urban modernity, where concerns for waste, water, air, externalities and so forth are abutted with the challenges of climate change. Pakistan ranks high on the list of countries most threatened by the impending effects of climate change. Numerous studies show that temperatures in certain parts of Asia will exceed habitable levels by end of the twenty-first century. According to a report published by the Asian Development Bank, a six-degree Celsius temperature increase is projected over the Asian landmass whereby countries like Pakistan could experience a significantly hotter climate. It is expected that the disruption in agricultural output and generally in the region's economy will trigger deepening vulnerabilities at various scales: from country, cities, and communities to households and individuals. In southern Pakistan, cities like Karachi, Hyderabad-Jamshoro, Sukkur and coastal cities such as Badin are already at the forefront of climate change-related impacts, ever more visible in the form of coastal storm surges, rising sea levels, hotter summers, unprecedented floods, human and livestock displacement, and unpredictable precipitation. Transforming South Asian cities into sustainable environments is the single biggest challenge that governments, policymakers, and entrepreneurs face today, and the ongoing political struggles over resources, infrastructures, amenities, and ecologies are shaping how cities play a role in climate adaption.

Notably, vulnerability and danger are already dominant factors that condition the permutations of urban life for ordinary citizens who are constantly put in harm's way. In urban Pakistan and India, the poor not only live near toxic waste streams, but are often threatened by beautification projects that would displace and relocate them rather than improve amenities. These harsh material conditions that constantly endanger the lives of the urban poor are not an outcome of climate change. The effects of decades of unpredictable urban planning, incompetent engineering, and the actions of greedy developers have compromised local urban ecologies that could otherwise withstand the shock of natural disasters. Negi and Srigyan's essay on contemporary Delhi's unremitting expansion, environmental changes, and its 'toxic urbanism' underscores the significance of ecology as it has come to the forefront of public discourse, policy, and governance in defining India's future. For South Asian cities to address the challenges of the climate crisis, in which the elements of air, water, and so forth have become artificial and politicised, they will need to redefine themselves beyond the logics of urban functionalism that has dismantled the commons, and produced an urbanity in which clichés like 'public space' have become deeply problematic as guarantors of democracy and collective well-being. After all, 'public space' pertains not only to the shared social space that is open and accessible to people, but also includes implicitly shared environmental resources such as waterways and forests and the urban commons constituted by parks, streets, plazas, sidewalks, markets, public transportation, architectural character, and more. As cities across the globe have become the most populated human environments, the functionalist approach of modern urban planning seems incapable of addressing crucial questions of air pollution, droughts, rising water levels, heat island effect, and deforestation.

As South Asian cities have become a crucial intersection between politics, ecology, and technology and where the balance between wealth, labour, resources, and energy necessitates retuning to address the failings of neoliberal economies, a key question is: how will the emergent politics alter the foundations of a neoliberal agenda in order to resolve an imminent ecological breakdown (Rifkin 2014)? For such political transformations to occur, the South Asian city appears not only as a site of ecological ruptures but also for bringing together unresolved tensions of hope and despair. Negi and Srigyan show that new possibilities are emerging in New Delhi. They discuss the role of different actors who have shifted towards environmental justice positions and responded to the critiques of a 'bourgeois environmentalism'. This has opened a space for a participatory urban governance that is gradually 'turning the tables on Delhi's car-owning elite'; a new politics is emerging that also refuses to label the city as 'world class'. While such interventions are hard-won and forged in challenging politico-economic situations, they, nevertheless, reveal that new possibilities for reconstructing the commons can emerge on a site of environmental uncertainty. This is an extremely important issue for the analysis of South Asian cities, and cities in general.

New Futures

What does it mean to lay claim to a future? An intimate relationship between risk, calculation, and speculation, the future can be understood as a horizon of anticipation. How might we write about new urban futures in South Asia? In this horizon of anticipation, how can we speak of mobilities, migrations, of new processes of urbanisation—of erasing the past, and the temporalities of destruction and (re)construction that reshape the built environment? What are the risks, uncertainties, and dangers that anticipate new futures of contemporary urbanism in South Asia? As Appadurai (2013) posits, humans are 'future makers' and it is within culture that ideas about the future are nurtured. Although, as Bunnell et al. (2017) show, futurity can also exceed Appadurai's framing agenda in terms of issues of spatiality and complex temporalities. These issues pertain not only to the aspirational futures of a rising middle class, for instance in Pakistan (Maqsood 2017) and India (Jodhka and Prakash 2016), but also to legalism and risk that may suggest ways that emphasise social relations of power, and the frameworks that address notions of environmental danger and new modes of governance (Anwar et al. 2019; Zeiderman 2016).

Futures are amenable to individual calculation and strategic action based on existing resources and social capital, as Muntasir Sattar demonstrates when discussing the educational aspirations of middle-class male migrants in Lahore. The aspirations of these male migrants and other actors, such as the property dealers in Karachi's periphery, peasant farmers contemplating land sales in Lahore's agrarian zones, and political brokers/*pradhans* mediating the delivery of services in New Delhi, cast the South Asian city as an active space where a multitude of futures are being prospected and performed through everyday practices and events.

Does the future of South Asian cities exhibit a radical instability premised on reproducing power structures, inequality, and ecological destruction?

Or will South Asian cities become devices for the common good? The contemporary experience in/of South Asian cities, and perhaps cities everywhere across the Global South, rests on the disjuncture between the planners' imaginary of the city as a coherent body with functional parts and its non-alignment with the proliferation of spaces that do not maintain the fiction of coherence. A common way to make sense of this non-alignment is in terms of an urban ontology that presumes this happens due to the politically-oriented and instrumental nature of residents' demands and actions that yield specific results (Boucher et al. 2009). But urban experiences in South Asia may be unfolding through ethical investments arising from new ways of relating to the future as a horizontal process in which new modes of subjectivation, for instance in the production of urban nature, are being developed to deal with instability. These are crucial questions that merit further investigations on the imminent South Asian city.

Dr Nausheen H. Anwar
Professor, City and Regional Planning
Director, Karachi Urban Lab
SSLA/IBA, Karachi

REFERENCES

Anderson, Ben, 'Preemption, Precaution, Preparedness: Anticipatory Action and Future Geographies', *Progress in Human Geography*, 34, 6 (2010), pp. 777–98.

Anwar, Nausheen H., 'Asian Mobilities and State Governance at the Geographic Margins: Geopolitics and Oil Tales from Karachi to Taftan', *Environment and Planning A*, 48, 6 (2016), pp. 1047–63.

———, Amiera Sawas, and Daanish Mustafa, 'Without Water, There is no Life': Negotiating Everyday Risks and Gendered Insecurities in Karachi's Informal Settlements', *Urban Studies*, 23 April, (2019), pp. 1–18.

Appadurai, Arjun, *The Future as Cultural Fact: Essays on the Global Condition*, London: Verso, 2013.

Benjamin, Solomon, 'Occupancy Urbanism: Radicalizing Politics and Economy beyond Policy and Programs', *International Journal of Urban and Regional Research*, 32, (2008), pp. 719–29.

Boucher, Nathalie, Mariana Cavalcanti, Stefan Kipfer, Edgar Pieterse, Vyjayanthi Rao, and Nasra Smith, 'Writing the Lines of Connection: Unveiling the Strange Language of Urbanization', International Journal of Urban and Regional Research, 32, 4 (2008), pp. 989–1027.

Bunnell, Tim, Jamie Gillen, and Elaine Ho, 'The Prospect of Elsewhere: Engaging the Future through Aspirations in Asia', *Annals of the American Association of Geographers*, 108, 1 (2018), pp. 35–51.

Ghertner, D. Asher, *Rule by Aesthetics: World-class City Making in Delhi*, Oxford University Press: New York, NY, 2015.

Jodhka, Surinder S., and Aseem Prakash, *The Indian Middle Class*, Oxford University Press, 2016.

Maqsood, Ammara, *The New Pakistani Middle Class*, Harvard University Press, 2017.

Rademacher, Anne M., and Kalyanakrishnan Sivaramakrishnan, *Ecologies of Urbanism in India: Metropolitan Civility and Sustainability*, 1, Hong Kong University Press, 2013.

Rao, Vyjayanthi, 'Slum as theory', *International Journal of Urban and Regional Research*, 30, 1 (2006), pp. 225–32.

Rifkin, Jeremy, *The Zero Marginal Cost Society: The Internet of Things, the Collaborative Commons, and the Eclipse of Capitalism*, St. Martin's Press, 2014.

Roy, Ananya, 'Why India Cannot Plan its Cities: Informality, Insurgence and the Idiom of urbanization', *Planning Theory*, 8, 1, pp. 76–87.

Zeiderman, Austin, *Endangered City: The Politics of Security and Risk in Bogota*, Duke University Press: Durham and London, 2016.

Index

215